Moral Hazard

Moral hazard is a core concept in economics. In a nutshell, moral hazard reflects the reduced incentive to protect against risk where an entity is (or believes it will be) protected from its consequences, whether through an insurance arrangement or an implicit or explicit guarantee system. It is fundamentally driven by information asymmetry, arises in all sectors of the economy, including banking, medical insurance, financial insurance, and governmental support, undermines the stability of our economic systems and has burdened taxpayers in all developed countries, resulting in significant costs to the community. Despite the seriousness and pervasiveness of moral hazard, policymakers and scholars have failed to address this issue. This book fills this gap.

It covers 200 years of moral hazard: from its origins in the 19th century to the bailouts announced in the aftermath of the COVID-19 outbreak. The book is divided into three parts. Part I deals with the ethics and other fundamental issues connected to moral hazard. Part II provides historical and empirical evidence on moral hazard in international finance. It examines in turn the role of the export credit industry, the international lender of last resort, and the IMF. Finally, Part III examines specific sectors such as automobile, banking, and the US industry at large.

This is the first book to provide an interdisciplinary analysis of moral hazard and explain why addressing this issue has become crucial today. As such, it will attract interest from scholars across different fields, including economists, political scientists, and lawyers.

Juan Flores Zendejas is an associate professor at the Department of History, Economics, and Society of the University of Geneva.

Norbert Gaillard is an economist and independent consultant, for more information visit his website at www.norbertgaillard.com.

Rick Michalek is a New York-based independent legal and financial consultant.

Routledge International Studies in Money and Banking

Capital and Finance
Theory and History
Peter Lewin and Nicolás Cachanosky

Democracy and Money
Lessons for Today from Athens in Classical Times
George C. Bitros, Emmanouil M. L. Economou, Nicholas C. Kyriazis

Monetary Policy after the Great Recession
The Role of Interest Rates
Arkadiusz Sieroń

Behavioural Public Finance
Individuals, Society, and the State
Edited by M. Mustafa Erdoğdu, Larissa Batrancea, and Savaş Çevik

The Economics of Cryptocurrencies
Edited by J. Mark Munoz and Michael Frenkel

Finance and Sustainable Development
Designing Sustainable Financial Systems
Edited by Magdalena Ziolo

The Financialized Economy
Alexander Styhre

Financialization, Financial Literacy, and Social Education
Edited by Thomas A. Lucey

Moral Hazard
A Financial, Legal, and Economic Perspective
Edited by Juan Flores Zendejas, Norbert Gaillard, and Rick Michalek

For more information about this series, please visit: www.routledge.com/Routledge-International-Studies-in-Money-and-Banking/book-series/SE0403

Moral Hazard

A Financial, Legal, and Economic Perspective

Edited by
Juan Flores Zendejas,
Norbert Gaillard, and
Rick Michalek

Routledge
Taylor & Francis Group
LONDON AND NEW YORK

First published 2022
by Routledge
2 Park Square, Milton Park, Abingdon, Oxon OX14 4RN

and by Routledge
605 Third Avenue, New York, NY 10158

Routledge is an imprint of the Taylor & Francis Group, an informa business

British Library Cataloguing-in-Publication Data
A catalogue record for this book is available from the British Library

Library of Congress Cataloging-in-Publication Data
A catalog record has been requested for this book

ISBN: 978-0-367-68833-2 (hbk)
ISBN: 978-0-367-68834-9 (pbk)
ISBN: 978-1-003-13924-9 (ebk)

DOI: 10.4324/9781003139249

Typeset in Bembo
by MPS Limited, Dehradun

Contents

List of Illustrations

Figures

Tables

Editors

Juan Flores Zendejas is an associate Professor at the Department of History, Economics and Society of the University of Geneva. He earned a PhD in economics from Sciences Po Paris. He has worked for the Mexican Government and as an external consultant to the private sector, the Mexican Senate, and international institutions. He was head of the Paul Bairoch Institute of Economic History between 2014 and 2018. Flores Zendejas' research focuses on the history of financial crises and sovereign defaults, the history of international financial organizations, and problems of economic development in Latin America. He has extensively published in journals such as *International Organization*, *European Review of Economic History*, *Journal of Economic History*, and the *Economic History Review*.

Norbert Gaillard is an economist and independent consultant. He studied at Sciences Po Paris and Princeton University. He has served as a consultant to the International Finance Corporation, the World Bank, the State of Sonora (Mexico), the OECD, the European Parliament, and various financial institutions (including a credit rating agency). He has taught at the Ecole Supérieure de Commerce de Paris, the University of Geneva and the Graduate Institute. He is a Euromoney Country Risk expert. His main areas of expertise are public debt and sovereign risk, local government debt and subnational risk, credit rating agencies, and country risk. He has authored more than 80 press articles. He has published 26 research articles/book chapters and five books since 2009. For more information visit his website at www.norbertgaillard.com.

Rick Michalek is a New York-based independent legal and financial consultant. He graduated from Columbia University with both a JD and an MBA. Rick is a former senior credit officer at the rating agency Moody's Investors Service in the structured derivatives group. He worked abroad as a securitization consultant to the New Zealand law firm Chapman Tripp and as an associate attorney in the New York office of Skadden Arps. He has consulted on a number of complex structured derivative litigation matters and continues to consult hedge funds and private equity investors on matters relating to the rating agencies and their processes. Rick has also assisted various US governmental agencies responsible for reforming the laws and regulations governing financial services.

Contributors

Giuseppe Bianco is an expert in international economic and financial law. Formerly at the Bank of Italy, he is currently a digital economy policy analyst at the OECD.

Cheryl D. Block is a professor of Law at Washington University in St Louis. Her research areas are basic federal income and corporate tax, federal tax policy, federal budget, and bailouts.

Rutger Claassen is a professor of Political Philosophy & Economic Ethics at Utrecht University. He works on socio-economic justice and defends a version of the capability approach.

Aline Darbellay is an assistant professor of Law at the University of Geneva. She has written extensively on credit ratings, financial markets, and FinTech issues.

Fumihito Gotoh is a lecturer in East Asian Studies at the University of Sheffield. His expertise includes East Asian and Japanese political economies and comparative capitalism.

Timothy J. Sinclair is an associate professor of International Political Economy at the University of Warwick. His research focuses on puzzles in the politics of credit ratings and global governance.

Stefano Ugolini is an associate professor of Economics at the University of Toulouse (Sciences Po Toulouse & LEREPS). He has developed strong expertise in the theoretical and historical aspects of central banking.

1 Moral hazard, a long-term perspective and challenges ahead

Juan Flores Zendejas, Norbert Gaillard, and Rick Michalek

Moral hazard is an elusive, yet commonly used term. An analysis of its origins and its diverse applications in different fields shows its theoretical and empirical relevance. This chapter introduces the main questions relating to moral hazard, beginning with the academic literature on insurance and finance. It provides a brief overview of the main challenges that have been raised in the context of moral hazard. It shows how public authorities have adjusted many of their decisions to intervene in the economy due to fears of moral hazard. Nevertheless, this chapter claims that moral hazard remains a major challenge for governments worldwide, given the financialization of the economy and the concentration of industry in different sectors. Moral hazard may lead to unintended and even perverse outcomes for societies, and thus, remains a major issue for scholars and policymakers.

In the Iliad, when Prince Paris of Troy decided to seduce Helen, queen of Sparta and wife of King Menelaus, he probably did not expect such an act to trigger a ten-year war between the two states. Paris's reckless behavior might have been related to his noble origins, leading him to believe that he was permitted to act as his willingness dictated. Another possibility, however, was the support granted by goddess Aphrodite, who had offered Paris the possibility to have the love of the most beautiful woman on earth. With this dream in mind, and with his back covered by Aphrodite, Paris's rash judgment might have been easily explained.

Some of today's economics texts would provide a straightforward explanation of Paris's behavior. Paris was exposed to moral hazard, a term now commonly used in contexts of asymmetric information. In the Iliad, Menelaus kindly welcomed Paris into his Palace. He did not know, nor could he know, about Paris's obscure reasons for his visit. Admittedly, ancient Greek relations between gods and humans might be more complex than today's concepts of divinity. Moreover, the struggles between Menelaus and Paris would more likely be considered a soap opera and would not trigger endless academic discussions. However, the example illustrates how the concept of moral hazard can encompass social, political, or economic interactions. Fortunately, not all moral hazard situations end up in armed conflicts.

DOI: 10.4324/9781003139249-1

Section 1 What is at stake?

According to the Oxford Dictionary, moral hazard can be defined as the "lack of incentive to guard against risk where one is protected from its consequences, e.g., by insurance."[1] While there is no consensus about the precise origins of the term, there is no doubt that it was largely preceded by situations in which individuals were confronted with moral hazard.[2] For at least the past two hundred years, scholars from different fields have analyzed, through a variety of approaches, the behavior of individuals, banks, and firms when facing situations of moral hazard. In fact, moral hazard might be present in all human actions (Emmett, 2011, p. 1150). This claim can be directly attributed to the fact that human interactions are characterized by uncertainty, and thus, individuals seek naturally to shift the burden from the consequences of their decisions onto others (McCaffrey, 2017). Yet, it is noteworthy that *economists* have devoted the most time analyzing the causes and consequences of moral hazard.

A rapid overview of moral hazard as an issue in the economic literature serves to understand why economists are so concerned. One major reason is the fact that moral hazard may create unnecessary costs to society and lead to distortionary effects. To give but the most illustrative examples of the kinds of moral hazard identified in the literature, we could mention the banking sector, government welfare programs, the automobile industry, and, of course, the insurance sector. Today's most commonly used theoretical framework underlying the problem of moral hazard is the neoclassical principal-agent theory (Mas-Colell, 1995). This theory attempts to describe a situation in which a principal hires an agent to accomplish a task. The principal and the agent have a different set of preferences. More importantly, the agent possesses superior information about the transaction (hidden information). The agent is also in a position where it could take actions that are unobservable to the principal (hidden actions). As a result, the principal cannot verify whether the agent acts according to what was agreed upon in the first place.

While problems of hidden information are frequently referred to as *adverse selection*, our view is that moral hazard involves situations of hidden actions.[3] Moral hazard reflects the agent's incentive to engage in [hidden] risky behavior offering a greater reward when it is (or believes it will be) protected from negative consequences, whether through an insurance arrangement or an implicit or explicit guarantee system. It is precisely in the insurance industry where scholars have mostly identified historical narratives on concerns relating to moral hazard. A first example dates back to the 11th century, when the losses that could be insured by a mutual-aid society in feudal France explicitly excluded covering losses that resulted from the negligence of the claimant (Moss, 2004). It is not surprising that the design of insurance contracts has been accompanied by endless discussions about the impact on an individual's disincentive to exercise caution, while increasing the proclivity to engage in careless or risk-seeking behavior (Djelic and Bothello, 2013, p. 592). Despite these concerns over individuals' misbehavior, the insurance business has expanded in both the public and the private sectors since the mid-19th century.[4]

Kenneth Arrow is now considered one of the most important contributors to the literature on moral hazard that emerged in the 1960s and 1970s. His first research works addressed medical insurance issues (Arrow, 1963) but his conception of moral hazard was not necessarily the one that is the most widely used today in the literature (Grignon et al., 2018). The variety of perspectives has led the insurance literature to distinguish between ex ante moral hazard – where an agent responds to changes in incentives by altering behavior affecting the risk of losses – and ex post moral hazard, which focuses on the effects of incentives – and disincentives – on claiming losses.[5] This distinction is relevant for understanding insurance contracts that do not necessarily prioritize minimizing the likelihood of having an accident, but rather reducing the amounts payable on insured claims.[6]

Another sector where moral hazard has been at the core of disputes is the financial sector. The emergence of entities having the capacity to provide lender-of-last-resort services triggered debates on their attitudes toward the riskiness of the projects that they decide to finance. Today, this issue involves primarily central banks, public entities, and multilateral organizations. It is interesting to note that when private entities provided such services, the mechanisms designed to eliminate moral hazard were not very different than those conceived by central banks in present times. These similarities are best illustrated in events during the 19th century.

In Britain, the evolution of the regulatory framework in the first decades of the 19th century prevented the Bank of England from acting on behalf of the British banking sector. In particular, the Bank Charter Act of 1844 imposed a 100-percent reserve on the Bank of England, thereby impeding the Bank from intervening in periods of financial difficulties (Fetter, 1965). This act had to be suspended given the gravity of the crises of 1857 and 1866. However, in order to avert moral hazard, the Bank of England reacted by gradually raising the quality requirements of the paper that could be utilized as collateral. The Bank also improved the information it held on potential users of their liquidity facilities (Bignon et al., 2012).

The U.S. banking system operated without a central bank during most of the 19th century. Clearing houses emerged as key actors that managed the co-insurance mechanisms to prevent contagious bank runs. Clearing houses acted as regulatory and supervisory agencies, and thus relied on a set of instruments that forced banks to respect certain basic, risk-management prescriptions (Winkler, 2011). Membership to this insurance mechanism was most useful for weaker banks that were more prone to engage in morally hazardous behavior (Dowd, 1994).

Yet, none of these frameworks sufficed to prevent occasional financial crises, nor even to completely mitigate moral hazard problems. In both cases, the institutional framework was to be either complemented by emergency measures (e.g., the 1890 Baring rescue in Britain) or even completely reformed as in the United States following the 1907 financial crisis, which led to the establishment of the Federal Reserve in 1913.

A long-term perspective on the 20th century tells a similar story. The fears arising from moral hazard appeared frequently in the aftermath of major financial crises. The introduction of the Federal Deposit Insurance Corporation (FDIC) aiming at protecting the "people's cold, hard-earned cash" drew criticism by the U.S. President F. D. Roosevelt as it would lead to "laxity in bank management and carelessness on the part of both banker and depositor" (Prins, 2009, pp. 138–139). Even so, Roosevelt signed the Glass-Steagall Act in June 1933, thereby implementing the deposit insurance scheme of which the FDIC would be in charge. Deposit insurance was designed to protect the interest of depositors and prevent banking runs, but moral hazard problems did not take long to materialize (see Grossman, 1992).

The debates that accompanied the failure of banks in the aftermath of the Bretton Woods collapse (see Schenk, 2014) suggest that moral hazard was becoming a key issue. In 1975, three economists – Paul Horvitz (director of research at the FDIC), Thomas Humphrey (economist at the Federal Reserve of Richmond), and Thomas Mayer (professor at the University of California, Davis) – wrote three independent articles in which they concluded that the rescue of banks was now among the top priorities of U.S. regulators. Mayer (1975, p. 604) even considered that "in the case of very large banks, it is widely believed, and probably correctly so, that the government would not allow them to fail, i.e., would not let them go into receivership." Such views proved prescient.[7] In 1984, after the Continental Illinois bank was bailed out by the Federal Reserve Bank of Chicago and the FDIC, the Comptroller of the Currency testified to the Congress that U.S. regulators would not let the top eleven multinational money center banks fail. In response, Congressman Stewart McKinney exclaimed that they had thus created a new kind of bank: the "too big to fail" (TBTF) bank.

This new environment had two noxious consequences that contributed to nurture moral hazard. First, financial institutions started a *race to bigness* in order to obtain the TBTF status and increase the likelihood to be rescued in the event of a severe crisis (Wilmarth Jr., 2002). Second, U.S. regulators, credit rating agencies (CRAs), and the Federal Reserve exacerbated (and are still exacerbating) the problems inherent to the TBTF phenomenon: financial sophistication, underestimation of credit risk, and growing indebtedness (Gaillard and Michalek, 2019). It seems clear that top policymakers accommodate TBTF banks not only for reasons of political campaign support but because they enable constituent households to maintain their standard of living and firms to continue their leverage strategies. In a nutshell, moral hazard would be the price to pay to preserve political survival, economic growth, and more fundamentally, to prevent systemic risk.

There are, however, dissonant perspectives, and one may wonder whether moral hazard constitutes a problem at all. The growth of the financial sector might have been unavoidable and its relevance in the development of today's rich countries has been recognized in the literature (Rousseau and Sylla, 2003). The history of financial institutions and capital markets has demonstrated that investors and banks have found different mechanisms to monitor their investments and have a voice in the decision-making process of the firms being financed (DeLong, 1991). The victory of finance has been connected to the victory of capitalism, and success stories of strong collaboration between banks and enterprises have been found in Western Europe, the United States, and more recently, in Japan and Eastern Asian countries. Furthermore, the principle of insurance and guarantee schemes has been expanding and constitutes a profitable business in most countries. This might generate moral hazard, but one should not disregard the positive effects of insurance and guarantee on economic activity. Anyway, in emergency situations, such as the onset of the Covid pandemic of 2020, one might conclude that the only solution is to "act fast and do whatever it takes" (Baldwin and Weder di Mauro, 2020).

Yet, it is unclear whether the recent actions implemented by the Fed were the most appropriate. They cut volatility in capital markets and restored confidence but the long-run consequence in terms of moral hazard remains to be seen (Bevilacqua et al., 2021). At the time of writing, governments worldwide are stepping in to provide support to households, banks, and firms. Although moral hazard has been largely overlooked so far, the burden to taxpayers and public finances will increasingly force authorities to identify those having inappropriately taken advantage of this support.[8] It raises the question about whether moral hazard is nested in contemporary capitalism. Sometimes, a last-resort loan or a bailout decision may be driven by close relationships between financiers and industrialists and government officials, especially in a context of "crony capitalism" (Rosas, 2006).

A final question is whether governments and central banks have the capacity and the tools to mitigate moral hazard. Banking theory has devoted considerable efforts to addressing moral hazard issues through a variety of mechanisms conditioning support. The Bagehotian rules are certainly a reliable recipe to fight moral hazard (see Bignon et al., 2012). Other approaches are conceivable. Freixas (1999) developed the term "constructive ambiguity" to describe a situation in which the uncertainty of a lender-of-last-resort intervention might eliminate ex ante moral hazard by encouraging market participants to limit risk-taking. However, this policy may not be credible in the eyes of investors because of the systemic importance of the failing institution. Besides, "constructive ambiguity" may be even counterproductive when such an institution delays borrowing to avoid stigma (Posner, 2018). In the case of the bailouts provided by the International Monetary Fund (IMF), there is a threat of *debtor* as well as *creditor* moral hazard. This double challenge has stirred controversy as it leads to a suboptimal use of public resources. The preferred creditor status of the lender of last resort and the conditionality it imposes on the borrower have proved efficient to prevent *debtor* moral hazard. The persistence of *creditor* moral hazard may be caused by domestic governments themselves, which makes fight against moral hazard even more difficult (see Altamura and Flores Zendejas, 2020). The frequent rescues of financial institutions since the 1970s have also convinced some economists to find alternatives to bailouts. Chennells and Wingfield (2015) explain why the use of "bail-ins" is likely to stabilize financial markets and contain moral hazard. At the very end, it seems that moral hazard cannot be fought efficiently unless policymakers reduce information asymmetry and promote greater transparency. This should undoubtedly call into question the excessive financialization of Western economies (Mattli, 2019; Ekeland and Rochet, 2020).

Despite the seriousness and pervasiveness of moral hazard, policymakers and scholars have failed to address this issue. To begin with, a government's decision to bailout a bank or a firm is a serious problem with a complex set of consequences for entire societies. Too few research works have been published to analyze what is at stake. This book intends to fill this gap. We have gathered a set of prestigious scholars from different fields including history, economics, law, and philosophy, to advance new insights and solutions to prevent or mitigate the effects of moral hazard. We provide a long-term, interdisciplinary perspective. Our point of departure is the recent evolution of the world economy: financialization and increased industrial concentration have led to situations of "too big to fail." The systemic importance of the banking sector poses increasing challenges to regulatory authorities and policymakers, while big corporations might affect public policies. This situation has reopened a set of questions that require prompt answers, including regulations, governmental intervention, and international cooperation.

Section 2 Outline of the book

The book is divided into three parts. Part I includes two chapters and is conceptual in nature, dealing with the ethics and other fundamental issues connected to moral hazard. Part II provides historical and empirical evidence on moral hazard in international finance. It examines in turn the export credit industry, the international lender of last resort, and the IMF. Finally, Part III deals with moral hazard in the financial and corporate areas. Chapter 10 provides a global conclusion and advances recommendations.

Chapter 2 deals with the role of ethics in moral hazard. Rutger Claassen analyzes how morality came to be intertwined with the term moral hazard. He shows that historically, the term "moral hazard" came with strong moral connotations, as moral *blame* was attached to those abusing insurance schemes. However, economists have taken moral hazard as a neutral, technical term, seeing individuals' risk-adjusting behavior simply as a rational calculated response to insurance and insured situations. But the question still lingers: is morally hazardous behavior – sometimes or always – immoral? Claassen discusses the debate in ethics about this question. He argues that moral hazard is pro tanto morally wrong. The analysis is grounded in the fact that insurance puts people in a fiduciary relationship. They then are under a moral duty to act on behalf of the others in their insurance pool and try to reach the optimum level of social risk. Yet, there are exculpating reasons which diminish moral responsibility. Finally, the policy implications are discussed, illustrated by the moral hazard posed by large banks in the financial crisis.

In Chapter 3, Stefano Ugolini disputes the commonly accepted idea that lending of last resort is necessarily conducive to moral hazard. His chapter questions this claim by tracking the evolution of monetary theory and practice over the very long term. While most economists have seen as inevitable the association between lending of last resort and moral hazard, others (especially Walter Bagehot) have claimed that the two may be separable if "constructive ambiguity" surrounds the conditions at which emergency liquidity may be provided to and accessed by banks. A brief overview of the practices adopted by monetary authorities over the centuries tends to confirm that the separability between lending of last resort and moral hazard may be attainable, but only through a correct and relevant design of banking regulation and liquidity-injecting operations.

In Chapter 4, Gaillard and Darbellay show how the actions undertaken by export credit agencies (ECAs) and export-import banks (EIBs) have encouraged moral hazard and induced risk-taking behaviors. They investigate how and why the legal and regulatory frameworks of ECAs and EIBs have contributed to reinforcing moral hazard. They explain that moral hazard has resulted from a combination of the fierce international competition and the information asymmetry between insurers/lenders, exporters and importers. Gaillard and Darbellay trace the practices of the U.S. Exim Bank in the 1970s. Their narrative suggests that in a context of massive lending to developing countries, this institution refrained from using a reliable country risk rating system and prioritized the foreign borrowers most capable of obtaining preferential treatment from their government. A major yet unsurprising outcome from this situation was that the percentage of non-performing loans soared during 1975–1982 and undermined the credibility of the U.S. Exim Bank.

Chapter 5 provides an overview of the efforts for international cooperation in pursuit of financial stability. Flores Zendejas and Gaillard argue that both creditor and debt moral hazard have undermined the actions of an international lender of last resort (ILOLR). They differentiate historical periods and demonstrate how, during the Pax Britannica years, the Bank of England and the Bank of France were de facto ILOLR and managed to contain both types of moral hazard. In the interwar years, the League of Nations developed new forms of last-resort loans but failed to prevent the Great Depression because of the lack of cooperation between top capital-exporting countries. Finally, since its establishment in 1944, the IMF granted various credit facilities conditioned on the recipient countries accepting macroeconomic stabilization. Flores Zendejas and Gaillard claim that the financial globalization process that started in the 1980s exacerbated *creditor* moral hazard. For them, this issue has been largely overlooked by the IMF but it should be a major source of concern for all policymakers.

Chapter 6 investigates how the IMF manages to fight moral hazard. Giuseppe Bianco describes how debt sustainability analysis and conditionality have been two key policy tools that limit debtor moral hazard. When necessary, a country is required to restructure its debt before being allowed to receive assistance. Next, in exchange for the IMF assistance, a country must commit to economic reforms: this conditionality is intended to ensure that the government "does its homework." The policies of lending into arrears (while taking a senior creditor position) and requiring financing assurances are designed to contain creditor moral hazard. They push private creditors toward a negotiated agreement with their sovereign debtor to solve the debt crisis and facilitate the IMF's intervention. The preferred creditor status of the Fund mitigates both types of moral hazard. This chapter highlights the strengths and inconsistencies in the use and application of these policies.

In Chapter 7, Gaillard and Michalek argue that the frequent bailouts observed during 1970–1984 paved the way to the present moral hazard era. In 1971, the bailout of Lockheed was passed by Congress by a narrow margin, reflecting policymakers' concerns over state interventionism. Yet, Gaillard and Michalek show that during 1974–1981, bailouts became a common policy tool. The size of the entity was clearly a key factor when public authorities had to decide whether to rescue or not (e.g., Chrysler in 1979). The institutionalization of the TBTF policy was completed during 1982–1984. In 1982, the Reagan administration asked for additional IMF quotas to support U.S. banks affected by the sovereign debt turmoil. In 1984, the Comptroller of the Currency established that major banks were now TBTF. For Gaillard and Michalek, this new paradigm encouraged risk-taking and gave birth to an insidious form of "big government."

In Chapter 8, Gotoh and Sinclair contend that the automobile industry has witnessed various examples of moral hazard because of its highly politicized nature. This chapter highlights two contrasting types of moral hazard: the liberal critique of state interventionism and the critical view of short-term financial capitalism. For Gotoh and Sinclair, the former type of moral hazard is seen mainly in coordinated market economies, where the government intervenes through industrial policy and bailouts. The authors present a striking illustration using the Nissan and Renault cases, which were subject to intervention by the Japanese and French governments. They argue that the latter type of moral hazard is observed primarily in liberal market economies, which emphasize short-term shareholder value and financial returns. The most telling example was the General Motors case where insufficient R&D investment and dependence on captive finance served to maintain large dividends and retiree benefits.

Chapter 9 by Cheryl Block addresses unique design and cost-estimation challenges regarding U.S. emergency responses to the 2007–2009 financial crisis and the 2020 COVID-19 pandemic. More specifically, she illustrates that the fragmented and insufficient U.S. emergency response infrastructure often requires rushed, ad hoc solutions to crisis, resulting in inefficient and sloppy solutions. This chapter compares relief and bailout-like intervention designs implemented by the Federal Reserve, other government agencies, and Congress in response to both crises, focusing in particular on the 2008 Emergency Economic Stabilization Act (EESA) and the 2020 Coronavirus

Aid, Relief, and Economic Security Act (CARES Act). It also considers specific budget costs that cannot be readily quantified, including potential moral hazards, indirect relief from special tax breaks, and relief from burdensome regulation.

In the concluding chapter, Gaillard and Michalek summarize the main arguments and findings presented in Chapters 2–9. Next, they advance recommendations to eliminate the roots of moral hazard, going beyond the 'fine tuning' of macroprudential and microprudential policies. First, the Federal Reserve should include the evolution of financial assets' prices in its monetary policy. Second, the strict separation of the deposit-taking function of universal banks from their capital markets activities is advocated. Third, TBTF banks could be compelled to hold a certain percentage of the securities they originate. Fourth, the number of times a security can be used as collateral should be cut dramatically. Fifth, a micro tax on all electronic payments could be implemented to penalize speculative transactions having asymmetric returns relative to their maximum risk. Sixth, certain types of financial products must be prohibited. Seventh, some "safe harbors" embedded within laws and regulations that facilitate morally hazardous behavior should be revisited.

Notes

1 https://www.lexico.com/definition/moral_hazard (last visited 22 June 2021).
2 On the debates on the genealogy of the concept, see Rowell and Connelly (2012).
3 For other authors, moral hazard arises when there is either hidden information or hidden actions, see Hart and Holmström (1987).
4 Zelizer (1979) attributes this evolution to different factors, including economic growth and deeper actuarial knowledge.
5 This differentiation is provided in Abbring et al. (2008, p. 2).
6 Ex ante moral hazard and adverse selection are close concepts, the difference being one of causality: adverse selection implies that an agent can be characterized by different levels of risk (which lead to different kinds of contracts), whereas in ex ante moral hazard, agents first choose the contract and thus, face different incentive schemes. For a comprehensive discussion on these terms see Chiappori (2000).
7 In fact, Horvitz (1975), Humphrey (1975), and Mayer (1975) mulled over how regulators and central bankers should organize to avert a financial crisis, and if necessary, how to provide last-resort loans.
8 See https://www.theguardian.com/us-news/2020/may/03/trump-coronavirus-wealthy-friends-donors-backers; https://www.bloomberg.com/opinion/articles/2020-04-29/ryanair-is-right-about-crack-cocaine-airline-bailouts

References

Abbring, J. H., Chiappori, P-A. and Zavadil, T. (2008) "Better Safe than Sorry? Ex Ante and Ex Post Moral Hazard in Dynamic Insurance Data," *Tinbergen Institute Discussion Paper No. 08-075/3.*

Altamura, C. E. and Flores Zendejas, J. (2020) "Politics, International Banking, and the Debt Crisis of 1982," *Business History Review*, Vol. 94, No. 4, pp. 753–778.

Arrow, K. (1963) "Uncertainty and the Welfare Economics of Medical Care," *American Economic Review*, Vol. 53, No. 5, pp. 941–973.

Baldwin, R. and Weder di Mauro, B. (2020) "Mitigating the COVID Economic Crisis: Act Fast and Do Whatever It Takes", *VOX, CEPR Policy Portal*, available at https://voxeu.org/content/mitigating-covid-economic-crisis-act-fast-and-do-whatever-it-takes.

Bevilacqua, M., Brandl-Cheng, L., Danielsson, J., Ergun, L. M., Uthemann, A. and Zigrand, J-P. (2021) "The Calming of Short-Term Market Fears and Its Long-Term Consequences: The Central Banks' Dilemma," available at 10.2139/ssrn.3774218.

Bignon, V., Flandreau, M. and Ugolini, S. (2012) "Bagehot for Beginners: The Making of Lending-of-Last-Resort Operations in the Mid-19th Century," *Economic History Review*, Vol. 65, No. 2, pp. 580–608.

Chennells, L. and Wingfield, V. (2015) "Bank Failure and Bail-In: An Introduction," *Bank of England, Quarterly Bulletin 2015*, pp. 228–241.

Chiappori, P-A. (2000) "Econometric Models of Insurance under Asymmetric Information," in Dionne, G. (Ed), *Handbook of Insurance*. Huebner International Series on Risk, Insurance, and Economic Security. Dordrecht: Springer Netherlands.

DeLong, J. B. (1991) "Did J. P. Morgan's Men Add Value? An Economist's Perspective on Financial Capitalism," in Temin, P. (Ed), *Inside the Business Enterprise. Historical Perspectives on the Use of Information*. Chicago and London: University of Chicago Press.

Djelic, M-L. and Bothello, J. (2013) "Limited Liability and Its Moral Hazard Implications: The Systemic Inscription of Instability in Contemporary Capitalism," *Theory and Society*, Vol. 42, No. 6, pp. 589–615.

Dowd, K. (1994) "Competitive Banking, Bankers' Clubs, and Bank Regulation," *Journal of Money, Credit and Banking*, Vol. 26, No. 2, pp. 289–308.

Ekeland, I. and Rochet, J-C. (2020) *Il faut taxer la spéculation financière*. Paris: Odile Jacob.

Emmett, R. B. (2011) "Frank H. Knight on the 'Entrepreneur Function' in Modern Enterprise," *Seattle University Law Review*, Vol. 34, No. 4, pp. 1139–1154.

Fetter, F. W. (1965) *Development of British Monetary Orthodoxy, 1797–1875*. Cambridge (MA): Harvard University Press.

Freixas, X. (1999) "Optimal Bail Out Policy, Conditionality and Creative Ambiguity," IDEAS Working Paper Series from RePEc.

Gaillard, N. and Michalek, R. J. (2019) "How and Why Moral Hazard Has Distorted Financial Regulation," in Hira, A., Gaillard, N. and Cohn, T. H. (Eds), *The Failure of Financial Regulation – Why A Major Crisis Could Happen Again*. International Political Economy Series. Cham: Palgrave Macmillan.

Grignon, M., Hurley, J., Feeny, D., Guindon, E. and Hackett, C. (2018) "Moral Hazard in Health Insurance," *Œconomia: History, Methodology, Philosophy*, Vol. 8–3, September, pp. 367–405.

Grossman, R. S. (1992) "Deposit Insurance, Regulation, and Moral Hazard in the Thrift Industry: Evidence from the 1930s," *American Economic Review*, Vol. 82, No. 4, pp. 800–821.

Hart, O. and Holmström, B. (1987) "The Theory of Contracts," in Bewlay, T. F. (Ed), *Advances in Economic Theory: Fifth World Congress*. Econometric Society Monographs. Cambridge: Cambridge University Press.

Horvitz, P. M. (1975) "Failures of Large Banks: Implications for Banking Supervision and Deposit Insurance," *Journal of Financial and Quantitative Analysis*, Vol. 10, No. 4, pp. 589–601.

Humphrey, T. M. (1975) "The Classical Concept of the Lender of Last Resort," *Economic Review, Federal Reserve Bank of Richmond*, January–February, pp. 2–9.

Mas-Colell, A. (1995) *Microeconomic Theory*. New York: Oxford University Press.

Mattli, W. (2019) *Darkness by Design: The Hidden Power in Global Capital Markets*. Princeton: Princeton University Press.

Mayer, T. (1975) "Should Large Banks be Allowed to Fail?," *Journal of Financial and Quantitative Analysis*, Vol. 10, No. 4, pp. 603–610.

McCaffrey, M. (2017) "The Morals of Moral Hazard: A Contracts Approach," *Business Ethics: A European Review*, Vol. 26, No. 1, pp. 47–62.

Moss, D. A. (2004) *When All Else Fails: Government as the Ultimate Risk Manager*. Cambridge (MA): Harvard University Press.

Posner, E. A. (2018) *Last Resort: The Financial Crisis and The Future of Bailouts*. Chicago and London: University of Chicago Press.

Prins, N. (2009) *It Takes a Pillage: An Epic Tale of Power, Deceit, and Untold Trillions*. Hoboken: John Wiley & Sons.

Rosas, G. (2006) "Bagehot or Bailout? An Analysis of Government Responses to Banking Crises," *American Journal of Political Science*, Vol. 50, No. 1, pp. 175–191.

Rousseau, P. L. and Sylla, R. (2003) "Financial Systems, Economic Growth, and Globalization," in Bordo, M. D., Taylor, A. M. and Williamson, J. G. (Eds), *Globalization in Historical Perspective*. Chicago: NBER and University of Chicago Press.

Rowell, D. and Connelly, L. (2012) "A History of the Term 'Moral Hazard'," *Journal of Risk and Insurance*, Vol. 79, No. 4, pp. 1051–1075.

Schenk, C. R. (2014) "Summer in the City: Banking Failures of 1974 and the Development of International Banking Supervision," *English Historical Review*, Vol. 129, No. 540, pp. 1129–1156.

Wilmarth Jr., A. E. (2002) "The Transformation of the U.S. Financial Services Industry, 1975–2000: Competition, Consolidation, and Increased Risks," *University of Illinois Law Review*, Vol. 2002, No. 2, pp. 215–476.

Winkler, A. (2011) "The Joint Production of Confidence: Lessons from Nineteenth-Century US Commercial Banks for Twenty-First-Century Euro Area Governments," *Financial History Review*, Vol. 18, No. 3, pp. 249–276.

Zelizer, V. A. R. (1979) *Morals and Markets: The Development of Life Insurance in the United States*. New York: Columbia University Press.

Part I

Conceptual and theoretical aspects of moral hazard

2 The ethics of moral hazard revisited

Rutger Claassen

Historically, the term "moral hazard" came with strong moral connotations, as moral blame attached to those abusing insurance schemes. However, economists have taken moral hazard as a technical term, seeing individuals' risk-adjusting behavior simply as a rational calculated response to insurance and insured situations. But the question still lingers: is morally hazardous behavior – sometimes or always – immoral? This chapter discusses the debate in ethics about this question. It argues that moral hazard is pro tanto morally wrong. The analysis is grounded in the fact that insurance puts people in a fiduciary relationship. They then are under a moral duty to act on behalf of the others in their insurance pool and try to reach the optimum level of social risk. Yet, there are exculpating reasons which diminish moral responsibility. Finally, the policy implications are discussed, illustrated by the moral hazard posed by large banks in the financial crisis.

Moral hazard refers to the tendency for persons to engage in higher levels of risk-taking if they know they are insured against losses. Without response, this may shift the burden of paying for the possible damage onto the shoulders of insurers and/or the other insured parties. They would then pay the price of such "less careful" behavior. A potential moral conflict is born. This phenomenon is ubiquitous in social and economic life. Here are three prominent examples.

The first illustration comes from the financial sector. Large banks, or other private financial institutions, can take high risks because they know that their actions are – implicitly – underwritten by a promise of governments to bail them out should they find themselves in heavy weather. The phenomenon is known as "too big to fail" (Stern and Feldman, 2004). Knowing this, they are likely to engage in riskier actions than they would have, had such an implicit guarantee not been in place. The sale and repackaging of subprime mortgages in the lead-up to the financial crisis of 2008 is one such example of risky actions (Dowd, 2009; Okamoto, 2009; Dow, 2012; Claassen, 2015). The government's motive for bailing out here is that banks are in a position of *systemic* power and importance (Cline, 1984). One bank's bankruptcy may have negative knock-on effects on other banks, given their close systemic

DOI: 10.4324/9781003139249-2

connections, and hence pose a threat to the functioning of the financial system as a whole. Taxpayers – who ultimately pay the bill in the form of higher taxes and/or a larger public debt – perceive the banks as imposing the costs of moral hazard on them.

A completely different context is that of welfare state benefits. Individuals may take fewer precautions than they otherwise would knowing they are insured in case of unemployment, illness, or workplace accidents. For example, they may spend less money and effort in increasing their personal skills to keep themselves employable, they may unreasonably speak up against their employers in cases of conflict being more willing to risk being fired, they may decrease their work efforts, and prioritize non-work activities. Whenever this leads to unemployment, the costs of their "more risky" behavior are shifted – in public welfare systems at least – unto the state, hence, again, the taxpayers. Many – especially conservative – politicians have argued since the 1980s that these effects are large and justify restricting access and generosity of welfare state schemes, so as to avoid overburdening them. The moral hazard argument has become part of the standard arsenal of those who want to roll back the welfare state (Stone, 2002; Heath, 2009).

Finally, a perhaps less familiar example is that of the legal structure of the business corporation (Djelic and Bothello, 2013). In the 19th century, industrialized countries adopted corporate laws which limited the liability of shareholders in a business corporation. Many businesses are now incorporated as Société Anonyme à Responsabilité Limitée (France), Limited Liability Company (U.S.), or Gesellschaft mit beschränkter Haftung (Germany). These arrangements were new at the time, and vehemently opposed by those who saw limited liability as a privilege diminishing responsible business behavior and encouraging high risk-strategies in business life. A businessman, according to these oppositional voices, should remain personally responsible for losses. This is what it means to be an entrepreneur (Ireland, 2010). In the end, the pressures to allow limited liability were too strong, and the practice was widely adopted. The parties onto whom the risk was shifted include a wide range of stakeholders, from employees of the business, creditors, consumers, third parties like local communities and taxpayers; basically, anyone who at some point may suffer losses due to businesses' risk-taking behavior. Regulations (work and safety regulation, environmental regulation, consumer protection regulation) may be seen as attempts to rein in the effect of a moral hazard enshrined into the very legal constitution of business corporations.

As these illustrations show, the phenomenon is wide-ranging. Discussion of moral hazard started in the 19th century, when life insurance and fire insurance were discussed (Baker, 1996). Health insurance became a prominent example when economists started debating the issue after Arrow's (1963) seminal article on the matter. New areas of application are constantly being opened up. For example, the concept has also been used to describe the effects of policies to save desperate refugees on future refugee numbers (Teitelbaum, 2015) and the effects of humanitarian interventions to protect rebellion groups against genocide on the likelihood of future rebellions (Kuperman, 2008). All these examples vary in their specific characteristics.

Economic analyses of the phenomenon focus on how strong the effect of moral hazard is: how much do individuals in a specific context change their behavior under the influence of insurance? My focus here is different. I assume that there is *some* level of moral hazard going on in examples like the above. It can be a lot, or less so, but for whatever level of moral hazard, we can ask a further, ethical question. This *ethical* question is whether such morally hazardous behavior is *immoral*. Is it merely an economically rational response to conditions or is it an instance of morally blamable behavior? The importance of this ethical question is that any *political* decision about whether or not to insure at all, and/or combat the moral hazards attending insurance, needs to combine economic analysis and ethical judgment. For every case, we need to know how prevalent moral hazard is, and whether it is a moral fault of the insured individual which insurers should be in the business of regulating.

There are only a handful of treatments by ethicists of this question. The leading one is by Benjamin Hale, who argues that moral hazard is *not* immoral. My purpose in this chapter is to argue that moral hazard *is* pro tanto morally wrong. I say pro tanto, because I also outline two important exculpating reasons, which excuse the person posing a moral hazard to others. In Section 1, I start with a brief recap of the debate about the "moral nature" of moral hazard. In Section 2, I introduce the legal category of fiduciary relationships. When people are in such a relationship, they have obligations to act in other-regarding ways. I argue relations under insurance should be seen as fiduciary. In Section 3, I reject Hale's argument, by showing how individuals are under a moral duty to act on behalf of the other people in their insurance pool and try to reach the optimum level of social risk. In Section 4, I discuss two important exculpating reasons, which can lead to diminished moral responsibility on the part of the person posing a moral hazard. In Section 5, I expand the analysis to deal with the special case of public insurance programs, with the bank bailouts as a leading example. Section 6 concludes.

Section 1 Moral hazard as economically rational and morally neutral

I begin with an overview of the debates about the moral nature of moral hazard. Let's start with some history (Baker, 1996; Rowell and Connelly, 2012; Leaver, 2015).

The term "moral hazard" gained traction in the 19th century to designate a certain class of risks for new forms of insurance, such as fire insurance and life insurance. Insurance itself suffered from a moral stigma, since it was associated with gambling and crime (Baker, 1996, pp. 255–259), and its acceptance was contingent, inter alia, on its effectiveness in dealing with moral hazard. 19th-century insurers reacted to moral hazard in two different ways, depending on the two sources of this tendency which they distinguished: character and circumstance. Some people believed simply to have "bad characters", would use every occasion for fraudulent or careless behavior. These people were to be left without insurance. Other people were in principle believed to be of good character, but nonetheless susceptible to temptation. These people could be insured, but the insurance contract had to be structured in such a way that the temptation to moral hazard was minimized (Baker, 1996, p. 241).

In the 19th century the moral lens was as important as the economic one. The best proof of this was that the standard economic solution for dealing with people of bad character – i.e., charging them higher premiums – was judged unacceptable:

> Not all of life, it seems, was to be ceded to the field of Hazard. What remained to be left outside was the realm of evil crime, fraud, and the suspicious "other". Thus, nineteenth-century life and fire insurers limited the insurance of moral hazards, not because of the complexity or for other technical reasons, but because of ideas about right and wrong, as the term "*moral* hazard" suggests. Insurance was a moral enterprise "deeply interested in the growth of public and private honor", and insurance men had a duty to "[g]uard against moral hazard from without" and "against moral perversion from within". Everyone in the enterprise, both insurer and insured, had an obligation to exclude the immoral. (Baker, 1996, p. 254).

Over the course of time, this moral lens on moral hazard has been lost, and an economic lens has become dominant. How did that happen?

From the economist's perspective, moral hazard is one example of a collective action problem, i.e., a situation in which behavior that is individually rational turns out to be collectively suboptimal. Moral hazard frequently occurs in the context of information asymmetries, as a consequence of what economists call "opportunistic behavior."[1] Individuals weigh costs and benefits, and insurance lowers the costs of a certain loss. This gives them an incentive to be less careful, with the predictable result that the insurance pool is overburdened with claims: "less loss from loss [for the individual] means more loss [for the collective]" (Baker, 1996, p. 270). In response, a fine-tuning of the terms of the insurance contract is needed, so as to minimize the opportunities for careless behavior. In the economist's hands, "moral hazard has become exclusively a property of insurance arrangements and not a property of the individuals who enter those arrangements" (Baker, 1996, p. 271). In the economic analysis, moral hazard is morally neutralized. It no longer denotes "bad character" of immoral persons, but simply refers to instrumentally rational action.

The best-known example of this economic approach is found in Mark Pauly's response to a famous 1963 paper by Kenneth Arrow. Arrow introduced the term with respect to medical insurance, as an example of decision-making under uncertainty (Arrow, 1963). This led Mark Pauly, in reply, to complain about the attitude of

> insurance writers' who 'have tended very strongly to look upon this phenomenon (of demanding more at a zero price than at a positive one) as a moral or ethical problem, using emotive words such as "malingering" and "hypochondria," lumping it together with outright fraud in the collection of benefits.

Instead, Pauly argued:

> the response of seeking more medical care with insurance than in its absence is a result not of moral perfidy, but of rational economic behavior. (Pauly, 1968, p. 535).

Arrow, in turn, replied to this by saying that:

> Mr. Pauly's wording suggests that "rational economic behavior" and "moral perfidy" are mutually exclusive categories. No doubt Judas Iscariot turned a tidy profit from one of his transactions, but the usual judgment of his behavior is not necessarily wrong. (Arrow, 1968, p. 538).

What both sides in this debate agree upon, then, is that moral hazard is an example of rational economic behavior. What they disagree on, is whether this is compatible with a judgment that such behavior is also morally wrong.

Most philosophers would agree with Arrow that conceptually there are two different standpoints. The judgment of immorality simply is made from a perspective of morality, which does not coincide with the perspective of instrumental rationality.[2] Arrow's disentanglement of economic rationality and (im)morality as two separate standpoints however merely opens up the possibility that the two may diverge in the case of moral hazard; it doesn't yet decide that matter. Pauly may still be right that all instances of moral hazard are morally unproblematic. Arrow has not given us a reason why some or all instances of moral hazard are morally problematic. To make such judgments, we need a more fine-grained ethical analysis. Therefore, we now turn to the ethicists' treatment of moral hazard.

There are only a handful of relevant contributions, the most important one being from Benjamin Hale.[3] His treatment vindicates Pauly's position: moral hazard is not immoral, it is morally neutral.

Hale's argument starts from the nature of insurance. The crucial point is that insurance is meant to *raise* people's level of risk-taking. For example, without car insurance, driving a car would be potentially very expensive. The costs of an accident being extremely high, everyone would stop driving or drive so slowly that the speed gains of having car traffic in society would be greatly diminished. With insurance, people can drive cars while assuming a higher risk profile (Hale, 2009, p. 11). Hale is not alone in emphasizing this. A similar argument has been made in the context of social risks. By insuring the accidents of modern industrial society, social insurance helped to make the development of such a society possible (Stone, 2002, p. 60). From this perspective, moral hazard is not a *moral* problem; on the contrary, higher levels of risk are the sought-after outcome of introducing insurance schemes.

This does not mean that there is no morally problematic behavior under insurance. Such behavior, however, according to Hale is immoral because of *other* reasons than its being the consequence of moral hazard. For example, insurance may give insured persons incentives to lie when filing an insurance claim. However, the wrongness of the moral hazard here is derivative of the wrongness of lying in general. Lying is morally wrong whether or not there is insurance in place (Hale, 2009, p. 9). In terms of the car example, we can perhaps see street drag-racing as an example of this, taking a deliberate chance of causing lethal accidents. This would be morally wrong whether or not there is insurance in place. Hence, we should distinguish three "zones" of risk-taking (my terminology), as summarized in Table 2.1. Insurance aims to get the behavior of those in the insured pool from the first zone ('A') to the second zone ('B'). However, it stays away from a third zone ('C'), which runs alongside A and B (fraudulent behavior is not a matter of taking higher levels of risk, but a qualitatively different kind of behavior, uncorrelated to any level of risk). Note that some of the behavior in zone C can still be *induced* by insurance (without insurance, lying when filing one's insurance claim would not be possible), but it is not morally wrong because of the mere assumption of a higher level of risk under insurance.

This bifurcation between moral and immoral behavior leads to a bifurcated response strategy on the part of the insurer. All behavior under insurance which is classified as moral, is to be legally permitted. All behavior classified as immoral should be ruled out as illegal. Individuals behaving immorally should be sanctioned by expulsion from the insurance pool. But the fact that insured individuals assume a higher risk profile as a matter of insurance is itself to be expected and is actually the very purpose of insurance. This assumes that we can in practice make a reasonable distinction between moral and immoral behaviors under insurance. Street drag-racers (zone C) risking their own and other people's lives can effectively be separated from careful drivers, and their drivers' licenses can be taken from them. By contrast, what we may call moral hazard (in zone B) is in fact morally acceptable behavior, for which an *economic* response is appropriate. This was exactly the conclusion Pauly also reached. At the same time Hale's argument does justice to the earlier "moralizing" approaches of insurers, by recognizing that intrinsically immoral

Table 2.1 Hale's Categorization of Risks (My Reconstruction)

	Zone A: low levels of risk-taking	*Zone B: high levels of risk-taking*	*Zone C: immoral behavior (irrespective of insurance)*
Example of car insurance	Very cautious driving	Normal driving	Street drag-racing
Response	No insurance needed	Insured against loss	Punished, or excluded from insurance

behavior under insurance may occur as much as outside the insurance context, and sometimes be even triggered by insurance (Zone C). Thus, his argument can be seen as an elegant synthesis of both approaches.

In an earlier paper, I accepted Hale's argument (Claassen, 2015, pp. 536–539) for standard private cases of insurance (and then explained that it did not apply in more complex cases, such as the government's relation to banks' position in the financial crisis). I now think Hale's argument was wrong.

Section 2 The moral basis: a fiduciary theory of insurance

My refutation of Hale's argument will be built on the legal theory of fiduciary relationships. Here I first argue that insurance relations are fiduciary relations. In such relations, individuals have moral obligations towards others to act in an other-regarding manner. This provides the groundwork for the argument in the next section.

In private law, many relationships are classified as contractual. In such relationships, private individuals follow their own purposes. In doing so, they generally do not have to take the purposes of others into account, other than as an informational input when trying to realize their own purposes. For example, a seller needs to know the purposes of his clients (to be able to effectively tailor his offer to their wishes, and be successful in business), but he does not have to optimize his clients' purpose-satisfaction himself. Even stronger, he may legitimately try to increase his own gain at the expense of his client, in a bargaining process over the price. Under contractual conditions, individuals act in a self-regarding manner.

Fiduciary relations (even if established through contract) are different. A fiduciary relation arises when one person, the fiduciary, exercises discretionary power over the interests of another, the beneficiary. Beneficiaries are vulnerable, dependent on their fiduciaries' judgments and actions (Frankel, 2011; Miller, 2014). For example, parents are acting as fiduciaries of their children. When doing so, the latter are vulnerable to the actions of the former. As a consequence, in fiduciary relations, the structure of moral obligations and expectations is different from typical contractual obligations. Fiduciaries have an obligation to act *on behalf of* their beneficiaries, in accordance with their best interests. Law expresses this in terms of two duties: a duty of loyalty and a duty of care. The fiduciary is bound to exercise her power in such a way that she does not betray the interests of her beneficiary, and exercise due diligence in the exercise of her mandate (both of these are 'obligations of means', versus the 'obligation of result', characteristic of contractual relations). Trust underlies the relationship as a whole. The beneficiary must have trust in the fiduciary, and the latter must act in a trustworthy manner, for the relationship to get off the ground, and be sustainable. Fiduciaries are expected to act in an *other-regarding* manner. In their actions, they need to adopt the ends of others as their own (Laby, 2008; Smith, 2014).[4]

It may be thought that this kind of relationship is only at home in the family, possibly extended to cover relations with friends, neighbors, and others to whom one is personally close (Frankel, 2011, p. 57). However, fiduciary relations are also an important part of professional and business life. Relations between professionals and clients are routinely described as fiduciary: doctors are fiduciaries for their patients, teachers for their students, lawyers for their clients. The relation between directors and shareholders is also a standard example of a fiduciary relationship, which brings the concept into the heart of economic life. It is interesting that some scholars are also describing the political relation as a fiduciary one: politicians, once elected or appointed to the role of representatives, are fiduciaries for their citizens. After all, they exercise discretionary power (governmental authority) over their citizens, who must obey the laws they make (Fox-Decent, 2011; Criddle et al., 2018). As this overview shows, fiduciary relations are widespread in all major spheres of life: personal, professional, economic, and political. At their origins lies an *incapacity* on the part of the beneficiary, which can be more principled or more pragmatic. Children simply do not have the skills and experience to raise themselves, patients do not have the knowledge to be their own doctors. Shareholders and citizens have neither the time nor the knowledge to govern their corporations and countries. Given such incapacities, it is more efficient or even the only possibility to have a fiduciary perform the actions which otherwise the beneficiary would have to execute. Note that some of these fiduciary relations are described as a *principal-agent* relationship, which is legally classified as one particular type of fiduciary relationship (Frankel, 2011, p. 42). Hence the introduction of fiduciary duties can often also be seen as answers to what economists refer to as "agency problems."

Turn now to moral hazard. Do insurance contracts create fiduciary relations? In law, when the question is raised at all, this is denied. However, I propose to revisit this judgment. There are two main reasons underlying the denial of fiduciary status to insurance relations; I would argue they are both unconvincing.

The first reason for the denial of fiduciary status focuses on the position of the insurer. Insurers, it is said, stand in contractual relations to their clients. This is necessarily so, since their interests are adversarial in the case of a claim. In order to maintain the viability of their business, insurers must critically scrutinize clients' claims, and reject them where appropriate. This adversarial structure impedes the attribution of fiduciary status. Insurers cannot act on behalf of their clients (Richmond, 1999). While this argument is right as far as it goes, it wholly focuses on the insurer-insured relation. However, I would argue that, most fundamentally, insurance is a relation between a set of insured persons, with the insurer serving merely as a hub. Individuals in the insurance pool insure *each other*; they spread risks amongst the members of the group. Insurance through the hub mobilizes the "law of large numbers" in statistics to capture efficiency gains from spreading risks (Heath, 2009; Landes, 2013).

Therefore, I would propose to see every insured person, with respect to her own actions, as being a fiduciary toward the others in the insurance pool, who are her beneficiaries. Vice versa, she is also a beneficiary with respect to each of these as fiduciaries, as far as their actions are concerned. Overall, the insurance pool can be seen as a web of mutual fiduciary-beneficiary relationships. For example, imagine I have bought cell phone insurance at a new insurance company, called Tom & Jerry's (the example comes from Braynen, 2014). I am now under an obligation (a duty of loyalty) to act on behalf of the other insured persons' interests in keeping the costs of coverage as low as possible. To do so, I must avoid actions that bring unnecessary risk to my cell phone (Questions such as "what is 'as low as possible'?" and "what is 'unnecessary' risk?" are addressed below).[5]

The second reason for denying fiduciary status to the insurance relation is that it seems counterintuitive to see everyday actions I undertake for myself as representing the interests of others. When I lie next to the swimming pool and pull my cell phone out of my bag (with some danger of it falling into the pool), I am seemingly performing a self-regarding action. It is hard to see this innocuous action in terms of "representing" other people's interests. Am I not merely after my own interests in such situations? However, this line of thinking suggests a dichotomy that needs to be firmly rejected. Actions can simultaneously be partly self-regarding *and* partly other-regarding. Insurance adds an invisible but real layer of other-regardingness to a whole range of self-regarding actions. Whether we like it or not, the insurance relation with my cell phone insurer is present in the background at every point in which I am performing self-regarding actions with my cell phone. It is my property, but the risk-sharing arrangement has woven a web of mutual dependence with the other cell phone owners in the pool. We now are a community sharing in the risks of cell phone ownership. The liabilities of cell phone ownership are partially socialized. This is not unlike situations where there is interdependence of interests without uncertainty (cooperative schemes that are not insurance schemes). For example, where a boat crew takes part in a sailing race, each is vulnerable to the others in the boat doing their part of the job (i.e., the main risk here is free riding).

Note how the analysis given in this section provides us with a precise handle on Arrow's intuition, that the same action can be economically rational *and* (potentially) immoral. The economically rational part refers to the self-regarding aspect of our actions, the immoral part to the other-regarding aspect. Immorality does not refer to a qualitatively different class of actions (as it did for Hale), but here becomes *a judgment on one aspect of the same action*. The analysis in terms of a fiduciary relationship has prepared the ground for such judgments of immorality, by showing that we are accepting a moral obligation to act on behalf of others when we are part of the same insurance pool. But note that whether we *actually* violate a moral obligation and act wrongfully when we expose ourselves to higher levels of risk still remains to be argued.

Section 3 The moral wrongness of moral hazard

Building on the analysis above, I will now argue that moral hazard is pro tanto immoral. As a first step, I will adjust Hale's conceptual scheme. Then I will argue that there is a pro tanto moral duty to avoid moral hazard.

Remember that Hale treats the issue in terms of three zones (see Table 2.1) where the purpose is to get society from the first zone (no insurance offered) to the second zone. This is socially optimal. I propose to adjust Hale's scheme in several ways. First, I leave out of consideration his zone C – the independently immoral actions, like insurance fraud. This is not because it does not exist, but because it is irrelevant to this analysis. Then I divide the field of his zones A and B into four zones (see Figure 2.1). Finally, I use a curved line instead of the more generic categories of "lower" and "higher" levels of risk; because the justification of moral hazard in terms of "making possible higher levels of risk" obscures three zones (new zones B, C, and D) which all permit higher risk levels than the original zone A without insurance, but are nonetheless very different.

The purpose of insurance, following Hale's argument, is to bring a group of persons from zone A to B. In zone A insurance is not worth having since individuals take very low risk (no demand). The costs outweigh the benefits of insurance. In zone D this is also the case, albeit for opposite reasons. Here individuals take excessive risks, and the costs outweigh the benefits too. Economically rational insurance would be worth having but insurers will not offer it (no supply). In zones B and C, benefits outweigh costs, and insurance will be offered. The shape of the curve is motivated by the idea that there is an optimal level of risk, represented by point S. Below this optimum, social welfare can still be enhanced by taking more risks (which will lead to more opportunities for socially beneficial innovations; but also more "peace of mind" on the part of the insured risk-takers, which is an intrinsic benefit of

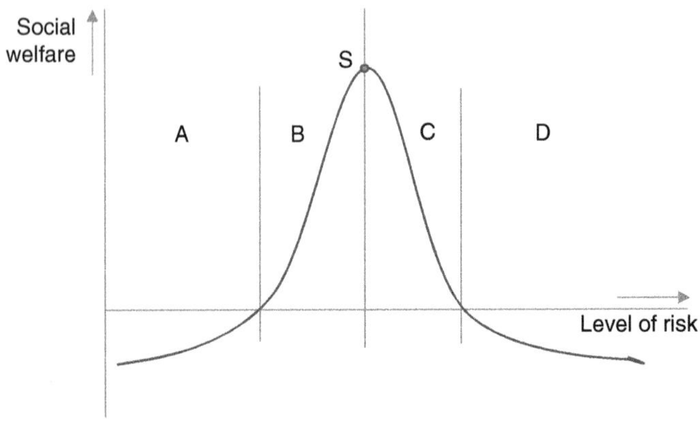

Figure 2.1 Moral Hazard Revisited.

insurance). Beyond the optimum, excessive risk-taking leads to a lower net gain from a social perspective, which at some point turns into a net loss.[6]

From the social point of view, individuals should target the level of risk they take to the social optimum, S. I define moral hazard as referring to the whole of zones B+C. Individuals pose a moral hazard to others *when (i) they increase their exposure to risk under insurance* (as was the intention of the scheme; hence there is a welfare improvement over zone A), *but (ii) they either take too little or too much risk, compared to the socially optimal level S.* They may have good reasons for doing this (i.e., they reach their personal optimum), but by doing so they shift the costs of their behavior to others. If we return to the example of car insurance, imagine that point S reflects the publicly determined speed limit. When all drivers orient their speed to this point, the car insurance system's ratio of social benefits (reduced time of transportation) and social costs (car accidents) is optimal. In zone C, drivers are breaking the speed limit. The speed limit helps individuals to orient their behavior as closely as possible to the optimum. In zone B, they drive too slowly, hence also foregoing some of the gains of the car insurance system. The analysis suggests this may be just as morally problematic, although this rarely is the focus of attention (in the following I will focus on zone C, since moral hazard is mostly thought of where people take too much risk).

All such behavior in zones B and C is *pro tanto* immoral. It may be only slightly immoral, if it is close to S, or very immoral, if further removed from S. I define the moral duty of individuals who are part of an insurance scheme as follows:

MORAL DUTY: Every individual in an insurance pool has a moral duty to target their level of personal risk-taking as closely as possible to point S.

But *why* is this a moral duty? In his article, Hale admits that welfarist doctrines in ethics can see the inefficiencies produced by moral hazard (which he does not question) as immoralities because for these doctrines the principle of efficiency is itself a moral principle. But he dismisses this line of reasoning without much argument (Hale, 2009, 4). In my view, the inefficiency of not reaching the optimum S can be evaluated as immoral (or at least "morally suboptimal", if one wants). Such judgments of immorality come in two different flavors, depending on the situation.

S is a moral requirement in a *weak sense* when the goal of the insurance scheme (i.e., an efficient scheme of cell phone insurance) is a collective goal shared by all the insured, but where this goal does not represent a moral requirement in itself. It is not as if the insured *owe* each other the existence of such an insurance scheme. It is not a moral requirement, but merely a pragmatic convenience for them to have one. In such cases, the moral requirement is generated by the *promise* made between the insured persons when creating their pool. Having opted in, you now have a moral obligation to organize your behavior toward the optimum as much as is possible for you. Nobody denies that breaking one's promises is pro tanto immoral. Here this is the basis of the claim that not targeting one's behavior toward S is immoral. Many private schemes of insurance fit this description, since the private sphere is characterized by voluntary interactions to reach goals that are themselves not morally mandatory.

S is a moral requirement in a *strong sense* where it is a matter of justice or fundamental rights to implement an insurance scheme in the first place. For example, arguably citizens owe each other insurance against major health risks. Similarly, I argued elsewhere that the government's rescue actions toward big banks, in the end, are at the service of a fundamental right of all citizens to an adequate standard of living (Claassen, 2015, pp. 530–534). Since matters of justice and fundamental rights often become matters of public concern and hence government action, most of the insurance schemes fitting into the strong sense are coercively imposed insurance schemes, located in the public sector (see Section 5 below for specific analyses of such schemes). Here the point is that in such cases, the promises, in the sense of collectively agreed public policies, merely serve to ratify, not to create, this underlying moral requirement. The order of justification hence is reversed, compared to the weak, private cases.

What is true for both weak and strong cases, is that there indeed is a duty of no-waste. The most optimal level (point S) is a moral requirement. Given scarcity of resources, anything less imposes an unnecessary claim on other people's private budgets or on public budgets (thereby representing an opportunity cost). The former should be at the free disposal of private persons themselves, while the latter can be better used to serve other urgent demands of justice. Note that my analysis shows that one does not need to be a welfarist to recognize the morality of efficiency. For private insurance, anyone accepting the basic morality of promises would be committed to the same viewpoint. For public insurance, anyone holding a non-welfarist theory of justice would also be committed to efficiently reaching the aims of that theory of justice.[7]

This general moral requirement is "distributed" over the individuals participating in the insurance pool, who each hold a part of the duty to realize a successful insurance scheme. Here the fiduciary character of the insurance relation kicks in. Each participant is vulnerable to the level of care observed by the others, but each participant also has a discretionary power with respect to their own behavior, to which the others are vulnerable. The duty of loyalty goes beyond duties to act honestly in contractual, adversarial relations, and asks each participant to see themself as a representative of these others, in the relevant respect. The duty does not prescribe particular well-specified courses of action. Rather, in unpredictable circumstances, the right course of action can only be well-judged by the participant themself. They must exercise their own *judgment* to decide what is in the best interests of their beneficiaries (Smith, 2014, p. 148). Fulfilling a fiduciary duty is a matter of having a loyal attitude (Laby, 2008, p. 146). From the perspective of the vulnerable others, this may be frustrating since they cannot control the fiduciary's actions as much as they perhaps would like to. It also leads to an important problem of uncertainty about what exactly is to be expected, which I discuss further below.

This finishes the explanation and defense of a pro tanto moral duty to avoid exploiting moral hazard at a cost to others. However, this is not the end of the story. As is familiar in ethics, a pro tanto duty is not the same thing as an all-things-considered duty. There may be countervailing considerations that cancel the immorality of moral hazard.

Section 4 Two exculpating reasons

From the definition of the moral duty above ("closely as possible"), it becomes clear that individuals can be excused whenever their level of risk was not under their (full) personal control. This is the basis for two major exculpating reasons. One is general and will be dealt with briefly; the other is particular to insurance relations and will be dealt with at length.

A very general reason, which holds true in and beyond insurance relations, is that one cannot be personally responsible for matters beyond one's control. There is an extensive philosophical literature on this. For example, luck egalitarians have argued that every action is either "a matter of chance" (or circumstance) or "a matter of choice" (or control). This chance/choice dichotomy structures, they argue, our moral landscape. Whenever something bad befalls an individual which was beyond his control ("bad brute luck"), society should compensate them. Whenever something bad happens for which individuals implicitly opted by taking their chances ("bad option luck"), no such compensation is due. Much debate has been waged on which factors belong in which category. For example, Ronald Dworkin (1981) argued that "preferences" (such as a preference for working few hours and shirking on the job) are always under one's control, while "talents" (such as marketable job-related talents) and handicaps are a matter of chance. Hence the untalented may get some compensation at the expense of the talented. Others have argued that the moral landscape should be carved up differently, with both preferences and talents sometimes under one's control, sometimes not (Cohen, 1989).

Regardless of these debates, the relevant point here is a more general one. Individuals who present a moral hazard sometimes cannot prevent themselves from doing so. In these cases, they bear less or even no personal responsibility. Their deviation from moral behavior is excused. This is important, because there is a substantial risk in assessments of moral hazard to "blame the victim." As Iris Young (2011) has convincingly argued in connection to U.S. debates about the welfare state, attributions of personal responsibility often ignore the structural constraints and background injustices under which welfare recipients must act. While I will not go into these matters here, I do think that they are incredibly important in weighing the appeals to moral hazard in policy debates.

The second exculpating reason relates more specifically to the insurance context. This is about information asymmetry, i.e., the difference between the "epistemic states" (Braynen, 2014, p. 43) of the insured and the insurer, and about who is responsible for this difference. One crucial question we have not addressed in the previous section is: how can an individual assess where point S lies? How does he/she know what it means to fulfill the moral duty identified above? Recall the example of the posted speed limit above, in the context of car insurance. Such a limit is an example of a clear, publicly known norm, about which little confusion arises. Hence one can clearly distinguish between those drivers who do, and those who do not target their behavior toward the social optimum. However, moral hazard often is the result of a vague norm, or even absence of norms, about how to behave. Braynen (2014, p. 44) gives the example of an imaginary "Tom and Jerry" company opening a cell phone insurance company, on the basis of flawless calculations indicating 4 in 100 cell phones break by accident. After insurance, the insured report 8 in 100 cell phones break down. There is no fraud, the increase is simply the result of less careful behavior. How can the situation be morally assessed?

The insurance contract is incomplete, to the extent that it doesn't specify acceptable or unacceptable actions to be undertaken with your cell phone. Imagine part of this epistemic uncertainty is disambiguated: Tom and Jerry find out that 25% of the increase is due to water-related accidents (cell phones in swimming pools, etc.), and they subsequently exclude water damage. This reduces reported accidents from 8 to 7 per 100. The insured have now been made morally (and legally) responsible for these 25% of cases. The new insurance contract has reduced the area of uncertainty, i.e., the area for which it is not clear whether the insured are *morally* to blame, because the behavioral expectations have not (yet) been made explicit. Reduced, but not eliminated. For example, is it reckless to do any of the following:

- i put your cell phone in the sun for two hours, causing overheating?
- ii put it on a low table where your two-year-old toddler can grab it?
- iii leave it in your jacket in the wardrobe in a restaurant?

Or are these the kinds of innocent behaviors that often end well, and that typify a more "worry-free" lifestyle, i.e., the kind of life which insurance is meant to make possible in the first place? In other words, are we in zone B, with these behaviors? Some would make a case that as long as a specific kind of behavior, such as (i) to (iii) above (an "action-type", as philosophers would say) has not been specified as problematic by the insurer, then it should be judged morally acceptable. Otherwise, it was up to the insurer to make regulations on the point. The whole of zones B and C should be exculpated in advance, because of this reason. This would make moral hazard morally justifiable after all (and validate Pauly's merely economic lens on the problem).

However, this in my view is flawed. The inability of the other insured persons in the insurance pool to specify all the act-tokens falling under the three action-types described above leaves the situation vulnerable to the judgment of the fiduciary. They have to maintain a standard of "reasonable carefulness" in their actions. The open-ended nature of the fiduciary's discretionary power and responsibility over the cell phone makes any pre-existing assessment by the vulnerable beneficiaries (the others in the pool) practically impossible. Consider that zone C could include each of the following actions:

(i-a)
one leaves one's cell phone in the sun for two hours, mid-spring in Spain (the phone survives);

(i-b)
one leaves one's cell phone in the sun for two hours, on a Caribbean cruise mid-summer (the phone is broken);

(ii-a)
one leaves one's phone on a low table; one's toddler has never violently smashed objects before, although they have by accident sometimes knocked objects over (the phone survives);

(ii-b)
one leave one's phone on a low table; one's toddler has a history of violently smashing objects against the wall (the phone is broken);

(iii-a)
one leaves the phone in a jacket in the wardrobe in a quiet village restaurant, where one knows the place and the owner;

(iii-b)
one leaves the phone in a jacket in the wardrobe in a trendy, crowded Manhattan restaurant that has a sign disclaiming risk to personal belongings.

In each of these three cases, one can argue that the fiduciary has broken a beneficiary's trust by engaging in behavior type-b. To be sure, type-a is also already "beyond the optimum," in that too many broken cell phones come out of type-a behaviors. But these are still to be excused, being reasonably close to S (i.e., in the targeted "zone" of S). Type-b behavior, however, clearly betrays an error of judgment. And in the given context, an error of judgment is a moral failure. There may be a grey zone but, at some point, there is a class of act-tokens about which most of the beneficiaries would say, in hindsight, that the fiduciary acted with insufficient care. This is the class of immoral actions under insurance, which triggers judgments that a person has exhibited morally hazardous behavior. Hence the discussion here makes a slight modification to the discussion in Section 3. Instead of seeing the optimum as a single point S, it rather is an area around S, a zone in which there is moral consensus.

Accordingly, a closer inspection of the problem of information asymmetry leads us to refine the analysis of Section 3. Moral hazard relates to behavior that falls outside of an area around S; within that area, one is exculpated. The refinement here leaves the analysis of the basic immorality of moral hazard intact while suggesting that there is some scope for behavior that is to be excused.

Section 5 The public context: the imposition of insurance

The analysis so far has explained how and why moral hazard, as defined, is immoral. This was demonstrated using a simple example of private cell phone insurance. This however is important for complex cases in public contexts, such as bank bailouts in financial crises, as well. Such cases build upon – and thus require – the foundational immorality explained so far. Immorality does not kick in *ex nihilo* in such cases; rather it is *aggravated* by these circumstances. To explain whether the public's moral outrage about the 2008–2009 bailouts was justified, we need both.

Public insurance has two special characteristics compared to private insurance. The first one we saw above, when analyzing the reasons for the immorality of moral hazard: public insurance is an answer to a moral requirement itself – in terms of social justice and/or fundamental rights of citizens. Hence the banks' excessive risk-taking generated the kind of moral blame which is always expressed by those in an insurance pool (the beneficiaries) when they find out one of them (the fiduciary) has been taking excessive risks (cf. leaving one's cell phone in the Caribbean sun). The second feature of public insurance is that it is mandatory and coercive: individual citizens are not allowed to opt out. The two features are related. Precisely because, say, health insurance or the stability of the banking system are moral requirements for the public, the costs of maintaining these schemes are imposed on all, through raising mandatory premiums or taxes (or budget cuts on social programs following the bailouts). I will now argue that this aggravates the immorality, because it reduces the response options for the rest of the pool.

To explain this, I first need to introduce some terminology. How to think about the response options of insurers (acting on behalf of all in the pool), in general, when they discover that one or several persons in their pool have been taking excessive risk?

In a perceptive article, Andrew Williams (2009, pp. 501–502) has introduced the idea of a public policy trilemma (I will give my own, idiosyncratic, reconstruction). This trilemma shows how there are three options to respond to moral hazard (see Figure 2.2). Imagine there is a basic requirement of social justice, called "personal health." All people in a society, as a matter of justice, are owed access to medical resources, up to some threshold level,

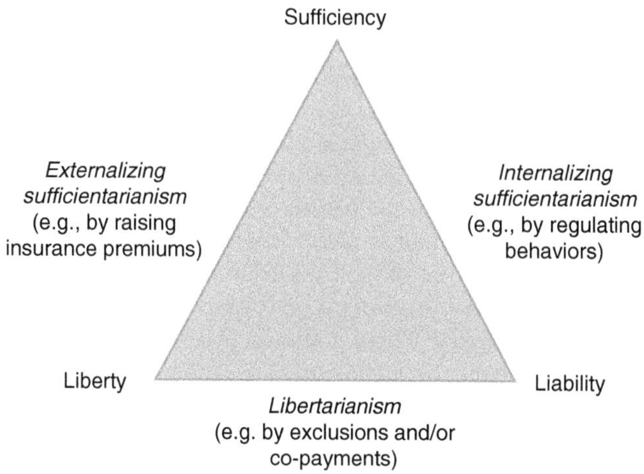

Figure 2.2 Public Policy Trilemma.

which we call "sufficiency." As a consequence, government implements public health insurance. Now a person's excessive risk-taking with one's health (discretionary lifestyle choices) may raise the costs of health care for all (moral hazard). In reply, government can do three things. It can maintain the person's liberty to engage in such risks, but hold him personally liable for this choice, and exclude him from insurance coverage; either altogether or exclusions for coverage of specified medical treatments (A financially based strategy with the same effect is to impose co-payments, co-insurance or deductibles). This will make him fall below the sufficiency threshold. This choice is called "libertarianism" (see Figure 2.2). If applied in the extreme, this abolishes the insurance scheme altogether. In a libertarian society, everyone is free to take the risks they want, but are also liable for the costs themselves. Alternatively, the government can maintain sufficiency for these persons: this is the "sufficientarian" view of justice. However, it can do so in two very different ways. One is by maintaining the person's liberty but canceling his liability. The costs are taken over by the collective. This is called "externalizing sufficientarianism", since the individual's costs are externalized. This will raise insurance premiums for all. The other, third way, is by imposing behavioral regulations and controls on the person, so that they cannot costlessly continue their risky ways. This is called "internalizing sufficientarianism", since they must now internalize the costs of their lifestyle themself. Their liability is maintained, their liberty restricted.[8]

We can learn from this trilemma that no strategy is without its own disadvantages. Out of the three basic moral values (sufficiency, liberty, and liability/responsibility), one can choose a combination of any two, but not all three. The trilemma indicates that an insurer has at least three different strategies at their disposal to react to moral hazard. The insurer can hence make a moral choice about which values to uphold and which value to give up (mixed strategies are thinkable, since one can position one's strategy anywhere within the areas indicated by the triangle, but any chosen point will involve compromises).

With this conceptual framework at hand, we can now better understand moral condemnations surrounding bank bailouts. Given the nature of the situation, out of the three available strategies, two were unavailable. The unavailability of libertarianism follows from the nature of public insurance itself. *If* one judged that it is a moral requirement to maintain a sufficiency level, then libertarianism is off the table. In the case of the bank bailout, some libertarians did argue that one should let financial institutions go bankrupt, since only this course of action would let liability fall where it should (Miron, 2009). Most people rejected this position, given the effects of such bankruptcies on the economy (hence all citizens), i.e., the systemic nature of the risks involved. But that means the government's only options were to consider internalizing or externalizing sufficientarianism (or a mixed policy of both). The further problem, however, is that internalizing sufficientarianism by its nature is a *forward-looking* strategy. It can only be implemented for future cases. Once some insured persons have engaged in excessive risks, the costs must be borne – either by themselves or by the insurance pool. Hence the only available option to deal with the financial crisis was to bail out distressed banks, thus externalizing sufficientarianism.

Moral condemnations of bank bailouts can be analyzed as a composite of two mutually reinforcing problems. First, moral condemnations of banks' excessive risk-taking have their basis in a violation of the contract to target one's own behavior as closely as possible to the social optimum. Second, the moral anger is aggravated by having no other option to resort to than to bear the costs of this collectively through the bailouts (which will increase public debt, lead to cuts in social programs and arguably inspire future morally hazardous behavior). While the example in this section has been the financial crisis of 2008–2009, one can suspect that a similar analysis applies to other cases of moral hazard which raise public concern. For example, similar concerns should be raised about the bailouts and rescue packages passed during the Covid-19 pandemic (see Block, Chapter 9 of this volume).

Section 6 Conclusion

This chapter has investigated the moral nature of moral hazard. My analysis supports the idea first suggested by Kenneth Arrow that increasing one's exposure to risk in the face of insurance can be immoral. However, it does so by addressing the important argument made in the ethical literature by Ben Hale: insurance schemes are socially beneficial exactly because they allow people to increase their risks. The way out of this conundrum is to recognize that there is a socially optimal level of risk-taking, which is not the maximal level. When insured persons fail to target their behavior sufficiently closely to this optimal level, they exploit the other members in the insured pool. When doing so, they fail to behave as good fiduciaries toward the others in the pool, thereby disincentivizing reflexive fiduciary behavior from such others.

This logic can become widespread, as illustrated by the financial crisis. If people start to exploit insurance schemes, such behavior may be infectious, i.e., others may be encouraged to do so too. This raises premiums for all and decreases the viability of the insurance pool itself. In the end, the insurance scheme will collapse. What is needed if we want to maintain insurance for all, especially in public policy contexts, is a strategy of what I have called "internalizing sufficientarianism", which regulates the behavior of the individual insured persons with the goal of reducing if not eliminating exploitative risk-taking. This will maintain the viability of the insurance pool, without asking others to pay the price.

Acknowledgment

I would like to thank Txai de Almeida Brito, Michael Bennett, Huub Brouwer, and Yara al Salman for their feedback and discussion. I thank Norbert Gaillard, Xavier Landes, and Maurits de Jongh for their extensive comments on an earlier draft. This work is part of the research program "Private Property and Political Power", with project number 360-20-390, which is financed by the Dutch Research Council (NWO).

Notes

1 For an illustration, see Darbellay and Gaillard, Chapter 4 of this volume.

2 Sometimes the latter standpoint is called "value rationality", following Max Weber's distinction between instrumental and value rationality (this terminology has the merit of making it clear that moral behavior is also rational, in its own way).

3 Besides Hale, only Braynen (2014) and McCaffrey (2017) aim to provide a new ethical argument about the morality of moral hazard. Heath (2009) and Landes (2013) have illuminating discussions of moral hazard, but do not provide a new argument. Claassen (2015) largely follows Hale, with an application to the financial crisis.

4 These two articles link the fiduciary duty to Kant's category of wide, imperfect duties.

5 This shows that we can see the insurer as a fiduciary, but only in the sense that he represents *all the other* insured persons' interests when he is critically examining whether *my* claim is worth accepting. Perhaps a more useful way to put this is that the insurer is a *judge*: he must arbitrate between me (fiduciary) and the others (beneficiaries) in deciding whether or not I have kept my duty of loyalty to them. This clears up another reason for denying fiduciary status to insurance contracts: that there is no concrete beneficiary. Indeed, there is a pool of beneficiaries on behalf of which I must take care. Multi-beneficiary schemes are a familiar figure in fiduciary law (Miller and Gold, 2015).

6 See also Pauly (2007) on the "optimal level of cost-sharing" in health insurance.

7 For my own theory of justice, see Claassen (2018).
8 The prudential rules imposed on financial institutions, especially the systemic ones, exemplify "internalizing sufficientarianism" strategies; see Flores and Gaillard, Chapter 5 of this volume.

References

Arrow, K. (1963) "Uncertainty and the Welfare Economics of Medical Care," *American Economic Review*, Vol. 53, No. 5, pp. 941–973.

Arrow, K. (1968) "The Economics of Moral Hazard: Further Comment," *American Economic Review*, Vol. 58, No. 3, pp. 537–539.

Baker, T. (1996) "On the Genealogy of Moral Hazard," *Texas Law Review*, Vol. 75, No. 2, pp. 237–292.

Braynen, W. (2014) "Moral Dimensions of Moral Hazards," *Utilitas*, Vol. 26, No. 1, pp. 34–50.

Claassen, R. (2015) "Financial Crisis and the Ethics of Moral Hazard," *Social Theory and Practice*, Vol. 41, No. 3, pp. 527–551.

Claassen, R. (2018) *Capabilities in a Just Society. A Theory of Navigational Agency*. Cambridge: Cambridge University Press.

Cline, W. (1984) *International Debt: Systemic Risk and Policy Response*. Washington, DC: Institute for International Economics.

Cohen, G.A. (1989) "On the Currency of Egalitarian Justice," *Ethics*, Vol. 99, No. 4, pp. 906–944.

Criddle, E., Fox-Decent, E., Gold, A., Kim, S. H. and Miller, P. (Eds) (2018) *Fiduciary Government*. Cambridge: Cambridge University Press.

Djelic, M-L. and Bothello, J. (2013) "Limited Liability and Its Moral Hazard Implications: The Systemic Inscription of Instability in Contemporary Capitalism," *Theory & Society*, Vol. 42, No. 6, pp. 589–615.

Dow, S. (2012) "Economics and Moral Sentiments. The Case of Moral Hazard," in Castro Caldas, J. and Neves, V. (Eds), *Facts, Values and Objectivity in Economics*. London/New York: Routledge.

Dowd, K. (2009) "Moral Hazard and the Financial Crisis," *Cato Journal*, Vol. 29, No. 1, pp. 141–166.

Dworkin, R. (1981) "What Is Equality? Part 2: Equality of Resources," *Philosophy & Public Affairs*, Vol. 10, No. 4, pp. 283–345.

Fox-Decent, E. (2011) *Sovereignty's Promise. The State as Fiduciary*. Oxford: Oxford University Press.

Frankel, T. (2011) *Fiduciary Law*. Oxford: Oxford University Press.

Hale, B. (2009) "What's So Moral About The Moral Hazard?," *Public Affairs Quarterly*, Vol. 23, No. 1, pp. 1–25.

Heath, J. (2009) *Filthy Lucre. Economics for People Who Hate Capitalism*. Toronto, Ontario: HarperCollins.

Ireland, P. (2010) "Limited Liability, Shareholder Rights and the Problem of Corporate Irresponsibility," *Cambridge Journal of Economics*, Vol. 34, No. 5, pp. 837–856.

Kuperman, A. (2008) "The Moral Hazard of Humanitarian Intervention: Lessons from the Balkans," *International Studies Quarterly*, Vol. 52, No. 1, pp. 49–80.

Laby, A. (2008) "The Fiduciary Obligation as the Adoption of Ends," *Buffalo Law Review*, Vol. 56, No. 1, pp. 99–167.

Landes, X. (2013) "The Normative Foundations of (Social) Insurance: Technology, Social Practice and Political Philosophy," *Working Paper-LPF 6*, Torino: Centro Einaudi & Laboratorio di Politica Comparata e Filosofia Pubblica.

Leaver, A. (2015) "Fuzzy Knowledge: An Historical Exploration of Moral Hazard and Its Variability," *Economy & Society*, Vol. 44, No. 1, pp. 91–109.

McCaffrey, M. (2017) "The Morals of Moral Hazard: A Contracts Approach," *Business Ethics: A European Review*, Vol. 26, No. 1, pp. 47–62.

Miller, P. (2014) "The Fiduciary Relationship," in Gold, A. and Miller, P. (Eds), *Philosophical Foundations of Fiduciary Law*. Oxford: Oxford University Press.

Miller, P. and Gold, A. (2015) "Fiduciary Governance," *William & Mary Law Review*, Vol. 57, No. 2, pp. 513–586.

Miron, J. (2009) "Bailout or Bankruptcy? A Libertarian Perspective on the Financial Crisis," *Cato Journal*, Vol. 29, No. 1, pp. 1–17.

Okamoto, K. (2009) "After the Bailout: Regulating Systemic Moral Hazard," *University of California Law Review*, Vol. 57, No. 1, pp. 183–236.

Pauly, M. (1968) "The Economics of Moral Hazard: Comment," *American Economic Review*, Vol. 58, No. 3, pp. 531–537.

Pauly, M. (2007) "The Truth about Moral Hazard and Adverse Selection," *Lourie Lecture Policy Brief No. 36/2007*. Syracuse: Syracuse University.

Richmond, D. (1999) "Trust Me: Insurers Are Not Fiduciaries to Their Insureds," *Kentucky Law Journal*, Vol. 88, No. 1, pp. 1–32.

Rowell, D. and Connelly, L. (2012) "A History of the Term 'Moral Hazard'," *Journal of Risk and Insurance*, Vol. 79, No. 4, pp. 1051–1075.

Smith, L. (2014) "Can We Be Obliged to Be Selfless?," in Gold, A. and Miller, P. (Eds), *Philosophical Foundations of Fiduciary Law*. Oxford: Oxford University Press.

Stern, G. and Feldman, R. (2004) *Too Big To Fail. The Hazards of Bank Bailouts*. Washington, DC: Brookings Institution Press.

Stone, D. (2002) "Beyond Moral Hazard: Insurance as Opportunity," in Baker, T. and Simon, J. (Eds), *Embracing Risk. The Changing Culture of Insurance and Responsibility*. Chicago: University of Chicago Press.

Teitelbaum, M. (2015) "The Truth About the Migrant Crisis. Tragic Choices, Moral Hazards, and Potential Solutions," *Foreign Affairs*. https://s.gifford.ucdavis.edu/uploads/filer_public/b9/28/b9284ac6-06fc-4588-ae30-2b8b38a39ffd/paper_teitelbaum_for-martin-seminar.pdf

Williams, A. (2009) "Liberty, Equality, and Property," in Dryzek, J., Honig, B. and Phillips, A. (Eds), *The Oxford Handbook of Political Theory*. Oxford: Oxford University Press.

Young, I. M. (2011) *Responsibility for Justice*. Oxford: Oxford University Press.

3 Moral hazard and lending of last resort

Stefano Ugolini

Nowadays, the idea that lending of last resort is necessarily conducive to moral hazard appears to be generally accepted. This chapter questions this received wisdom by tracking the evolution of monetary theory and practice over the very long term. While most economists have seen as inevitable the association between lending of last resort and moral hazard, others (especially Walter Bagehot) have claimed that the two may be separable if "constructive ambiguity" surrounds the conditions at which emergency liquidity may be accessed by banks. A brief overview of the practices adopted by monetary authorities over the centuries tends to confirm that the separability between lending of last resort and moral hazard may be attainable, but only through a correct design of banking regulation and liquidity-injecting operations.

On the very eve of the United Kingdom's departure from the European Union in February 2020, a YouGov poll found that the majority of Scottish voters had now shifted in favor of independence, yet by far the most popular reason advocated in favor of remaining in the U.K. was that "if Scotland faced financial problems, the U.K. would have the resources to help."[1] In all likelihood, behind this preoccupation stood the memory of the dramatic 2008 bailouts by the U.K. government of Scotland's two banking behemoths, Royal Bank of Scotland (RBS) and Halifax Bank of Scotland (HBOS); in fact, on the eve of the 2014 referendum, RBS had explicitly threatened to leave an independent Scotland.[2] Threats by banks to move their headquarters from an independence-seeking region in order to secure the assistance of public authorities are not specific to Scotland – Québec[3] and Catalonia[4] shared in that experience. Yet, a priori, should not the chance of no longer having to potentially implement very costly interventions to support ailing banks be a reason in favor of independence rather than against it? This paradox shows how the principle of unconditional support to unsound financial institutions has become deeply rooted in the public opinion of our time. But is this strict association between liquidity assistance and financial misbehavior really inevitable? How did we get there? And is not there any alternative available? To shed light on these questions, this chapter will reconstruct the genesis of the

DOI: 10.4324/9781003139249-3

debate on the relationship between lending of last resort and moral hazard. It will also track the historical evolution of the monetary practices aimed to assist the banking sector in times of emergency.

The modern literature has often tended to conflate the two forms of ex-post intervention to ensure financial stability – viz. *lending of last resort* (assistance to illiquid but solvent intermediaries) and *bailout* (assistance to illiquid and insolvent intermediaries) – in view of the fact that illiquidity and insolvency may not be separable phenomena (see, e.g., Goodhart, 1999).[5] Despite the actual inseparability of illiquidity and insolvency, lending of last resort and bailout arguably remain different kinds of policies – lending of last resort being a rule-based intervention, while bailout being a discretionary one. The question of the moral hazard implications of bailouts is hardly an interesting one, as the literature has universally acknowledged these to be substantial. That is why this chapter will only focus on the subtler and more controversial question of the moral hazard implications of lending of last resort, which is (unlike bailouts) universally recognized as a welfare-maximizing policy *per se* (Ugolini, 2017, pp. 107–118). After all, bailouts require the deep pockets of taxpayers and therefore are a matter for fiscal authorities. In this chapter, the focus will be kept on monetary rather than fiscal authorities.

In the remainder of this chapter, I will proceed as follows. First, I will reconstruct the original arguments of the debate on the relationship between lending of last resort and moral hazard, as they were set in the 1860s by the famous Bagehot-Hankey controversy. Second, I will show how the debate evolved in recent decades, following the adoption of the conceptual framework originally developed by insurance theory. Third, I will discuss the limits of the current state of the debate, especially in what concerns the question of the alleged inseparability between lending of last resort and moral hazard. Fourth, I will present a very synthetic historical outline of the evolution of the practices aimed at minimizing the moral hazard potentially associated with liquidity provision by monetary authorities. The chapter will end with some general conclusions.

Section 1 The origins of the debate: Bagehot vs Hankey

The main arguments of the debate on the relationship between lending of last resort and moral hazard were notoriously first established in mid-Victorian Britain, with the famous Bagehot–Hankey controversy (Fetter, 1965; Goodhart, 1988; Bignon et al., 2012; Awrey, 2020).[6] The controversy took place in the context of the violent financial crisis of 1866. In May 1866 Overend, Gurney & Co Ltd, London's biggest bill broking company (the 19th-century equivalent to a modern-day money market fund), found itself in deep insolvency and sought support from the Bank of England. The Bank refused to bail out the company, thus leaving it to fail. News of Overend's failure sparked a huge panic and a rush to liquidity on the London money market. The Bank's standing facility was inundated with demands for credit.

As monetary creation was strictly limited by Peel's Act of 1844, in order to be able to meet all demands, the Old Lady of Threadneedle Street had to ask the government for a temporary suspension of the Act – as it had already been forced to do in the two preceding crises of 1847 and 1857. The government immediately agreed: once granted the ability to create unlimited amounts of money, the Bank promptly met all eligible demands for credit, but at very high interest rates (Flandreau and Ugolini, 2014).

It was during those days of big financial turmoil that *The Economist* magazine, whose leading editor was Walter Bagehot,[7] started to publish a series of articles criticizing the Bank's attitude during the crisis. The articles did not question the refusal to engineer a bailout for Overend Gurney (which, to the contrary, they warmly approved), nor did they deny that the Bank was rightly behaving as a lender of last resort – as it had already been doing in 1857 (Bignon et al., 2012). What the magazine did criticize was the Bank's communication strategy. As a matter of fact, Threadneedle Street was trying to maintain an extreme form of "constructive ambiguity":[8] while ready to act as a lender of last resort, it was not willing to let money market participants take its support for granted. In Walter Bagehot's view, this very uncertainty about the fact that liquidity might be obtained (at a positive yet finite price) needlessly exacerbated the severity of panics. This is why he maintained that the Bank should have firmly pre-committed to the implementation of lending of last resort (at a very high, but less than infinite interest rate) in any possible state of the world.

The Economist's campaign was not well received in central banking circles. Although the Bank of England did not react officially, some months later one eminent member of its board, Thomson Hankey,[9] took the initiative of replying to it in the preface to a new edition of his treatise on banking. Hankey put his opposition to Bagehot in very bold terms:

> *The Economist* newspaper has put forth what in my opinion is the most mischievous doctrine ever broached in the monetary or banking world in this country; viz., that it is the proper function of the Bank of England to keep money available at all times to supply the demands of bankers who have rendered their own assets unavailable. Until such a doctrine is repudiated by the banking interest, the difficulty of pursuing any sound principle of banking in London will be always very great. [...] I can only express my regret that the Bank, from a desire to do everything in its power to afford general assistance in times of banking or commercial distress, should ever have acted in a way to encourage such an opinion. The more the conduct of the affairs of the Bank is made to assimilate to the conduct of every other well-managed bank in the United Kingdom, the better for the Bank, and the better for the community at large. [...] I have alluded to the prevailing opinion that, by some management or other (though what that management should be no one has yet defined), the Bank of England might have the power, which *The Economist* thinks

> desirable, of coming to the rescue whenever any financial difficulty may arise; and especially that good bills of exchange – that is, bills of an undoubted character – *ought at all times to be discountable at the Bank of England.* One of the grounds alleged as a reason why this should be the case has been the public character of the institution of the Bank. Supposing that this reason had any sound basis, it does not appear to have occurred to those who advocate the right of holders of bills of exchange to claim ready money from the Bank in exchange for future engagements, that there are many other parties in England who are engaged in carrying on works of great public importance who might equally put in their claim to be as much considered as holders of bills of exchange. [...] What is really asked for by the advocates of the right of the holders of bills of exchange to have their bills at all times discounted at the Bank of England is that one class in the country shall be benefited at the expense of the rest of the community. (Hankey, 1867, pp. 25–26 and 29–30).

Hankey situated his reasoning at a normative level. First, he argued that providing banks with the certainty that they would receive liquidity assistance during crises would have incentivized them to take excessively leveraged positions. Second, he stated that doing so amounted to granting a privilege to some actors at the expense of the rest of the economy, thus generating distributional effects from the real sector to the financial sector.

In his best-selling book *Lombard Street* (first published in 1873), Walter Bagehot took aim at firing back at Hankey, thus vehiculating the controversy to the history of economic thought. Bagehot's reply to Hankey was articulated into four points:

> I am scarcely a judge, but I do not think Mr. Hankey replies to *The Economist* very conclusively.
>
> First. He should have observed that the question is not as to what 'ought to be', but as to what is. *The Economist* did not say that the system of a single bank reserve was a good system, but that it was the system which existed, and which must be worked, as you could not change it.
>
> Secondly. Mr. Hankey should have shown 'some other store of unused cash' except the reserve in the Banking Department of the Bank of England out of which advances in time of panic could be made. These advances are necessary, and must be made by someone. The 'reserves' of London bankers are not such store; they are used cash, not unused; they are part of the Bank deposits, and lent as such.
>
> Thirdly. Mr. Hankey should have observed that we know by the published figures that the joint stock banks of London do not keep one-third, or anything like one-third, of their liabilities in 'cash'. [...]
>
> Fourthly. Mr. Hankey should have observed that, as has been explained, in most panics, the principal use of a 'banking reserve' is not to advance to

> bankers; the largest amount is almost always advanced to the mercantile public and to bill-brokers. (Bagehot, 1873, pp. 171–172).

In front of Hankey's normative reasoning, Bagehot explicitly chose to put forward only strictly positive arguments. On the one hand, he did not deny that in non-crisis times banks would be tempted to over-leverage. He merely stated that banks would do so regardless of the central bank's official stance, betting on the inevitability of liquidity assistance during crises.[10] In his view, the Bank of England's refusal to officially acknowledge its role as lender of last resort only had a negative impact in crisis times, while it did not have any impact in non-crisis times. On the other hand, Bagehot did not deny that lending of last resort would generate distributional effects. He merely pointed out that given the nature of the monetary instrument used by the Bank to implement its monetary operations (i.e., the bill of exchange),[11] the economy at large (and not only the financial sector) did benefit from liquidity injections.

Although Bagehot is universally considered to have won the controversy (Fetter, 1965), it is worth noting that in his direct reply to Hankey, he did not really address his opponent's theoretical arguments about moral hazard. To the contrary, he indirectly admitted that they were well-founded, but concluded that the central bank had no choice anyway. Although (as we shall see in Section 3), Bagehot did provide other relevant insights elsewhere in *Lombard Street*, his failure to cope directly with Hankey's arguments from a normative viewpoint would allow later economists to talk squarely about a "Bagehot problem" (Hirsch, 1977). In turn, it is worth noting that in his rebuttal of Bagehot, Hankey only focused on one dimension of moral hazard – i.e., excessive leverage. In fact, Hankey's objections to Bagehot could have been easily addressed through the introduction of reserve requirements, which did not exist in England at the time (Ugolini, 2017, pp. 131–143).[12] As a result, the Bagehot–Hankey controversy was somewhat of a dialogue of the deaf: in modern parlance, we might say that while Bagehot was arguing for the need of a better "forward guidance" to manage bankers' expectations, Hankey was arguing for the need for macroprudential regulation to limit banks' risk-taking. While from a practical viewpoint both claimants eventually proved somewhat right (as both unconditional lending of last resort and macroprudential regulation came to be jointly adopted by all central banks in the course of the 20th century), from a theoretical viewpoint none managed to specifically address the opponent's argument, thus falling short of satisfactorily settling the controversy.

Section 2 Central banking as insurance: vindicating Hankey?

For more than one century after the Bagehot–Hankey controversy, the literature did not experience any significant improvement. The early-20th-century reference work on the lending of last resort, Ralph Hawtrey's *The Art of Central Banking* (Hawtrey, 1932), provided contradictory answers on how monetary authorities might have mitigated moral hazard (Moore, 1999, pp. 454–455). According to Moore (1999), by the end of the 20th century the literature had basically proposed to central bankers four alternative practical solutions to fix the problem. The first and more popular one was a mere restatement of Bagehot's (1873) guidelines: eliminating uncertainty about universal liquidity assistance by a single public institution but limiting it to a previously-established list of eligible securities. The second one, proposed by Kindleberger (1978), was the opposite to Bagehot's: creating uncertainty about liquidity assistance, to be provided in an uncoordinated fashion by a number of different public institutions. The third one, most prominently defended by Goodhart (1988), consisted of coupling liquidity assistance with other microprudential and macroprudential tools – most notably, capital and reserve requirements. And the fourth one, sketched by Hirsch (1977), consisted of coupling liquidity assistance with strong social sanctions to misbehavior. All solutions revolved around the elements already put forward in the Bagehot–Hankey controversy, without however developing a strongly compelling rationale.

The literature took a new turn only when, in the last quarter of the 20th century, it gradually started to integrate insights from insurance theory. This process took place in a number of successive steps. First, the conceptual framework developed to study insurance schemes was applied to the analysis of deposit insurance. Insurance theory had long started to tackle the question of moral hazard (Rowell and Connelly, 2012), and deposit insurance was just another plain application of the general framework: introducing deposit insurance created incentives for insured agents to misbehave. The second step was due to Merton (1977), who showed that providing a guarantee as the one supplied by deposit insurance was economically equivalent to selling a put option. The third and crucial step was accomplished by Solow (1982), who argued that there was no economic difference between lending of last resort and deposit insurance: the central bank's commitment to provide liquidity assistance to banks under any state of the world amounted, in his view, to the provision of an insurance clause. The fourth step then naturally consisted of interpreting lending of last resort as the supply of a put option – and therefore, as a contingent liability for the central bank (Blejer and Schumacher, 2000).[13] The fifth and last step eventually consisted of concluding that the provision of such a put option precipitated the central bank into a regime of "financial dominance." In the aftermath of the "Great Inflation" of the 1970s, Sargent and Wallace (1981) had famously argued that the commitment to support the public debt put the central bank into a regime of "fiscal dominance", depriving it of the possibility to set the monetary stance appropriately; in the aftermath of the "Great Financial Crisis" of 2008, Brunnermeier and Sannikov (2012) noted that commitment to support the banking system had the very same kind of effect.[14] As much as a regime of "fiscal dominance" provides no incentives for fiscal discipline, a regime of "financial dominance" provides no incentive for financial discipline: as a result, lending of last resort is inevitably conducive to moral hazard and to a "redistributive monetary policy" – a result that can only be mitigated through the application of macroprudential tools (Brunnermeier and Sannikov, 2012).

Therefore, the application of the conceptual framework developed for insurance to the domain of central banking has led to more theoretically-founded, very pessimistic conclusions: lending of last resort inevitably generates moral hazard and distributional effects from the real sector to the financial sector, and this can only be solved indirectly through the introduction of macroprudential tools. Ironically, these conclusions closely resemble those to which Thomson Hankey had come 150 years earlier. Does this mean that recent theoretical developments fully vindicate the positions defended by Hankey in his controversy with Bagehot? As a matter of fact, things are slightly more complicated than they might first appear.

Section 3 The varying liquidity indemnity: vindicating Bagehot?

The gradual process of transposal of insurance theory to central banking has implied some distortions of the mobilized conceptual framework, thus generating confusion. While deposit insurance can legitimately be seen as a form of insurance, application of the same conceptual framework to lending of last resort requires at least some adaptations. In fact, there appears to be at least one main difference between "classical" insurance contracts and the alleged "liquidity insurance" policy provided by the central bank: while insured agents know in advance the sum they will be entitled to receive in case an insurance claim is filed, borrowers from the central bank can never be sure about how much cash they will receive in exchange for their collateral, as the lender is not committed in advance to guarantee any specific lending conditions. By modifying either discount rates or haircuts, central banks can actually modify quite substantially the amount of liquidity actually provided upon presentation of each given unit of collateral – something an insurer will not be entitled to do. This means that, if put option there is, it is quite a special one, as its "strike" (i.e., the price at which collateral can be exchanged on demand against cash) is undisclosed.[15] This detail is particularly important, because it reintroduces an element of uncertainty that has the potential to downsize moral hazard: banks will be certain to receive liquidity assistance in case of panic, but they will be uncertain about the exact amount of liquidity they will be able to receive against their collateral.

It is noteworthy that despite criticizing the Bank of England's extreme form of "constructive ambiguity", Walter Bagehot had not denied the need for some level of uncertainty: indeed, he had been adamant on the fact that last-resort lending should take place at "high rates", in order to "prevent the greatest number of applications by persons who do not require it" (Bagehot, 1873, p. 197).[16] And Thomson Hankey had himself mobilized the very same argument, writing that the central bank had "to fix such a high rate of interest as would prevent applications from those whose demands were not pressing" (Hankey, 1867, p. 27). Therefore, Bagehot and Hankey had agreed on the fact that liquidity assistance by the central bank should be reserved to those whose demand for cash had a very low price elasticity. But in Bagehot's view (and in stark contrast to Hankey's), this was a sufficient condition for discouraging free riding on central bank liquidity, and thus excessive risk-taking by commercial banks:

> The 'unsound' people are a feeble minority, and they are afraid even to look frightened for fear their unsoundness may be detected. The great majority, the majority to be protected, are the 'sound' people, the people who have good security to offer. (Bagehot, 1873, p. 198).

Thus, trying to extract some normative message from Bagehot's positive thinking, we might say that he was arguing as follows: lending of last resort and moral hazard were potentially separable dimensions, but in order for this to be the case, the terms at which the "put option" was made available to borrowers had to be disadvantageous and unforeseeable.

This very important point has been extensively overlooked by most of the literature, which has tended to look at the three Bagehotian rules ("lend freely", "on good collateral", "at high rates") as three separable entities rather than as a whole (Bignon et al., 2012). In particular, the third rule has generally been interpreted as valid for a country adopting a fixed exchange regime (as Britain used to be in Bagehot's times, when it adhered to the classical gold standard), but no longer relevant in the context of a floating exchange regime in which the central bank can freely create unlimited amounts of money (see, e.g., Martin, 2009). As a result, in recent episodes of crisis lending, central bankers happened to do the very opposite of what Bagehot had prescribed concerning interest rates (Hogan et al., 2015).

Central bankers' willingness to keep interest rates at a level that is compatible with macroeconomic needs during a slump can well be understood. However, interest rates are not the only instrument allowing to modify the "exchange rate" at which collateral can be swapped for cash at the central bank: this can also be impacted by modifications in haircuts (margins). Of course, an interest payment and a margin deposit are two different things, which are supposed to have different functions: interest rates are intended to remunerate the lender's capital (and thus to provide incentives to borrowers), while haircuts are intended to protect the lender's capital from potential losses on collateral value (in case the borrower does default). On the one hand, interests are permanently lost to the borrower; while on the other hand, margins are fully recovered by the borrower as soon as the loan is repaid. Yet, in the short term (i.e., for as long as the loan does not mature), the application of a high interest rate and the application of a high margin do produce exactly the same effect on borrowers: viz., they both diminish the amount of cash that can be immediately obtained upon presentation of each unit of collateral. Haircuts also present the advantage of being easily differentiable for different classes of collateral, thus allowing for the maintenance of laxer borrowing conditions on less risky collateral (esp. government bonds).

In *Lombard Street*, Walter Bagehot was silent about haircut policy. To all likelihood, this was due to the fact that in the mid-19th century, the liquidity-injecting operation *par excellence* consisted not of loans on securities, but of discounts of bills of exchange.[17] Discounts did not imply haircuts because bills of exchange "disappeared" ("self-liquidated") at maturity: unless in case of default, they were not returned to the borrower at maturity, and their market price always converged with their face value (Jobst and Ugolini, 2016). In a world where central banks only inject liquidity through discounts, interests and margins are therefore functionally undistinguishable from each other. But in a world where central banks inject liquidity through loans on securities, increasing margins allows benefiting from the advantages of high rates put forward by Bagehot (fixing an unfavorable "exchange rate" between collateral and cash), without however suffering from its disadvantages (imposing prohibitive borrowing costs in dire macroeconomic contexts).

This means that, through the adoption of a conservative haircut policy, the Bagehotian rationale for high rates may be reconciled with the macroeconomic rationale for low rates in crises, thus allowing for a dissociation between lending of last resort and moral hazard. As the actual haircut policy put in place by central banks during recent crises so far remains completely undisclosed, we still do not know whether central bankers were indeed faithful to Bagehot's spirit and set sizable haircuts for their liquidity-injecting operations. Available indirect evidence, however, appears to suggest that they were not (Gorton et al., 2020).

To sum up, the conceptual framework interpreting lending of last resort as a form of insurance is only appropriate if the conditions at which banks are allowed to swap collateral with cash at the central bank are advantageous and foreseeable. In view of his insistence on the fact that interest rates should be "high" (and therefore, volatile) during crises, Walter Bagehot might be interpreted as having argued that such conditions should not be advantageous and foreseeable: if the "strike" of the "put option" cannot be systematically anticipated by banks, lending of last resort will be separable from moral hazard. The central bank has the possibility of modifying the "exchange rate" between collateral and cash by changing either the discount rate (as Bagehot advocated) or, in alternative, the haircuts imposed on collateral. In recent crises, however, central bankers appear to have violated the spirit of Bagehot's prescriptions, supplying liquidity at low rates and with small haircuts on collateral. It was precisely this leniency that created the conditions for the existence of an actual "put option" – sometimes described in the literature as the "Greenspan put"[18] or "Fed put" (Miller et al., 2002). In such circumstances, lending of last resort and moral hazard will no longer be separable, and the central bank will find itself stuck in a regime of "financial dominance" (Brunnermeier and Sannikov, 2012).

Section 4 The tamer's tools: a brief historical overview

In the previous sections, we have seen that since the mid-19th century, the theoretical literature has been split concerning the question of the separability between lending of last resort and moral hazard. On the one hand, Hankey (1867) argued that borrowers' certainty that they will always receive liquidity assistance from the central bank does inevitably encourage them to behave imprudently. Adopting the conceptual framework developed by insurance theory, late-20th-century economists denounced the central bank's provision of a "put option" to the financial sector, generating a regime of "financial dominance" (Hirsch, 1977; Solow, 1982; Blejer and Schumacher, 2000; Brunnermeier and Sannikov, 2012). On the other hand, Bagehot (1873) suggested that lending of last resort and moral hazard could be separated if "constructive ambiguity" concerned not the provision of liquidity in crisis times, but the conditions at which liquidity is provided: these were supposed to be tough and unforeseeable for borrowers *ex ante*. However, we also noted that monetary practice in recent decades has consisted precisely of what Hankey and his followers had feared – i.e., an unconditional provision of cash at favorable and foreseeable conditions, thus incentivizing banks to free-ride on central bankers' liquidity assistance.

This opens the question of the practical design of liquidity-injecting intervention. Does the current design stand in continuity with or in contrast to previous practice? In this section, we will very briefly outline the evolution of the approaches adopted in Europe, over the very long run, in order to "tame" moral hazard. Even though the principle of last resort lending was only formally established in Bagehot's times (Fetter, 1965), the problem of the provision of liquidity support by monetary authorities and of their implications for financial stability is a hardy perennial, having manifested itself since Antiquity (Calomiris et al., 2016). As the banking business started to become increasingly sophisticated in the late Middle Ages, the question of how to minimize liquidity shocks while also minimizing moral hazard naturally emerged.

Of course, the problem of moral hazard in banking is not limited to the question of lending of last resort. A banker acts as an "agent" on behalf of her "principals" (i.e., the depositors who have entrusted their money to her), and this delegation is a classical example of the principal–agent situation that is conducive to moral hazard (Stiglitz, 1989). Early banking regulation was essentially focused on this kind of agency problem. The solution universally adopted to tackle the problem was the maintenance of unlimited liability: bankers' personal wealth would therefore systematically act as collateral to their bank's liabilities. To reinforce this principle, legislation often included harsh sanctions to delegation: a banker could be punished for leaving her books or her seals to her clerks, as she was always held as ultimately responsible for all operations accomplished by her bank. Moreover, high barriers-to-entry existed in the banking sector, so that only people with certified financial and reputational capital would be admitted to exercise the profession. Most of these provisions remained in force throughout Europe until the first half of the 19th century (Ugolini, 2017, pp. 119–121).

While such regulations to tackle agency problems in banking were uniformly adopted everywhere, some more sophisticated financial centers gradually started to implement additional rules, in an attempt at keeping under control the growing concern of banking instability. One of Europe's most prominent financial centers during the medieval and early modern era, Venice was the first place to develop a complex banking legislation that covered all three "pillars" of nowadays' Basel Accords: i) legal restrictions on banks' operations, ii) supervision, and iii) disclosure. The "first pillar" included reserve requirements, capital requirements, as well as activity restrictions (i.e., bans on some specific kinds of operations). The "second pillar" consisted of the creation of the first dedicated supervisory body in the world: the Provveditori sopra Banchi ("bank superintendents"), instituted in 1524. The "third pillar" featured the introduction of a principle of publicity of bank books, which were considered as public records and made accessible to everyone upon request (Ugolini, 2017, pp. 122–126).

The existence of a number of restrictions aimed at minimizing moral hazard *ex ante* explains why, in late medieval and early modern Europe, the first episodes of liquidity support from authorities to banks took place at particularly favorable conditions. This is particularly evident in the case of Venice, where lending-of-last-resort operations were implemented with mild conditions even before the creation of a public bank. During the very violent financial crisis of 1499, when the whole Venetian banking system edged toward the brink of collapse, the Treasury transferred all of its coin reserves to banks against immediate cancellation of its liabilities with them, which allowed some of them to survive a run by depositors (Lattes, 1869, pp. 15–20). Following this episode, a more formalized mechanism for providing liquidity against deposit of collateral was created through the Mint. During the 1576 crisis, for instance, the Mint lent its coin reserves to banks upon security of public debt at 4% interest. If such conditions were somewhat tougher than in 1499, they were still very mild, as the charged interest rate was lower than the market rate. Yet, there is no evidence that such moves encouraged less prudent strategies among bankers (Mueller, 1997, pp. 126–127).

In the 17th century, public banks were founded in a number of European cities – including Venice (1587), Amsterdam (1609), Hamburg (1619), and London (1694). These new, state-sponsored organizations gradually assumed the function of lenders to the private sector (Bindseil, 2019, pp. 108–135). The defining moment in which lending of last resort first started to be implemented on a large scale was the second half of the 18th century, when a wave of successive crises (1763, 1773, and 1781) was handled via the intervention of the monetary authorities in support of private bankers. In London, liquidity assistance was extended directly by the Bank of England (Kosmetatos, 2019), while in Amsterdam and Hamburg the respective public banks provided a liquidity backstop to a government-sponsored mutual guarantee fund

(Uittenbogaard, 2009, pp. 127–137; Bindseil, 2019, pp. 144–154). Being a privately-owned joint-stock bank with substantial equity, the Bank of England had capital buffers to absorb potential losses; by contrast, the public banks of Amsterdam and Hamburg, working with no paid-up capital, could not afford to do the same. Still, lending conditions proved relatively mild: in Bindseil's (2019, p. 147) words, "none of the supposed 'Bagehot rules' was followed: neither was credit only granted against what is accepted as good collateral in normal times, nor was the price of loans high." And yet, losses appear to have been limited in the end.

Therefore, the emergence of last-resort lending operations within a context of unlimited liability and tight regulation was not particularly conducive to moral hazard. But in the course of the 19th century and following the rise of *laissez-faire* ideology, the banking system evolved rapidly, especially in England. By the 1860s, limited-liability banking had become widespread and free-entry; capital and reserve requirements had disappeared; banking supervision had basically become nonexistent; and only very thin transparency rules were in place (Turner, 2014; Ugolini, 2017, pp. 131–134). This was the "brave new world" in which the Bagehot–Hankey controversy took place: such a context explains why both Hankey and Bagehot agreed on the fact that lending of last resort should occur at very high interest rates in order to limit risk-taking by unregulated banks. This new policy of high rates was now made possible by the abolition, in the mid-19th century, of another important piece of financial regulation: i.e., usury laws, which had previously prevented the deployment of such a strategy. In the half century preceding the outburst of the First World War, this new policy of free lending at very high rates appears to have worked reasonably well. It must be underlined, however, that if the Bank of England managed to minimize losses on last-resort lending (Bignon et al., 2012), this was also due to the development of sophisticated micro-prudential tools allowing the Bank to monitor the accumulation of fragilities in the financial system (Flandreau and Ugolini, 2014).

The 19th-century model of unregulated banking came to an end in the interwar years. During these years, lending-of-last-resort facilities were taken for granted by the banking sector, while the pre-war discipline of lending at high rates was jeopardized by macroeconomic and political considerations, forcing central bankers to keep interest rates at low levels (Eichengreen and Flandreau, 2012). This situation then became conducive to moral hazard, and substantial fragilities started to build in the financial system. In 1931, the herculean efforts to keep overleveraged banks afloat in a number of countries led to the collapse of the international monetary system (Ugolini, 2017, pp. 138–143). As a result, the 1930s ushered in the age of "financial repression", in which moral hazard was tamed through much more radical tools – sometimes coming to full nationalization of banking systems (Toniolo and White, 2016). In this new age, interest rates completely ceased to be seen as an instrument aimed at fostering financial stability: they only became an instrument aimed at fostering macroeconomic stability, and their level started to be fixed in view of growth rates.

When a new era of financial liberalization started in the 1970s, therefore, the experience of the previous generations in managing the delicate relationship between lending of last resort and moral hazard had been lost for decades. In particular, the rationale that had led to the introduction of the high-rate policy in the 19th century had been totally forgotten in the meantime. As it had been the case in the interwar period, a combination of lax banking regulation and lax lending-of-last-resort conditions proved, again, to be conducive to moral hazard (Gaillard and Michalek, 2019). The outcome of this explosive mix manifested itself with the spectacular crisis initiated in 2008. In stark contrast with the 1930s, however, the 2010s did not lead to a complete rebuttal of pre-crisis practices (Helleiner, 2014). Lending of last resort continued to be made accessible at very favorable and foreseeable conditions (Hogan et al., 2015; Gorton et al., 2020), while public opinion apparently resigned itself to the alleged inseparability of lending of last resort and moral hazard.

Section 5 Conclusions

Currently, the belief that lending of last resort and moral hazard are indissociable elements is a very widespread one, and public opinion appears to have surrendered to the idea that unconditional support to the financial sector is inevitable. In this chapter, I have tried to put this belief under scrutiny by retracing the historical evolution of theory and practice over the very long term. I have first shown that the Bagehot–Hankey controversy of the 1860s already contained, in a nutshell, all the main arguments subsequently developed about the separability (Bagehot) or inseparability (Hankey) of lending of last resort and moral hazard. I have then illustrated how the transposal of the conceptual framework of insurance theory to the monetary domain apparently vindicated Hankey's position. Hence, I have pointed to the approximations of such a transposal, underlining that the price of the alleged "put option" supplied to the banking system is (at least, in theory) undisclosed. In this respect, I have maintained that Bagehot's plea for "high rates" of discounts (i.e., for keeping the "exchange rate" between collateral and cash unfavorable and unpredictable to banks) is the very source of the separability between lending of last resort and moral hazard, and that the same result can also be attained by charging varying haircuts on collateral while leaving interest rates low. Having ascertained that current practice does not respect these requirements, I have asked whether past practice mirrored contemporary choices. I have concluded that this was not the case, as monetary authorities found in the past a number of different devices to tame the moral hazard associated with liquidity assistance. The only other period in which both banking regulation and the conditions for accessing emergency liquidity were lax was the interwar – indeed, another period of mounting financial fragilities.

In sum, the main take-home message of this chapter is that the ability to dissociate lending of last resort from moral hazard strictly depends on the concrete design of liquidity-injecting operations and of the regulatory environment in which they take place – or, differently said, that the devil is (as always) in the detail. Such a design still considerably varies across countries to date (Ugolini, 2017, pp. 152–155; Awrey, 2020), yet margins for improvement arguably exist in all of them.

Notes

1 See https://yougov.co.uk/topics/politics/articles-reports/2020/01/30/scottish-independence-yes-leads-remainers-increasi
2 See https://www.theguardian.com/business/2014/sep/11/rbs-will-leave-scotland-yes-vote
3 See https://www.ft.com/content/7ba064e4-3a61-11e4-bd08-00144feabdc0
4 See https://www.ft.com/content/daada4cc-a9b4-11e7-93c5-648314d2c72c
5 Lending of last resort at the international level is analyzed by Flores and Gaillard, Chapter 5 of this volume. The bailout issue is addressed in Gaillard and Michalek (Chapter 7), Gotoh and Sinclair (Chapter 8), and Block (Chapter 9) in this volume.
6 To be precise, similar arguments had already been advanced by earlier writers (esp. Henry Thornton), but the Bagehot–Hankey controversy definitively set the terms of the debate (Moore, 1999).
7 Walter Bagehot (1826–1877) was one of the most influential writers in mid-Victorian Britain. The son of a managing director of Stuckey's Bank (one of the most important country banks in England), he first started a banking career with his father. After becoming the son-in-law of *The Economist*'s founder and owner, James Wilson (1805–1860), Bagehot took up the role of editor-in-chief of the magazine in 1861. Besides his journalistic activity, Bagehot authored several essays on evolutionary politics and social change (including his famous treatise on *The English Constitution*, first published in 1867), thereafter considering him one of the founders of Social Darwinism. Bagehot's most renowned contribution to economics, *Lombard Street* (first published in 1873), can be seen as the application of his evolutionary thought to the financial realm (Ugolini, 2017, pp. 5–7).
8 "'Constructive ambiguity', it is argued, can allow a central bank to step in when systemic crisis threatens, while maintaining pressure on banks to act prudently since they cannot be certain of being rescued. The doctrine of constructive ambiguity is a way of dealing with the *time-inconsistency* problem. The time-inconsistency problem arises because it is in the interests of the authorities to deny, *ex ante*, willingness to provide a safety net, but to step in if a crisis nevertheless develops" (Crockett, 1996, p. 549). Also see Freixas et al. (2000).
9 Thomson [Jr] Hankey (1805–1893) was a London-based merchant and politician. A partner in his father's house Thomson Hankey & Co (which was involved in the West Indies and slave trade), he was first elected to the board of directors of the Bank of England in 1835, and in 1851–1852 he served as governor. From 1853 to 1868, and again from 1874 to 1880, he was the Liberal MP for the city of Peterborough. As a member of the House of Commons as well as of the Political Economy Club, he delivered a number of speeches on financial topics; some of these were later reworked into written essays, as it was the case for his *Principles of Banking* (first conceived as a speech in 1858, then published in four successive editions between 1860 and 1887).
10 Bagehot based this on the idea that the central bank and its borrowers are interdependent, as the central bank's power strictly depended on borrowers' willingness to hold the money it created: "But if the Bank had not made these advances, could it have kept its reserve? Certainly it could not. It could not have retained its own deposits. A large part of these are the deposits of bankers, and they would not consent to help the Bank of England in a policy of isolation. They would not agree to suspend payments

themselves, and permit the Bank of England to survive, and get all their business. They would withdraw their deposits from the Bank; they would not assist it to stand erect amid their ruin" (Bagehot, 1873, p. 191). Note that this is a rather different argument than the contemporary "put option" argument (see Section 2). Moreover, Bagehot's argument appears to be fully valid in a world where central bank money is *not* the only form of domestic legal money (which was the case under the classical gold standard, where gold coins were indeed legal money), but much less so in modern-day fiat money regimes.

11 On the nature of sterling bills of exchange in the 19th century, see Accominotti et al. (2021).

12 See Section 4.

13 For an application of this conceptual framework to Bagehot's times, see Calomiris (2011). This interpretation is discussed by Flandreau and Ugolini (2014).

14 To be precise, the concept of "financial dominance" had already circulated before in academic and central banking circles (see Diessner and Lisi, 2020, pp. 318–320).

15 See, e.g., Bank for International Settlements (2014, p. 6). This is acknowledged by Calomiris (2011, p. 126, ft 18), who recognizes that describing lending of last resort as the provision of a put option is "a bit of an overstatement": if the central bank can change the interest rate at which it lends on the collateral, then the price of the option becomes "a moving target."

16 On this point, see also Freixas et al. (2000, pp. 74–76) and Bignon et al. (2012, pp. 603–605).

17 Although mid-19th-century commentators only focused on discounts, in truth "advances" (loans on securities) were already a major type of liquidity-injecting operation in those times. Even archival evidence is particularly scanty, however, for what concerns the haircuts the Bank of England used to apply on advances (Bignon et al., 2012).

18 The term "Greenspan put" refers to the extraordinary monetary intervention implemented by the Federal Reserve under the instigation of its then President, Alan Greenspan, to support the financial system following the stock market crash of October 1987. See also Flores and Gaillard, Chapter 5 of this volume.

References

Accominotti, O., Lucena-Piquero, D. and Ugolini, S. (2021) "The Origination and Distribution of Money Market Instruments: Sterling Bills of Exchange during the First Globalization," *Economic History Review*, forthcoming. https://onlinelibrary.wiley.com/doi/epdf/10.1111/ehr.13049

Awrey, D. (2020) "The Puzzling Divergence of the Lender of Last Resort Regimes in the US and UK," *Journal of Corporation Law*, Vol. 45, No. 3, pp. 597–658.

Bagehot, W. (1873) *Lombard Street: A Description of the Money Market*. London: Henry S. King.

Bank for International Settlements (2014) "Re-Thinking the Lender of Last Resort," *BIS Papers No. 79*.

Bignon, V., Flandreau, M. and Ugolini, S. (2012) "Bagehot for Beginners: The Making of Lending-of-Last-Resort Operations in the Mid-19th Century," *Economic History Review*, Vol. 65, No. 2, pp. 580–608.

Bindseil, U. (2019) *Central Banking before 1800: A Rehabilitation*. Oxford: Oxford University Press.

Blejer, M. I. and Schumacher, L. (2000) "Central Bank Use of Derivatives and Other Contingent Liabilities: Analytical Issues and Policy Implications," *IMF Working Paper No. 00/66*.

Brunnermeier, M. K. and Sannikov, Y. (2012) "Redistributive Monetary Policy," *paper presented at the Jackson Hole Symposium, Federal Reserve Bank of Kansas City*.

Calomiris, C. W. (2011) "Banking Crises and the Rules of the Game," in Wood, G., Mills, T. C. and Crafts, N. (Eds), *Monetary and Banking History: Essays in Honour of Forrest Capie*. London: Routledge, pp. 88–132.

Calomiris, C. W., Flandreau, M. and Laeven, L. (2016) "Political Foundations of the Lender of Last Resort: A Global Historical Narrative," *Journal of Financial Intermediation*, Vol. 28, pp. 48–65.

Crockett, A. (1996) "The Theory and Practice of Financial Stability," *De Economist*, Vol. 144, No. 4, pp. 531–568.

Diessner, S. and Lisi, G. (2020) "Masters of the 'Masters of the Universe'? Monetary, Fiscal and Financial Dominance in the Eurozone," *Socio-Economic Review*, Vol. 18, No. 2, pp. 315–335.

Eichengreen, B. and Flandreau, M. (2012) "The Federal Reserve, the Bank of England, and the Rise of the Dollar as an International Currency, 1914–1939," *Open Economies Review*, Vol. 23, No. 1, pp. 57–87.

Fetter, F. W. (1965) *Development of British Monetary Orthodoxy, 1797–1875*. Cambridge (MA): Harvard University Press.

Freixas, X., Giannini, C., Hoggarth, G. and Soussa, F. (2000) "Lender of Last Resort: What Have We Learned since Bagehot?," *Journal of Financial Services Research*, Vol. 18, No. 1, pp. 63–84.

Flandreau, M. and Ugolini, S. (2014) "The Crisis of 1866," in Dimsdale, N. and Hotson, A. (Eds), *British Financial Crises since 1825*. Oxford: Oxford University Press, pp. 76–92.

Gaillard, N. and Michalek, R. J. (2019) "How and Why Moral Hazard Has Distorted Financial Regulation," in Hira, A., Gaillard, N. and Cohn, T. H. (Eds), *The Failure of Financial Regulation – Why A Major Crisis Could Happen Again*. International Political Economy Series. Cham: Palgrave Macmillan, pp. 111–151.

Goodhart, C. A. E. (1988) *The Evolution of Central Banks*. London and Cambridge, MA: MIT Press.

Goodhart, C. A. E. (1999) "Myths about the Lender of Last Resort," *International Finance*, Vol. 2, No. 3, pp. 339–360.

Gorton, G., Laarits, T. and Metrick, A. (2020) "The Run on Repo and the Fed's Response," *Journal of Financial Stability*, Vol. 48. doi: 10.1016/j.jfs.2020.100744.

Hankey, T. (1867) *The Principles of Banking, Its Utility and Economy*. London: Effingham Wilson.

Hawtrey, R. G. (1932) *The Art of Central Banking*. London: Longmans Greene.

Helleiner, E. (2014) *The Status Quo Crisis: Global Financial Governance after the 2008 Meltdown*. New York: Oxford University Press.

Hirsch, F. (1977) "The Bagehot Problem," *Manchester School of Economics and Social Studies*, Vol. 45, No. 3, pp. 241–257.

Hogan, T. L., Le, L. and Salter, A. W. (2015) "Ben Bernanke and Bagehot's Rules," *Journal of Money, Credit and Banking*, Vol. 47, No. 2–3, pp. 333–348.

Jobst, C. and Ugolini, S. (2016) "The Coevolution of Money Markets and Monetary Policy, 1815–2008," in Bordo, M. D., Eitrheim, Ø., Flandreau, M. and Qvigstad, J. F. (Eds), *Central Banks at a Crossroads: What Can We Learn from History?* New York: Cambridge University Press, pp. 145–194.

Kindleberger, C. P. (1978) *Manias, Panics and Crashes: A History of Financial Crises*. Basingstoke: Macmillan.

Kosmetatos, P. (2019) "Last Resort Lending before Henry Thornton? The Bank of England's Role in Containing the 1763 and 1772–1773 British Credit Crises," *European Review of Economic History*, Vol. 23, No. 3, pp. 299–328.

Lattes, E. (1869) *La libertà delle banche a Venezia dal secolo XIII al XVII*. Milan: Valentiner & Mues.

Martin, A. (2009) "Reconciling Bagehot and the Fed's Response to September 11," *Journal of Money, Credit and Banking*, Vol. 41, No. 2–3, pp. 397–415.

Merton, R. C. (1977) "An Analytic Derivation of the Cost of Deposit Insurance and Loan Guarantees: An Application of Modern Option Pricing Theory," *Journal of Banking and Finance*, Vol. 1, No. 1, pp. 3–11.

Miller, M., Weller, P. and Zhang, L. (2002) "Moral Hazard and the US Stock Market: Analysing the "Greenspan Put'," *Economic Journal*, Vol. 112, No. 478, pp. 171–186.

Moore, G. (1999) "Solutions to the Moral Hazard Problem Arising from the Lender-of-Last-Resort Facility," *Journal of Economic Surveys*, Vol. 13, No. 4, pp. 443–476.

Mueller, R. C. (1997) *The Venetian Money Market: Banks, Panics, and the Public Debt, 1200–1500*. Baltimore, MD: Johns Hopkins University Press.

Rowell, D. and Connelly, L. B. (2012) "A History of the Term 'Moral Hazard'," *Journal of Risk and Insurance*, Vol. 79, No. 4, pp. 1051–1075.

Sargent, T. J. and Wallace, N. (1981) "Some Unpleasant Monetarist Arithmetic," *Federal Reserve Bank of Minneapolis Quarterly Review*, Vol. 5, No. 3, pp. 1–17.

Solow, R. (1982) "On the Lender of Last Resort," in Kindleberger, C. P. and Laffargue, J. (Eds), *Financial Crises: Theory, History and Policy*. Cambridge: Cambridge University Press, pp. 237–248.

Stiglitz, J. E. (1989) "Principal and Agent," in Eatwell, J., Milgate, M. and Newman, P. (Eds), *Allocation, Information and Markets*. London: Palgrave Macmillan, pp. 241–253.

Toniolo, G. and White, E. N. (2016) "The Evolution of the Financial Stability Mandate: From Its Origins to the Present Day," in Bordo, M. D., Eitrheim, Ø., Flandreau, M. and Qvigstad, J. F. (Eds), *Central Banks at a Crossroads: What Can We Learn from History?* New York: Cambridge University Press, pp. 424–492.

Turner, J. D. (2014) *Banking in Crisis: The Rise and Fall of British Banking Stability, 1800 to the Present*. Cambridge: Cambridge University Press.

Ugolini, S. (2017) *The Evolution of Central Banking: Theory and History*. London: Palgrave Macmillan.

Uittenbogaard, R. (2009) "Lending by the Bank of Amsterdam (1609–1802)," in Van Nieuwkerk, M. (Ed), *The Bank of Amsterdam: On the Origins of Central Banking*. Arnhem: Sonsbeek, pp. 120–131.

Part II

Moral hazard and sovereign risk

4 Moral hazard in the export credit industry

Aline Darbellay and Norbert Gaillard

This chapter shows that the actions undertaken by export credit agencies (ECAs) and export-import banks (EIBs) have encouraged moral hazard and induced risk-taking behaviors. Section 1 investigates how and why the legal and regulatory frameworks of ECAs and EIBs have contributed to reinforcing moral hazard. In fact, moral hazard results from a combination of the fierce international competition and the information asymmetry between insurers/lenders, exporters, and importers. Section 2 explores the practices of the U.S. Exim Bank in the 1970s. In a context of massive lending to developing countries, this institution refrained from using a reliable country risk rating system and prioritized the foreign borrowers most capable of obtaining preferential treatment from their government. It is not surprising that the percentage of non-performing loans soared during 1975–1982 and undermined the credibility of the U.S. Exim Bank.

The export credit industry developed in the aftermath of World War I. In a context of international monetary turmoil, gloomy economic growth, and an increasing trend toward protectionism, major European governments started subsidizing their exporting firms in order to promote the competitiveness of their national economies. Export credit agencies (ECAs) and export-import banks (EIBs) were established to fulfill this goal.[1] Such measures were supposedly temporary, but they were maintained even after World War II. Export credit schemes contributed to spur international trade in the 1950s and 1960s, but they also burdened developing countries with short- and medium-term debts. In the meantime, only big firms in capital-exporting nations managed to obtain guarantees and/or credits for their foreign clients. The growing competition from Japanese and Taiwanese firms in the 1970s exacerbated competition among ECAs and EIBs, which sacrificed country risk analysis to preserve their core business. The world debt crisis of 1982 jeopardized the future of these institutions. Most of them were subsequently reorganized or privatized. They implemented reliable country risk ratings and revised their insurance, guarantee, and lending policies. Despite that, their role has remained ambiguous since the 1980s: ECAs and EIBs are still a foreign policy tool and their programs continue to benefit only very few economic sectors.

DOI: 10.4324/9781003139249-4

This chapter sheds new light on an important, yet overlooked, source of moral hazard at the international level. Conducting a legal and economic analysis, we examine how the actions undertaken by ECAs and export-import banks have not only distorted competition in international trade and finance, but also encouraged moral hazard and induced risk-taking behaviors. Our argument is based on the traditional liberal doxa, such as expressed by Melitz and Messerlin (1987) who advocate that export subsidies are "distortionary at a microeconomic level in ways which more than offset any macroeconomic advantage." Yet, we go further in our analysis as we focus on the principal-agent and moral hazard problems in the export credit industry. On the one hand, ECAs and EIBs are *agents*, acting on behalf of their government.[2] On the other hand, especially in their roles as insurers and guarantors, they are expected to monitor the actions of *two* types of insured parties (i.e., the domestic exporters and the foreign importers) in order to eliminate information asymmetry and avert excessive risk taking. In this idiosyncratic environment, the export credit business is likely to get involved in conflicts of interest, face multiple and possibly contradictory objectives, and encourage moral hazard. This chapter investigates these tricky issues and highlights to what extent the various dimensions of moral hazard have contributed to the system of "corporate welfare."

Section 1 shows how the untrammeled expansion of export credit programs has increased information asymmetry between the insurers/lenders, home governments, domestic exporters, and foreign importers, nurtured moral hazard, and led to a misallocation of financial resources. Section 2 can be considered a case study. We examine how the policy of the Exim Bank – especially in the 1970s – magnified moral hazard and contributed to undermining the credibility of the institution. Section 3 concludes.

Section 1 The export credit industry: an obstacle to economic efficiency

1.1 The export credit industry since 1919

The export credit industry emerged a century ago,[3] but it appears that ECAs played a prominent role in the international trade and financial architecture primarily between the 1950s and the 1970s (see Gaillard, 2020a, pp. 45–47). The services offered may range from insurance and guarantees to loans granted to foreign importers. In some jurisdictions, ECAs restrict their support to insurance and guarantees, leaving export credits to the banking system, while in others, ECAs have been set up as public institutions that facilitate export credits by providing loans (Camino and Cardone, 1997, p. 415). In so doing, governments end up assuming a significant proportion of the credit risk on loans to foreign buyers of exported goods and services (Fleisig and Hill, 1984, pp. 321–322). Although official ECAs should be distinguished from private ECAs, the latter frequently have strong ties to their governments (see

Fourcade et al., 2008). While the problem of moral hazard is relevant to both official and private ECAs, it is worth noting that official ECAs may be more prone to engage in collusive practices with borrowing states as insurance policies and loans are backed by their governments.

The history of ECAs can be split in two distinct periods: the era of export subsidies and competitive incentives (1920–1980) and the era of professionalization and multilateralism (1980–2020).

From the 1920s to the early 1980s, the expansion of ECAs' activities consisted of subsidizing the export industry. Concretely, through their insurance and guarantee schemes, ECAs charged premium fees significantly lower than those justified by the actual risk, while export-import banks granted loans at below-market rates. For both types of export promotion programs, subsidization could also involve abnormally long terms as well as guarantees and credit extensions.

The first government export credit insurance programs were designed to stimulate exports following the collapse of international trade and alleviate the lack of private credit insurance schemes (Hanna, 1931, p. 541; Dietrich, 1935). In the 1930s, within a context of growing protectionism, the development of the export credit industry accelerated as the exporter that awarded the longest payment term enjoyed a key competitive advantage and was very likely to obtain the deal (Bonin, 2002, p. 345).

In the interwar years, the development of export credit was thought to be a temporary measure leading to trade recovery. Yet, ECAs flourished in most European countries and the subsidization of exporters intensified. In addition, ECAs and export-import banks were instrumentalized to reach foreign policy goals.[4] These policies increased competition between major capital-exporting nations such as the United States, the United Kingdom, and France. They were particularly keen on lending to the clients of their national champions (Bonin, 2002, p. 347), which distorted international trade.

In the early years of export credit insurance, the main challenges were scarce information and the lack of reliable credit ratings to set adequate premium rates (Hanna, 1931, p. 548). For example, blindsided with its initial objective of promoting French exports, the Société française d'assurance-crédit (SFAC) encountered financial difficulties as early as 1930 (i.e., three years after its establishment). It appeared that the SFAC had covered risky and insolvent importers because it had failed to assess their creditworthiness efficiently (Bonin, 2002, p. 350).[5] This concern was even more pronounced after World War II. Starting in the 1960s and until 1982, the huge amounts lent by the Exim Bank to foreign firms and governments for the purpose of buying U.S. industrial goods were made possible by a very lax risk assessment policy (see Gaillard, 2020a, p. 50 and Section 2 below).

In the 1960s and 1970s, western ECAs offered a wider array of financial services, including political risk guarantees. These schemes enabled exporters to sell their products in new, risky importing countries without bearing any significant financial consequences. Consider the case of Coface, the French state-owned ECA established in 1946 (for an exhaustive discussion, see Saul, 2002 and 2010). Between 1957 and 1967, the total amount of French exports benefiting from medium-term guarantees against natural disasters, political risk, and transfer risk rose by a factor of 8 (Saul, 2010, p. 172).[6] This boom was driven by the rapid expansion of the insurance coverage. During 1963–1967, Coface announced it insured against corporate default risk, lowered premia, increased the maximum guarantee threshold from 90% to 95% for transactions exceeding five years, and covered foreign loans and foreign direct investments provided they were connected to export activities (Saul, 2002, p. 364). This system reinforced the ties between major exporters and their governments. The favorable treatment granted to multinational firms resulted in a system of "corporate welfare" (see also Gaillard and Michalek, Chapter 7). As the ECAs located in other countries followed similar strategies, it became obvious that the global outcome of the export credit industry was a zero-sum game.

So, it is not surprising that some rules needed adjustment to bring more discipline to the export credit industry, particularly in light of the growing competition from Hong Kong, Japan, Singapore, South Korea, and Taiwan. The members of the Organisation for Economic Co-operation and Development (OECD) expressed their willingness to expand international rules to limit the possibility of governmental subsidization of domestic exporters and mitigate competition (Alvarez and Flores Zendejas, 2014, p. 129). They ultimately adopted the OECD Arrangement on Guidelines for Officially Supported Export Credits in 1978 (1978 Arrangement). In a context of heightened multilateralism, participating countries agreed to refrain from giving an unfair advantage to their domestic firms.

The 1978 Arrangement contributed to transition into a new era. The default of Mexico in 1982 (see Flores and Gaillard, Chapter 5; Gaillard and Michalek, Chapter 7) had repercussions worldwide and affected the export credit industry. In the early 1980s, major exporting countries (except Germany and Japan) had to sustain growing trade deficits attributable to insufficient export credits. More dramatically, some key players such as the Exim Bank and Coface posted structural losses, reflecting the exhaustion of their business model. Inevitably, an era of deregulation was to start where the state would reduce its involvement (see Becker and McClenahan, 2003, pp. 269–279; Saul, 2010, pp. 176–180).

The "professionalization era" starting in the 1980s was driven by three fundamental changes: the privatization of many ECAs, the extensive use of country risk ratings, and the ongoing promotion of multilateralism to prevent distortions in the export credit industry.

A major evolution in the last two decades of the 20th century was the wave of privatization of ECAs, largely caused by the losses experienced in the late 1970s and early 1980s. For example, the ECGD, COSEC (the Portuguese export credit agency), Coface, and the Israeli Credit Insurance Company were privatized in 1991, 1992, 1994, and 2002, respectively.[7] Traditional ECAs also gained autonomy and were allowed to acquire foreign competitors. However, regardless of their status,

ECAs have kept strong ties to their governments. In the meantime, private insurance companies entered the political risk insurance business.

Country risk methodologies and ratings have developed and refined remarkably since the 1980s.[8] ECAs have become reliable country risk experts whose ratings are extensively used by exporters as well as international investors. In 2020, Credendo (the Belgian export credit agency) published several types of ratings assessing short-term political risk, medium/long-term political risk, political violence risk, expropriation and government action risk, currency inconvertibility, and transfer restriction risk.[9] Other ECAs, such as Atradius, Coface, and Euler Hermes, have set up quite similar country risk ratings.[10] These additional indicators enable investment decisions to be made much more confidently than several decades ago.

The 1980s heralded an era of multilateralism with the increasing importance of OECD legal instruments. An agreement on premium for export credits (the so-called Knaepen Package) was reached and incorporated in the OECD Arrangement in 1997 (OECD, 2008). A classification was established for the purpose of setting minimum risk premium rates: countries are rated on a scale of 0 to 7, where 0 represents the least risky countries and 7 the riskiest (Gaillard, 2020a, p. 199). The OECD country risk classification results from a consensual decision from an expert group composed of ECA representatives.[11] The OECD norms have also aimed to promote responsible lending practices, including human rights and environmental issues (Darbellay, 2021).[12] Most notably, in 1998, the OECD developed the Recommendation on Common Approaches for officially supported export credits, which were approved in 2003 and have been revised several times since then.

1.2 The various sources of moral hazard in the export credit industry

The issue arises as to what extent the export credit industry has not only distorted competition among exporters but also induced risk-taking behaviors, thus encouraging moral hazard.

Broadly speaking, moral hazard describes the phenomenon of excessive risk-taking due to the presence of insurance. A fundamental theoretical assumption is that moral hazard is contingent upon the existence of a hidden action, i.e., a riskier behavior by the "insured" which is unknown to the "insurer." Two distinct types of moral hazard can be identified. *Ex-ante* moral hazard, which occurs when an insured party has incentives to conduct risky activities affecting the probability of loss before an insurance event, should be distinguished from *ex-post* moral hazard, which occurs when an insured party has incentives to conduct risky activities that affect the magnitude of losses after an insurance event (Götze and Gürtler, 2020, pp. 758–759).

The remainder of this chapter focuses on *ex-ante* moral hazard, which may materialize when an "insurer" has multiple duties, is involved in conflicts of interest, and/or fails to monitor the insured party adequately. ECAs and export-import banks are precisely in such position. They have close relationships with their respective governments, promote the products of major domestic exporters, and are the guarantor and/or creditor of foreign importers and foreign governments. In addition, ECAs are assigned various duties: they subsidize the export industry (possibly to the detriment of their profitability), contribute (in principle) to cut the trade deficit, and play an active (but unofficial) role in the foreign policy of their government. It is not surprising that this combination may result in morally hazardous behaviors on the "insured" side.

In fact, there are several potential sources of moral hazard in the export credit industry. First, the interdependence between several insured parties may encourage moral hazard because of the mutualization of risk. Indeed, an insured exporter may be willing to take risk at the expense of other insured exporters. For example, the exporters of industrial goods – generally considered more strategic by the ECA or the export-import bank – are more likely to obtain low premia, enhanced guarantees, and/or longer-term financing for their clients than the exporters of consumer goods. This discrepancy explains why export credit schemes have long benefited only very few sectors (e.g., aircraft, energy, and machinery). These findings are largely documented for several countries and different periods (see Feinberg, 1982, pp. 34–35; Godinot, 2009, pp. 22–25; Kidwell, 2015, pp. 10–12).

Second, *debtor* moral hazard may arise in the relationship between ECAs and export-import banks, on the one hand, and borrowing firms and states, on the other. Concretely, the former provide massive guarantees and/or loans at subsidized rates to the latter. In engaging in permissive lending practices without conditionality, they implicitly allow that part of the debt burden will be eventually restructured or will lead to additional loans. Seck and Chimisso dos Santos (2018, pp. 97–99) show how ECA-supported activities are likely to burden debt service payments. The export credits granted in the 1960s and 1970s are striking illustrations (see Gaillard, 2020a, p. 46). More recently, Coface faced criticism owing to its lax practices in the 2000s. From 2002 to 2006, the write-off of Coface claims increased by 395% to reach EUR 2.05 billion (Fourcade et al., 2008, p. 96). Concerns were raised about reclassifying, *ex post*, Coface's distressed commercial loans into official development aid (Fourcade et al., 2008). Such deplorable policies, disconnected from any commonsense country risk analysis, support the view that (i) some loans were granted for diplomatic or political purposes and (ii) their full repayment was never expected. It is noteworthy that these practices occurred several years after Coface was privatized.

Third, moral hazard may develop in the relationship between *official* ECAs and export-import banks, on the one hand, and their home government and/or parliament, on the other. Official ECAs may be incentivized to provide specific risky loans with a view to fostering a public policy agenda (e.g., support to a specific sector, preservation of jobs, etc.). They may end up needing additional financing and even a bailout from the government. Here, moral hazard materializes in a novel manner as the export credit industry is the "agent" who overlooks risk or increases his risk-taking and deceives the "principal" (i.e., public authorities and, ultimately, taxpayers). The strategy of the Exim Bank in the late 1970s illustrates this type of moral hazard (see Section 2).

Fourth, moral hazard may stem from the relationship between ECAs and exporters. Consider, for example, the government that encourages its exporters to conquer new foreign markets. The credit position of the potential importers is likely to be so low that the exporters and private insurers will be reluctant to bear such risk themselves (Camino and Cardone, 1997, p. 423). However, the existence of a state-owned ECA or export-import bank offering subsidized guarantees or loans will lead the domestic firm to export to the risky country. Once the supported firm realizes that the export credit scheme enables it to take greater risks, moral hazard takes roots. This vicious circle perfectly mirrors the close connection between subsidy and moral hazard.[13]

Section 2 The failure of the Exim Bank and the three dimensions of moral hazard

This section scrutinizes the Exim Bank's policy since the Cold War. The utter failure of the Exim Bank observed in 1982–1983 occurred in the context of the economic recession and the less developed countries' (LDC) debt crisis. The Washington-based institution had not only failed to cut the U.S. trade deficit,[14] but it had also posted a record-high percentage of delinquent loans, which jeopardized its existence. Several factors combined to undermine its credibility, from permissive lending practices to excessive subsidization to big industrialists.

Here, we argue that moral hazard did play a key role in the failure of the Exim Bank. We contend that the bank's strategy encouraged moral hazard among foreign buyers as well as U.S. exporters. More dramatically, moral hazard materialized in the relations between the Exim Bank and the U.S. Congress. These issues are tackled in turn. The final sub-section shows how the rising tensions between the United States and China have contributed to reinvigorate the institution since 2019. This new context is likely to encourage risk taking and possibly moral hazard.

2.1 Establishment and development of the Exim Bank

The *First* Export-Import Bank was established in Washington in February 1934 to facilitate trade with the Soviet Union. A few weeks later, the *Second* Exim Bank was created to assist economic relations with Cuba, but its activities were soon extended to all countries, except Russia. Following the breakdown of debt negotiations between Russia and the United States, the Second Bank was liquidated, and the First Bank was allowed to take over its activities. Since 1936, there has been a single Exim Bank: it is the United States' official ECA (Patterson, 1943). Over the past 85 years, the institution was reauthorized with bipartisan support in Congress 17 times, despite several fierce controversies, especially in the 1980s and in the mid-2010s (see below).

Although the agency was designed to create jobs in the United States by promoting the exports of U.S. firms, it has fulfilled other missions. For example, it was urged to counter the subsidized financing of other ECAs. The Exim Bank also played a prominent role to support U.S. foreign policy. The various tasks assigned to the agency have made it difficult for policymakers and scholars to assess its efficiency.

The Exim Bank offers three major types of financial services: direct loans, loan guarantees, and export credit insurance. After granting loans exclusively until the mid-1950s, the agency increasingly used guarantees and insurance to meet the needs of its customers. The share of these two services combined rose from less than 1% in 1955 to 54% in 1975, 87% in 1995, and more than 99% in 2015.[15]

The main recipient countries have been major developing and emerging economies, such as Argentina, Brazil, India, Indonesia, Mexico, the Philippines, South Korea, and Turkey. China and Russia joined this list in the 1990s.[16] The top beneficiaries of Exim Bank operations have long been the aircraft, oil and gas, and manufacturing sectors (see Feinberg, 1982, pp. 34–35 and Kidwell, 2015, pp. 10–12). The U.S. Exim Bank served as model for several governments eager to develop their own export credit schemes, including the export-import banks of South Korea, India, and China, established in 1976, 1982, and 1994, respectively.

2.2 The Exim Bank and its foreign debtors

The presumption of morally hazardous behaviors between the Exim Bank and its debtors must be examined very carefully because of the nature of the bank's activity. In fact, the Exim Bank provides *project* loans, guarantees, and insurance to private and public entities. Considering that there is seldom a unique borrower or insured entity within a given country, one could conclude that the "too-big-to-fail" (TBTF) problem does not arise as when investors lend massively to the same borrower (typically a government) for general purpose (see Flores and Gaillard, Chapter 5). Despite that, systemic risk does exist for two reasons.[17] In autocratic and socialist countries, the state is often the guarantor of all deals signed by private firms. Besides, inconvertibility risk remains a serious impediment to *all* transactions in a foreign country. This is because, in some countries, the credit position of private and public debtors and insured entities is largely contingent on the capacity and willingness of the government to preserve its own credit position and maintain capital mobility.

The next (perhaps utmost) challenge consists of substantiating possible debtor morally hazardous strategies. Such evidence can be provided in few cases. As a result, we analyze primarily the actions performed by the Exim Bank and the elements of the environment from the 1960s through the 1980s that were *likely* to encourage debtor moral hazard.

The first factor was undoubtedly the *junior* creditor status of the Exim Bank. The wave of sovereign debt restructurings announced in the 1960s shows that the type of external debt most frequently subject to consolidation involved suppliers' credits, such as those granted by ECAs (World Bank, 1969). The reason was that their higher interest rates and shorter maturities increased debt service payments. This junior status meant that the dubious debtors had an incentive to borrow from the Exim Bank rather than from the World Bank, which enjoyed a *senior* status. Thus, it is hardly surprising that the number of Exim Bank loans classified as delinquent rose from 15 in 1960 to 32 in 1967, and 54 in 1972. More importantly, the ratio of delinquent loans to total loans (in volume) soared in the second part of the 1970s and in the early 1980s (see Figure 4.1). Two explanations can be advanced. First, Bohn (1986) contends that, like other ECAs, the Exim Bank seems to have vacillated between its export-promoting function and its role as a potential source of development assistance support. Second, Alvarez and Flores Zendejas (2014) find that export credit schemes were used as leverage to lead LDCs to sign stand-by agreements with the International Monetary Fund (IMF).

Turn now to another issue. The Congress has long used the Exim Bank as an instrument to pursue U.S. foreign policy. For example, the Foreign Assistance and Related Agencies Appropriations Act of 1964 prohibited the Exim Bank from lending to any communist country, except Yugoslavia. In 1971, the Export Expansion Finance Act removed this prohibition to stimulate East-West trade. However, if one wants to find some elements of debtor moral hazard, it is necessary to examine the Exim Bank policy regarding U.S. allies.

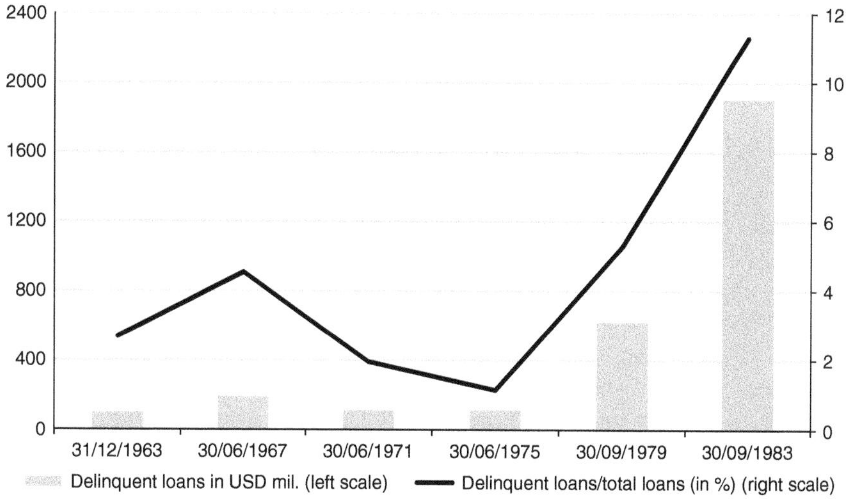

Figure 4.1 Exim Bank's Delinquent Loans, 1963–1983.

Source: Authors calculations based on Exim Bank's annual and semiannual reports (various years).

The Western economies do not seem to have raised any concern. After getting massive loans in 1945–1948 for their reconstruction, these countries joined NATO and thrived on their own.[18] For example, the Exim Bank's exposure to Belgium, France, Germany, Italy, Netherlands, and the United Kingdom declined from 28% in 1959 to 10% in 1967, and 7% in 1982.[19] None of these governments defaulted on their loans to the agency.

In fact, some forms of debtor moral hazard may be identified among what Pipes and Garfinkle (1991) call "friendly tyrants." Several of these allies had significant bargaining power with Washington and managed to obtain fresh loans from the Exim Bank amid a complex geopolitical context and opaque business conditions. Different strategies were implemented to do so; two deserve examination here.

In a certain number of deals, the LDC government claimed cost overruns to get additional financing and guarantees. This strategy enabled the Philippines and Zaire to finance expensive projects: a nuclear plant and a hydroelectric plant, respectively.[20] In other cases, Exim Bank's loans served as a sweetener in negotiations over the renewal of American military bases, as happened in Spain and Turkey in 1976.[21]

The outcomes of these massive capital flows were incredibly diverging. On the one hand, Spain and the Philippines piled up debt, guarantees, and insurance which accounted for more than 8% of the Exim Bank exposure in 1982.[22] Both governments were solvent when the world debt crisis erupted that year. On the other hand, the Exim Bank rescheduled certain loans to Zaire and Turkey as early as 1977–1978. What is remarkable is that the two countries got additional loans shortly after their default! This "policy" undoubtedly encouraged debtor moral hazard; it also reflected poor monitoring efforts.

Here is the third factor that distorted the relations between the Exim Bank and its debtors: namely, the weak country risk assessment performed by the institution.

The Exim Bank's lending policy was based on several criteria but the top one was certainly the borrower's status and its capacity to obtain preferential treatment, such as a state guarantee, a complementary state loan, tax concessions, and/or subsidies. The agency's country risk rating system was rudimentary: the key determinants were the risk of balance-of-payments problems, the level of indebtedness, and the repayment performance of previous loans, especially Exim Bank loans[23] (see Gaillard, 2020a, pp. 49–52, for an analysis of country risk rating methodologies used in the 1970s).

The Washington-based institution used to rate countries on a 4-notch scale but this rating system was discontinued in 1977 (Feinberg, 1982, p. 46). Its risk assessment policy was very lax. In several annual reports, the agency stated that the risk of loss on loans, guarantees, and insurance was not susceptible to accurate measurement because of the unpredictable nature of future economic and political conditions throughout the world (Exim Bank, 1969, p. 21; 1979, p. 28). It is therefore not surprising that the share of loans classified as delinquent increased inexorably in the second half of the 1970s and in the early 1980s (see Figure 4.1).

The junior status of the Exim Bank, its opaque role in the U.S. foreign policy, and its poor country risk rating system combined to undermine the credibility of the agency. The 1982–1983 debt crisis only hastened its decline. It is obvious that the policy followed by the financial institution in the 1970s paved the way to some forms of debtor moral hazard. The agency lent massively to countries like Turkey and Zaire. Despite their default, those countries bargained their "geostrategic" position and managed to get fresh loans from the Exim Bank. Here is what can surely be considered "creeping bailouts" driven by debtor moral hazard.

2.3 The Exim Bank and U.S. exporters

In a business world with no export credit program, the exporter has two objectives: to find a customer (i.e., an importer) and to get paid for the goods delivered. The exporter has thus a commercial and financial responsibility. Once an export credit scheme is set, the financial risk is mainly borne by the ECA. Thus, the firm aims to supply as many goods as possible, regardless of the credit position of the importer. The exporter has a clear incentive to exploit a bullish economic environment struggling with information asymmetry. This environment was observed in the United States during 1977–1981.

At the time, the catalyst for a proactive role of the Exim Bank was the perceived necessity to cut the U.S. trade deficit. During the fourth quarter of 1975, the trade balance was an $8.9 billion surplus. One year later, it had become a deficit of $14.4 billion. During the fourth quarter of 1977, the deficit had widened to $35.5 billion (for an exhaustive analysis, see Lawrence, 1978). The low growth of U.S. exports was identified as a major cause for this trend. That is the reason why, shortly after taking office in May 1977, Exim Bank president John Moore announced that he intended to spur U.S. exports by an aggressive lending policy.[24] Indeed, the total amount of loans granted jumped from $1.2 billion for FY1977 to $4.5 billion for FY1979 and $5.4 billion for FY1981 (Exim Bank, 1977; 1979; 1981).

This lending boom was unorthodox as the Exim Bank lent at below-market rates. Boyd (1982) finds that the average interest rate for 1977–1980 was remarkably stable around 8.3% whereas Fed Funds rate started soaring in 1978.[25] This strategy was a boon for exporters as well as foreign importers, but it threatened the profitability of the institution (see below).

The expansion of the Exim Bank operations at subsidized interest rates distorted market dynamics and encouraged excessive risk taking. The case of Boeing – a top beneficiary of Exim Bank programs – is very telling. In order to preserve its international market share, the Seattle-based firm managed to convince the Exim Bank to finance jet sales to companies located in risky countries including Niger and Tanzania in 1978; Cameroon and Ethiopia in 1979; Guinea and Honduras in 1980.[26] It is interesting that the credit conditions offered to these airline companies were comparable to those of New Zealand, France, or Canada (Exim Bank, 1978; 1979; 1980).

It is not difficult to consider that Boeing followed a morally hazardous behavior. This assumption is supported by several prominent facts. First, during FY1975–FY1977, Boeing's foreign clients were airline companies located in industrial and major emerging economies exclusively. These countries had strong credit position or were traditional debtors to the Exim Bank. Second, the aircraft company knew that, year after year, it could enjoy a permanent subsidy from the agency. Third, by mid-1977, the bank had expressed its willingness to boost U.S. exports by overlooking the credit position of importers and offering subsidized interest rates. In this propitious context, Boeing had a unique opportunity to get deals with new and risky importing countries.[27]

By subsidizing a small group of privileged sectors (e.g., the aircraft, nuclear, and transportation equipment industries),[28] the Exim Bank acted as a lender of *first* resort and consolidated the lobbying power of a few industrialists. It is not surprising that the financial institution got abused by some major exporters.[29]

2.4 The Exim Bank and the Congress

The most striking illustration of moral hazard involving the Exim Bank was its relations with the Congress and, thus indirectly, with U.S. taxpayers. In the 1970s, the agency was in a headlong rush to promote exports and expand its operations. This increasingly costly strategy relied on the belief that the U.S. Congress would perpetually lift authorized lending ceilings. Several factors support our view.

During the first half of the 1970s, the Exim Bank faced a maturity mismatch because it financed long-term loans with short-term borrowings (General Accounting Office – GAO, 1975, p. i). This flaw was largely fixed by 1980 (GAO, 1982, p. 26) but another problem was exacerbated: Exim Bank's borrowing costs. In fact, the agency's borrowing rate was consistently higher than its lending rate. During 1974–1980, this spread was around 2 percentage points and it exceeded 3 percentage points by 1982 (GAO, 1975, p. 3; 1980, p. 12; 1983, p. 2). In the medium-long term, this dangerous trend could lead to the depletion of the bank's reserves.

In 1980, the bank had become unable to promote exports on a self-sustaining basis. A few weeks prior to the end of FY1980, President J. Moore informed the administration that the bank had pierced its authorization ceiling by $1.1 billion. Fred Bergsten (Assistant Treasury Secretary for International Affairs) and top budget officials convinced the Congress to vote $1.1 billion in guarantees to finance some of the Exim Bank commitments. The Congress passed this off-budget item but discovered shortly after that these guarantees were in fact direct loans.[30] The Exim Bank had obtained opaque additional funding to continue its risky lending policy. The problem was the bank would have to tap capital markets to get the $1.1 billion, which included higher interest rates than if the sum had been funded through the Treasury. At last, the Exim Bank's morally hazardous strategy came to light. In several letters sent to J. Moore in August 1980, President Carter's budget director expressly demanded that the bank limit its direct loans until FY1985 and respect approved budget availabilities.[31]

The Carter administration's determination to fight the U.S. trade deficit, the growing foreign competition – especially from France, Japan, and the United Kingdom (GAO, 1980, p. 4) – and the unwavering support of big manufacturers had led the Exim Bank to grant even more loans at subsidized interest rates to riskier importers. In 1980, the agency urgently needed appropriations to continue its business and announced it would not pay a dividend to the U.S. Treasury[32]: more than ever, the bank had become a bottomless financial pit for the Congress and, therefore, for U.S. taxpayers.

2.5 The Exim Bank since the 1980s

The 1980s marked the inescapable decline of the Exim Bank. Two key factors combined to weaken the institution.

First, the Reagan administration, which came into power in January 1981, was eager to impose a neoliberal agenda. David Stockman, the Director of the Office of Management and Budget, targeted the bank's direct lending program and proposed cutting back its operations by 20% for the current FY1981 and another 20% for FY1982. He argued that the agency was too costly in the then context of massive fiscal deficit. He also complained that two-thirds of the loans granted in 1980 went to seven companies: Boeing, Combustion Engineering, General Electric, Lockheed, McDonnell Douglas, Western Electric, and Westinghouse. Despite the resistance by some in the Congress and big exporters, the Exim Bank had lost its momentum by 1985.[33]

Second, the LDC crisis tarnished the reputation of the bank, whose cumulative losses reached $1.1 billion during FY1982 through FY1985.[34] The worrisome reports published by the GAO in the preceding years were well founded. The problem was that the world economic recovery was slow. The austerity measures imposed on developing and emerging countries by the IMF and major creditor governments depressed international demand and prevented the bank from resuming its full activities. For example, during FY1983–FY1986, the credits authorized by the agency were around 30% of the levels budgeted.[35] Exim Bank President William Draper reacted by promoting in 1985 a new program called "I-Match." Under this program, the institution would make up the difference between the subsidized loan rates offered by competing ECAs and higher market rates. This initiative was opposed by major exporters and traditional Exim Bank supporters because subsidies could be easily identified and estimated. A watered-down program was eventually adopted because there was nothing better to expect from the Reagan administration (Becker and McClenahan, 2003, pp. 210–211). The golden age of the Exim Bank was over.

Starting in the 1980s, the Exim Bank played the traditional role of an ECA by offering mainly guarantees and insurance schemes. It is interesting that, in 2007, the Congress enacted legislation that made the Exim Bank a self-sustaining entity no longer requiring a direct appropriation to fund its operations (Exim Bank, 2008, p. 3). Despite this historic move, the controversy about the efficiency of the institution did not diminish. In 2012, the Exim Bank's charter reauthorization was reduced from five years to two years and, in 2014, its authority was extended for only nine months, through June 30, 2015. On July 1, 2015, its full authority lapsed, which meant that the agency was prohibited from engaging in any business activities. A few months later, the Export-Import Bank Reform and Reauthorization Act of 2015 reauthorized the bank through September 30, 2019. However, due to a lack of quorum for the transaction of business by its Board of Directors, the institution was unable to authorize any long-term transactions. As a result, the total amount of authorizations (including loans, guarantees, and export credit insurance) declined from $20.5 billion in 2014 to $5 billion in 2016 and $3.3 billion in 2018 (Exim Bank, various years).

In May 2019, the quorum of the board was restored and allowed the bank to again offer its full range of financing. Shortly later, the Trump administration granted the Exim Bank a seven-year reauthorization. Kimberly Reed, the Exim President, recently explained that her institution had the mandate to take on Chinese exporters on behalf of U.S. businesses.[36] In a brief, the Exim Bank went even further, stating that "China challenges American power, influence, and interests, attempting to erode American security and prosperity."[37] The Exim initiative called "Program on China and Transformational Exports" is designed to (i) neutralize China's export subsidies for competing goods and services financed by official export credit or tied to aid and (ii) support American innovation and technological standards, through direct exports in key industries (e.g., artificial intelligence, biotechnology, biomedical sciences, wireless communications equipment, quantum computing, renewable energy, energy efficiency, and energy storage, semiconductor and semiconductor machinery manufacturing, emerging financial technologies, water treatment and sanitation, and high-performance computing).

In this exacerbated context, it is not surprising that the bank might support risky projects. In September 2019, it approved a $5 billion loan for Mozambique, the largest direct loan in the history of the bank. Its purpose is to provide equipment and services for the development and construction of an integrated liquefied natural gas (LNG) project. The principal supplier was Anadarko Petroleum Corp., a Texas firm which was acquired by Occidental Petroleum Corp. during the summer of 2019.[38]

The loan to Mozambique increased markedly the weighted-average risk rating for export credit authorizations for FY2019 to 6.9, compared to 5.5 in FY2018 (Exim Bank, 2019, p. 41).[39] The agency indicates that it generally does not authorize new credits that would be rated worse than "8", which is equivalent to B– on Standard & Poor's (S&P) rating scale. Yet, the FC rating assigned to Mozambique by S&P was in the "selective default" category when the loan was approved. Consequently, it seems clear that the $5 billion loan was granted regardless of Mozambique's credit position mainly because it thwarted China's ambitions. President K. Reed stated that the bank was told that

> China and Russia were slated to finance this deal before our Exim board quorum was restored by the U.S. Senate. The project now will be completed without their involvement and instead with 'Made in the USA' products and services. This is a win for our nation.[40]

The heightened rivalry between the United States and China is likely to encourage moral hazard, quite similar to what was observed in the second half of the 1970s. The Exim Bank has much more leeway than five or ten years ago and its new mission allows it to take more risks. American manufacturers as well as developing economies are aware of this changing environment. The former could be tempted to convince the agency to cover exports to risky foreign countries. The latter might threaten the bank with a shift to China if they do not get additional financing and/or debt rescheduling. It is too early to check whether moral hazard has materialized but the present context should raise concern.

Section 3 Conclusion

This chapter explores how the export credit industry has distorted international trade and, more dramatically, encouraged moral hazard. The noxiousness of export credit programs is encapsulated in the policy followed by the Exim Bank, especially in the 1970s and early 1980s.

Since the deregulation of the 1980s and 1990s, moral hazard issues have been partly addressed by new domestic and multilateral paradigms. Export-import banks and ECAs are more efficient but some flaws persist. Political interference has been observed in European countries as well as in the United States, especially to support big domestic industrialists and preserve diplomatic influence.

In fact, additional remedies can be advanced to fight moral hazard. The top priority consists of reducing information asymmetry. Export credit firms should be as transparent as possible regarding their exposure and the beneficiaries of their programs (sectors, firms, countries). Next, they must monitor carefully the credit position of domestic exporters as well as foreign importers. This entails robust corporate and country risk methodologies and ratings, which should be used to discriminate among applicants and set premium rates and/or interest rates. Lastly, governments and parliaments must increase supervision of ECAs and export-import banks, transform them into self-sustaining agencies, or, more radically, privatize them and ensure that the entity will not be bailed out in case of financial distress.

Other issues deserve examination. It is illusory to believe that ECAs and export-import banks successfully reduce trade deficit or improve the competitive position of a country. Competitiveness is fundamentally based on relevant research and development, efficient outsourcing, and reasonable debt strategy. A firm benefitting frequently from export credit subsidies should be considered highly politically connected but, at the same time, vulnerable in the medium/long term. Boeing and General Electric are two striking illustrations. These two major multinational companies have obtained massive Exim Bank loan guarantees for decades (Feinberg, 1982, p. 35; Kidwell, 2015, p. 12) but they have been unable to preserve their international market share and saw their credit position weaken significantly.[41] Why? Because in a globalized world economy, subsidies are short-term, second-best options that not only disincentivize the beneficiary from enhancing its competitiveness but also encourage excessive risk-taking.

Since the 2000s, moral hazard incentives in the credit export industry have waned. Central banks' accommodative monetary policies (see Flores and Gaillard, Chapter 5, and Gaillard and Michalek, Chapter 10 of this volume), recurrent bailouts in case of financial crisis (see Block, Chapter 9 of this volume), and inflated credit ratings (see Gaillard, 2014; Gaillard and Harrington, 2016) have become much more serious issues. However, the last few years have shown that multilateralism is increasingly questioned by populist movements, protectionism is spreading, and many countries may be tempted to subsidize massively their exporting firms. In the nascent *post-globalization* era (Gaillard, 2020b), a resurgence of moral hazard in the export credit industry is probable.

Notes

1 For example, the Export Credits Guarantee Department (ECGD, United Kingdom), the Nederlandsche Credietverzekering Maatschappij, and the Société française d'assurance-crédit were established in 1919, 1925, and 1927, respectively. The Export-Import Bank of the United States ('Exim Bank' thereafter) was set up in 1934.
2 We assume here that ECAs and export-import banks are *de jure* or *de facto* state agencies.
3 For an analysis of the first credit export scheme launched in Great Britain, see Dietrich (1935). Other prominent research works can be mentioned: Segré (1958) studies the activities of British, French, and German ECAs in the 1930s–1950s while Feinberg (1982) and Becker and McClenahan (2003) investigate the role of the Exim Bank. For a literature review on export promotion programs between the 1960s and the 2000s, see Gianturco (2001) and Freixanet (2012). For an overview of the present export credit industry, see https://www.eca-watch.org.
4 The establishment of the Exim Bank in 1934 was driven by financial as well as diplomatic motives, see Section 2.
5 It is important to recall that Moody's assigned sovereign ratings since 1918 (see Gaillard, 2011, p. 4).
6 During the same period, the aggregated inflation rate was around 60% only; see https://france-inflation.com/inflation-depuis-1901.php.
7 See https://www.icisa.org/members-public.
8 For an analysis of the accuracy of such indicators, see Gaillard, 2020a, pp. 191–256.
9 See https://www.credendo.com/fr/country-risk. Appendix 4.1 lists Credendo's medium/long-term political risk ratings as of 1st January 2021.
10 Atradius and Euler Hermes are Dutch and French-German ECAs, respectively.

11 The lowest possible fees for a transaction are determined by the OECD country risk classification (Gonter, 2011, p. 223). This mechanism prevents ECAs from charging excessively low premium fees to risky borrowers. Appendix 4.1 lists the OECD country risk classifications as of 1st January 2021.
12 For an analysis of the societal responsibility of multinational firms (especially regarding human rights), see Bernaz (2017).
13 In a complementary analysis, Altamura and Flores Zendejas (2020) find that the decisions of commercial banks to lend to foreign governments in the late 1970s were based on their home governments' preferences, competition, and the assumption that home governments and international organizations would intervene as lender of last resort if necessary.
14 Recall that, in 1970, Henry Kearns – then Chairman of the Exim Bank – believed that the institution could generate enough exports sales to erase the U.S. balance-of-payments deficit. See P. Shabecoff, "Ex-Im Bank Adopts Hard Sell," *New York Times*, 13 December 1970.
15 Authors calculations based on Becker and McClenahan (2003) and Exim Bank (2015).
16 It is important to recall that, along with the Marshall Plan, Exim Bank's loans enabled Western Europe to recover from World War II.
17 For a focus on the concept of systemic risk, see Gaillard and Michalek, Chapter 7 of this volume.
18 The North Atlantic Treaty Organization (NATO) was established in 1949.
19 Authors' calculations based on Exim Bank's annual and semiannual reports (various years).
20 See "Ex-Im Bank Sets Loan, Guarantees Credits For Zaire Power Line," *Wall Street Journal*, 11 June 1979; "Ex-Im Bank to Back Loans to Philippines For Nuclear Facility," *Wall Street Journal*, 25 March 1981; "Ex-Im Bank to Back $204.5 Million Loan For Philippines Plant," *Wall Street Journal*, 15 September 1982.
21 See M. Acoca, "U.S., Spain Sign Pact on Defense: Accord on Bases Sets $1.3 Billion," *Washington Post*, 25 January 1976; Howard (1976, p. 309); Exim Bank (various years).
22 Authors' calculations based on Exim Bank (1982, pp. 34–35).
23 This criterion is hardly credible in light of what we have just described.
24 "Ex-Im Bank Plans More Lending to Spur Exports," *Los Angeles Times*, 3 August 1977.
25 The effective Fed Funds rate increased from 4.61% in January 1977 to 10.07% in January 1979, and 18.90% in December 1980; see https://fred.stlouisfed.org/series/FEDFUNDS.
26 For three of the six countries (namely, Niger, Cameroon, and Ethiopia), the amount of the loan exceeded the Exim Bank exposure at the end of the previous fiscal year.
27 Our analysis is consistent with Fitzgerald and Monson (1989, pp. 93–94) who investigate the conditions in which moral hazard is likely to appear in an export credit insurance contract.
28 See Minyard (1976) and U.S. Senate (1983).
29 In the specific case of Boeing, our suspicion of moral hazard appears all the more credible as, during the same period, the Federal Trade Commission documented that the aircraft giant had recently paid bribes to foreign officials to secure the sale of its jets; see J. Landauer, "U.S. Files Allege That Boeing Co. Bribed Foreign Officials to Win Sales Contracts," *Wall Street Journal*, 27 April 1979. The concomitance of moral hazard and corruption practices tends to support the immoral feature of moral hazard (see Claassen, Chapter 2 of this volume), thus requiring legal means to fight it.
30 J. F. Berry, "Ex-Im Financing Becoming Classic Off-Budget Case," *Washington Post*, 14 September 1980.
31 J. F. Berry, "Carter Tells Ex-Im Bank to Put Lid on Its Budget," *Washington Post*, 30 September 1980.

32 "Ex-Im Bank Says It Won't Pay Treasury A Dividend for 1980," *Wall Street Journal*, 16 December 1980. The dividend had amounted to $35 million in 1979.
33 C. H. Farnsworth, "Ex-Im Bank vs. Budget Cutters," *New York Times*, 13 February 1981; G. Lardner Jr., "House Stuns Administration by Defeating Ex-Im Bank Fund Cuts," *Washington Post*, 19 May 1981; and Becker and McClenahan (2003), pp. 210–211.
34 Authors' calculations based on Exim Bank's annual reports.
35 Authors' calculations based on Becker and McClenahan (2003), p. 223.
36 See https://www.theafricareport.com/29796/us-exim-we-have-a-new-mandate-to-take-china-on-around-the-world.
37 See https://www.exim.gov/who-we-serve/external-engagement/china-and-transformational-exports-program/fact-sheet.
38 In September 2019, Anadarko sold its 26.5% operated interest in the Mozambique LNG project to Total. The other operators were ENH Rovuma Área Um, S.A. (15%), Mitsui E&P Mozambique Area1 Ltd. (20%), ONGC Videsh Ltd. (10%), Beas Rovuma Energy Mozambique Limited (10%), BPRL Ventures Mozambique B.V. (10%), and PTTEP Mozambique Area 1 Limited (8.5%). See https://www.total.com/media/news/press-releases/total-closes-acquisition-anadarkos-shareholding-mozambique-lng.
39 The Exim Bank classifies credits into 11 risk categories, with '1' being the lowest risk and '11' the highest.
40 See https://www.exim.gov/news/exim-approves-5-billion-finance-exports-mozambique-lng-project.
41 Moody's rating of the two firms slipped from the 'Aaa'–'Aa' categories in 1998 to the 'Baa' category in 2020.

References

Altamura, C. E. and Flores Zendejas, J. (2020) "Politics, International Banking, and the Debt Crisis of 1982," *Business History Review*, Vol. 94, No. 4, pp. 753–778.

Alvarez, S. and Flores Zendejas, J. (2014) "Trade Finance and Latin America's Lost Decade: The Forgotten Link," *Economic History Research*, Vol. 10, No. 2, pp. 127–139.

Becker, W. H. and McClenahan, Jr. W. M. (2003) *The Market, The State, and The Export-Import Bank of the United States, 1934–2000*. Cambridge: Cambridge University Press.

Bernaz, N. (2017) *Business and Human Rights, History, Law and Policy – Bridging the Accountability Gap*. Abingdon: Routledge.

Bohn, Jr. J. A. (1986) "Eximbank's Role in International Banking and Finance: Loans, Reschedulings, and Development," *The International Lawyer*, Vol. 20, No. 3, pp. 829–836.

Bonin, H. (2002) "Aux origines de l'assurance-crédit en France (1927-1939): La création et l'essor de la SFAC et le repli de ses concurrentes," *Histoire, Économie et Société*, Vol. 21, No. 3, pp. 341–355.

Boyd, J. H. (1982) "Eximbank Lending: A Federal Program That Costs Too Much," *Federal Reserve Bank of Minneapolis, Quarterly Review*, Winter, Vol. 6, No. 1, pp. 1–17.

Camino, D. and Cardone, C. (1997) "The EU Proposal for a Council Directive on Export Credit Insurance: A Critical Evaluation," *Geneva Papers on Risk and Insurance*, Vol. 22, No. 84, pp. 413–425.

Darbellay, A. (2021) "Responsible Lending: Export Credit Agencies as Drivers of Human Rights," in Bantekas, I. and Stein, M. A. (Eds), *The Cambridge Companion to Business and Human Rights Law*. Cambridge: Cambridge University Press.

Dietrich, E. B. (1935) "British Export Credit Insurance," *American Economic Review*, Vol. 25, No. 2, pp. 236–249.

Exim Bank (various years) *Annual Report*. Washington, DC: Exim Bank [for 1967 and later].

Exim Bank (various years) *Semiannual Report*. Washington, DC: Exim Bank [for the years prior to 1967].

Feinberg, R. E. (1982) *Subsidizing Success – The Export-Import Bank in the U.S. Economy*. Cambridge: Cambridge University Press.

Fitzgerald, B. and Monson, T. (1989) "Preferential Credit and Insurance as Means to Promote Exports," *World Bank Research Observer*, Vol. 4, No. 1, pp. 89–114.

Fleisig, H. and Hill, C. (1984) "The Benefits and Costs of Official Export Credit Programs," in Baldwin, R. E. and Krueger, A. O. (Eds), *The Structure and Evolution of Recent U.S. Trade Policy*. Chicago: University of Chicago Press.

Fourcade, J-P., Charasse, M. and Hervé, E. (2008) *Rapport d'information fait au nom de la commission des Finances, du contrôle budgétaire et des comptes économiques de la Nation sur l'enquête de la Cour des comptes relative aux procédures publiques gérées par la COFACE*. Sénat, Session ordinaire de 2008-2009, No. 95. Paris: Sénat.

Freixanet, J. (2012) "Export Promotion Programs: Their Impact on Companies' Internationalization Performance and Competitiveness," *International Business Review*, Vol. 21, No. 6, pp. 1065–1086.

Gaillard, N. (2011) *A Century of Sovereign Ratings*. New York: Springer.

Gaillard, N. (2014) "How and Why Credit Rating Agencies Missed the Eurozone Debt Crisis?," *Capital Markets Law Journal*, Vol. 9, No. 2, pp. 121–136.

Gaillard, N. (2020a) *Country Risk – The Bane of Foreign Investors*. Cham: Springer.

Gaillard, N. (2020b) "Le COVID-19, accélérateur de la post-mondialisation," *Politique Etrangère*, Vol. 85, No. 3, pp. 59–70.

Gaillard, N. and Harrington, W. (2016) "Efficient, Commonsense Actions to Foster Accurate Credit Ratings," *Capital Markets Law Journal*, Vol. 11, No. 1, pp. 38–59.

General Accounting Office (1975) *Weakened Financial Condition of The Export-Import Bank of The United States*. Report to the Congress by the Comptroller General of the United States. 17 October. Washington, DC: General Accounting Office.

General Accounting Office (1980) *Financial and Other Constraints Prevent Eximbank From Consistently Offering Competitive Financing For U.S. Exports*. Report to the Congress by the Comptroller General of the United States. 30 April. Washington, DC: General Accounting Office.

General Accounting Office (1982) *Examination of the Export-Import Bank's Fiscal Year 1981 Financial Operations and Related Issues*. Report to the Congress by the Comptroller General of the United States. 18 November. Washington, DC: General Accounting Office.

General Accounting Office (1983) *Examination of The Export-Import Bank's Financial Statements for The Fiscal Years Ended September 30, 1982 and 1981*. Report to the Congress by the Comptroller General of the United States. 10 June. Washington, DC: General Accounting Office.

Gianturco, D. E. (2001) *Export Credit Agencies, The Unsung Giants of International Trade and Finance*. London and Westport, CT: Quorum Books.

Godinot, S. (2009) *2001–2008: qui bénéficie des garanties COFACE?* Montreuil: Les Amis de la Terre.

Gonter, M. (2011) "Premium: The Least Understood Rules of the Arrangement," in Organisation for Economic Co-operation and Development, *Smart Rules for Fair Trade, 50 Years of Export Credits*. Paris: OECD.

Götze, T. and Gürtler, M. (2020) "Risk Transfer and Moral Hazard: An Examination on the Market for Insurance-Linked Securities," *Journal of Economic Behavior and Organization*, Vol. 180, pp. 758–777.

Hanna, J. (1931) "Credit Insurance," *University of Pennsylvania Law Review*, Vol. 79, No. 5, pp. 521–548.

Howard, H. N. (1976) "The Bicentennial in American-Turkish Relations," *Middle East Journal*, Vol. 30, No. 3, Bicentennial Issue, Summer, pp. 291–310.

Kidwell, G. (2015) *Policy Analysis: Export-Import Bank.* Arlington: Charles Koch Institute.

Lawrence, R. Z. (1978) "An Analysis of the 1977 U.S. Trade Deficit," *Brookings Papers on Economic Activity*, Vol. 1, pp. 159–189.

Melitz, J. and Messerlin, P. (1987) "Export Credit Subsidies," *Economic Policy*, Vol. 2, No. 4, pp. 149–167.

Minyard, R. E. (1976) *The Export-Import Bank: Implications for The Federal Budget and The Credit Market.* Washington, DC: Congressional Budget Office.

Organisation for Economic Co-operation and Development (2008) *The Export Credits Arrangement, 1978–2008.* Paris: OECD.

Patterson, G. (1943) "The Export-Import Bank," *Quarterly Journal of Economics*, Vol. 58, No. 1, pp. 65–90.

Pipes, D. and Garfinkle, A. (1991) *Friendly Tyrants: An American Dilemma.* New York: St. Martin's Press.

Saul, S. (2002) "L'État et l'assurance des risques à l'exportation: la COFACE (1946-1966)," *Histoire, Économie et Société*, Vol. 21, No. 3, pp. 357–375.

Saul, S. (2010) "La COFACE: des opérations avec garantie de l'État au risque pays," *Les cahiers Irice*, Vol. 2010/2, No. 6, pp. 169–195.

Seck, S. L. and Chimisso dos Santos, D. (2018) "Export Credits, Sovereign Debt, and Human Rights," in Bantekas, I. and Stein, M. A. (Eds), *Sovereign Debt and Human Rights.* Cambridge: Cambridge University Press.

Segré, C. (1958) "Medium Term Export Finance," *Banca Nazionale del Lavoro Quarterly Review*, Vol. 11, No. 45, pp. 113–271.

United States Senate (1983) *Export-Import Bank Programs and Policies.* Hearings before the Subcommittee on International Finance and Monetary Policy of the Committee on Banking, Housing, and Urban Affairs – September 14 and 16, 1982. Washington, DC: U.S. Senate.

World Bank (1969) *Multilateral Debt Renegotiations: 1956–1968.* Washington, DC: World Bank.

Appendix 4.1: Credendo Political Medium/Long-Term Ratings and OECD Country Risk Classifications as of 1st January 2021

Countries	*Credendo political medium/long-term ratings*	*OECD country risk classifications*	*Countries*	*Credendo political medium/long-term ratings*	*OECD country risk classifications*
Afghanistan	7	7	Lesotho	5	6
Albania	5	5	Liberia	7	7
Algeria	4	5	Libya	7	7
Andorra	1	NC	Liechtenstein	1	NC
Angola	6	6	Lithuania	1	NC

(Continued)

Countries	*Credendo political medium/long-term ratings*	*OECD country risk classifications*	*Countries*	*Credendo political medium/long-term ratings*	*OECD country risk classifications*
Antigua & Barb.	6	7	Luxembourg	1	NC
Argentina	7	7	Macau	2	2
Armenia	6	6	Macedonia	5	5
Aruba	5	5	Madagascar	6	7
Australia	1	NC	Malawi	7	7
Austria	1	NC	Malaysia	2	2
Azerbaijan	4	5	Maldives	6	7
Bahamas	4	4	Mali	7	7
Bahrain	6	5	Malta	1	NC
Bangladesh	4	5	Marshall Islands	7	NC
Belarus	6	6	Mauritania	7	7
Belgium	1	NC	Mauritius	3	3
Belize	6	NC	Mexico	3	3
Benin	5	6	Micronesia	6	NC
Bhutan	6	6	Moldova	6	7
Bolivia	5	5	Monaco	1	NC
Bosnia & H.	6	7	Mongolia	7	7
Botswana	3	3	Montenegro	6	7
Brazil	5	5	Morocco	4	3
Brunei	2	NC	Mozambique	7	7
Bulgaria	2	3	Myanmar	6	6
Burkina Faso	6	7	Namibia	6	6
Burundi	7	7	Nauru	5	NC
Cambodia	6	6	Nepal	6	6
Cameroon	6	6	Netherlands	1	NC
Canada	1	NC	New Zealand	1	NC
Cabo Verde	6	6	Nicaragua	6	7
Central Afr. Rep.	7	7	Niger	7	7
Chad	6	7	Nigeria	6	6
Chile	3	NC	Norway	1	NC
China	2	2	Oman	6	5
Colombia	5	4	Pakistan	6	7
Comoros	7	NC	Palau	6	NC
Congo, Dem. R.	7	7	Panama	4	4
Congo, Rep.	7	7	Papua New G.	5	6
Costa Rica	3	4	Paraguay	4	5
Côte d'Ivoire	5	6	Peru	3	3

(*Continued*)

Countries	*Credendo political medium/long-term ratings*	*OECD country risk classifications*	*Countries*	*Credendo political medium/long-term ratings*	*OECD country risk classifications*
Croatia	3	4	Philippines	3	3
Cuba	7	7	Poland	2	NC
Curaçao	5	5	Portugal	1	NC
Cyprus	4	NC	Qatar	4	3
Czech Republic	1	NC	Romania	2	3
Denmark	1	NC	Russia	4	4
Djibouti	7	7	Rwanda	6	6
Dominica	6	NC	Sao Tome & P.	7	NC
Dominican Rep.	4	4	Saudi Arabia	3	2
Ecuador	6	7	Senegal	5	5
Egypt	5	5	Serbia	4	4
El Salvador	5	5	Seychelles	5	NC
Eq. Guinea	7	7	Sierra Leone	7	7
Eritrea	7	7	Singapore	1	0
Estonia	1	NC	Slovakia	1	NC
Ethiopia	6	7	Slovenia	1	NC
Fiji	5	5	Solomon Islands	6	NC
Finland	1	NC	Somalia	7	7
France	1	NC	South Africa	4	4
Gabon	5	6	Spain	1	NC
Gambia	7	7	Sri Lanka	5	6
Georgia	6	6	St. Kitts & Nevis	5	NC
Germany	1	NC	St. Lucia	6	NC
Ghana	5	6	St. Vincent & G.	6	NC
Greece	5	NC	Sudan	7	7
Grenada	6	NC	Sudan (South)	7	7
Guatemala	4	4	Suriname	6	7
Guinea	7	7	Swaziland	5	6
Guinea-Bissau	7	7	Sweden	1	NC
Guyana	6	6	Switzerland	1	NC
Haiti	7	7	Syria	7	7
Honduras	4	5	Taiwan	1	1
Hong Kong	2	3	Tajikistan	7	7
Hungary	3	NC	Tanzania	5	6
Iceland	2	NC	Thailand	3	3
India	3	3	Timor-Leste	6	6
Indonesia	3	3	Togo	6	6

(*Continued*)

Countries	*Credendo political medium/long-term ratings*	*OECD country risk classifications*	*Countries*	*Credendo political medium/long-term ratings*	*OECD country risk classifications*
Iran	7	7	Tonga	6	NC
Iraq	6	7	Trinidad & T.	3	3
Ireland	1	NC	Tunisia	6	6
Israel	3	NC	Turkey	5	5
Italy	1	NC	Turkmenistan	6	7
Jamaica	5	6	Tuvalu	7	NC
Japan	1	NC	United Arab E.	3	2
Jordan	6	5	Uganda	6	6
Kazakhstan	5	5	Ukraine	6	6
Kenya	7	6	United Kingdom	1	NC
Kiribati	7	NC	United States	1	NC
Korea (North)	7	7	Uruguay	3	3
Korea (South)	1	NC	Uzbekistan	5	5
Kosovo	6	6	Vanuatu	6	NC
Kuwait	3	2	Venezuela	7	7
Kyrgyzstan	6	7	Viet Nam	4	4
Laos	6	7	Yemen	7	7
Latvia	2	NC	Zambia	7	7
Lebanon	7	7	Zimbabwe	7	7

Sources: https://www.credendo.com/country-risk and http://www.oecd.org/trade/topics/export-credits/arrangement-and-sector-understandings/financing-terms-and-conditions/country-risk-classification

Note: Credendo rates countries on a scale of 1 (least risky) to 7 (most risky). The OECD rates countries on a scale of 0 (least risky) to 7 (most risky). High-income OECD and eurozone countries are not classified (NC) by the OECD.

5 The international lender of last resort between Scylla and Charybdis

Juan Flores Zendejas and Norbert Gaillard

This chapter provides a historical overview of the efforts for international cooperation in pursuit of financial stability. We argue that there are two fundamental threats likely to undermine the actions of an international lender of last resort (ILOLR): debtor *moral hazard and* creditor *moral hazard. During the Pax Britannica years, the Bank of England and the Bank of France were de facto ILOLR and managed to contain both types of moral hazard. In the interwar years, the League of Nations developed new forms of last-resort loans but failed to prevent the Great Depression because of the lack of cooperation between top capital-exporting countries. Since its establishment in 1944, the International Monetary Fund (IMF) has granted various credit facilities conditioned on the recipient countries accepting macroeconomic stabilization. The financial globalization process that started in the 1980s has exacerbated creditor moral hazard. This issue, largely overlooked by the IMF, should be a major source of concern for policymakers.*

In his *Art of Central Banking*, first published in 1932, R. G. Hawtrey wrote that an international central bank could contribute to the stability of the monetary system, mainly through a cooperation mechanism that would eventually be coordinated by the then recently formed Bank for International Settlements. According to Hawtrey, this cooperation was necessary given the incapacity of an international central bank to issue currency. He identified two main obstacles. First, the potential pressure on the available resources in face of a global crisis affecting several countries at once. This involved that the international lender would have to coordinate with central banks from unaffected countries, meaning that it would not act as a lender of last resort, but rather as a coordinator and an additional lender. The second obstacle was the uncertain capacity of this new international body to distinguish the central banks affected by payments imbalances from those which were imprudent or resorted to inflation.

Hawtrey was preoccupied with the challenges stemming from the Great Depression. For example, he aimed at mitigating the sources of the fluctuations in the value of gold – the keystone of the Genoa monetary system set up ten years earlier. Although no adequate institution was established to reach this

DOI: 10.4324/9781003139249-5

goal, his proposals foreshadowed the international agreements reached a decade later at Bretton Woods. Today, the limitations and fragilities of the international monetary and financial system remain a hot topic, as suggested by the vast literature on systemic risk and last-resort lending that flourished in the aftermath of the 2007–2008 subprime crisis (see, among others, Evanoff et al., 2009; Bank for International Settlements, 2014; Broz, 2015).

In this chapter, we present an overview of the quest for institutional monetary and financial cooperation since the mid-19th century. We focus on historical experiences that show that coordinated efforts to provide last-resort loans have led to positive benefits for both debtors and creditors. While such actions failed to be institutionalized until the interwar period, coordinated official intervention became necessary to achieve certain stability to the financial architecture. However, these interventions encouraged either debtor or creditor moral hazard. Our long-term perspective investigates how contemporaries dealt with moral hazard in different periods. We observe a major shift in the discussions and actions of major international lenders, going from a preoccupation mainly on debtor moral hazard to one on creditor moral hazard. This shift has several drivers, including regulatory changes, concentration in the U.S. financial sector, and political cooption by the financial sector. As we contend, a major obstacle that emerged three decades ago is the growing size of the financial sector, a feature that might hinder the potential capacity of an international lender of last resort (ILOLR) to intervene efficiently.

Therefore, it is striking that economists' opinions are especially divergent. To begin with, not everybody is convinced that there is a need for an international lender of last resort. The obvious candidate, the International Monetary Fund (IMF), seems to have fallen into disfavor (Schadler, 2014). In the recent European debt crisis, it was accused of waiving its own rules, opening the box to further fiscal indiscipline, encouraging discretionary behavior in its lending decisions, and turning a blind eye on political interference (see Bianco, Chapter 6 of this volume). These kinds of arguments echo those raised almost two decades ago by Rogoff,[1] who suggested that the Fund should give up its lending activities, as it encourages borrowers' (and lenders') moral hazard and does not have sufficient financial resources in the event of a global financial crisis.

It is noteworthy that Rogoff's arguments contrast with those advanced by Hawtrey. Rogoff's concerns were largely related to a highly interconnected financial system, one in which the financial sector occupies a prominent place, a reality that differs radically from Hawtrey's times. Next, few economists promote today a return to fixed exchange rates, although disputes still rage over the appropriate exchange rate regimes. However, we are convinced that, like in the early 1930s, our financial system is now threatened by an unprecedented systemic crisis. We agree with Rogoff about the limited resources of the IMF, but we suggest that he may be looking in the wrong place. In this chapter, we argue that the focal point of a reform of the IMF – as a lender of last resort – should rather take into account the exorbitant size of the financial sector and thus address the inherent creditor moral hazard issue.

How should an ILOLR operate with limited financial resources and without inducing moral hazard? Fischer (1999) provides some parallels with the literature on lending of last resort in the banking sector, where a lender or crisis manager may intervene only in specific circumstances, leading to a situation in which a "constructive" ambiguity would encourage lenders and borrowers to negotiate a debt restructuring – under the assumption of no official support – bringing back to the market the defaults' disputes and optimizing the need for official intervention.[2] However, unnecessary ambiguity may enhance the risk of disorderly defaults. Such a situation, in which ILOLR does not intervene despite market expectations of the contrary, may be highly costly to the economy and lead to a systemic crisis. Therefore, Fischer (1999) concludes that an ILOLR should spell out its rule to the extent possible.

This chapter is structured as follows. Focusing on the Pax Britannica years, Section 1 analyzes how the Bank of England and the Bank of France were de facto ILOLR and managed to contain debtor as well as creditor moral hazard. Section 2 investigates the policies implemented by two new international organizations: the League of Nations and the Bank for International Settlements (BIS). They developed innovative forms of last-resort loans but failed to prevent the Great Depression because of the lack of cooperation between top capital-exporting countries. Section 3 examines the role of the IMF during 1944–1973. A remarkable feature of this period was that IMF stand-by agreements were generally accompanied by debt restructurings. Section 4 shows how and why the globalization process starting in the 1980s has exacerbated *creditor* moral hazard.[3] This trend has been overlooked by the IMF, which placed much greater emphasis on preventing *debtor* moral hazard. Section 5 concludes.

Section 1 During the Pax Britannica, an evolving international financial architecture, with no ILOLR

During the 19th century, international trade and capital flows increased considerably. This economic and financial integration implied that a recession in one country could lead to a decline in the economic activity at the international level.[4] This was particularly true for the bigger, central countries, such as Great Britain and France. Not surprisingly, international economic and financial crises occurred frequently (e.g., in 1866, 1873, 1890, and 1907). Banking, debt, and currency crises took place in different places simultaneously, obliging governments, private banks, and central banks to cooperate.

1.1 1870–1914: a liberal framework

Wherever they were established, national central banks fulfilled lending of last resort functions. Bignon et al. (2012) describe how the Bank of England's operations evolved during the crises of 1847, 1857, and 1866. According to these authors, the support by the Bank of England was selective during the first crisis, while the rates at which liquidity was provided were lower than those offered in the market. In the following crises, the Bank began providing liquidity more extensively at above-market discount rates, as it was later advocated by Walter Bagehot in his book *Lombard Street.* According to Bignon et al., the evolution from credit rationing to massive liquidity provision was also paralleled by the Bank of France around the same years (see also Ugolini, Chapter 3 of this volume). Moral hazard was taken into consideration by the two central banks, but it did not emerge as a major problem as the two institutions tightened their prudential standards as a prerequisite for granting access to their rediscounting operations.

While the central banks' role as lender of last resort was still in the making in the 19th century, international crises requiring coordinated action or cooperative behavior were more limited. The examination of the financial crises listed in Kindleberger (1978) shows that most crises ended up with the intervention of a *national* lender of last resort. The exceptions were the crises of 1836–1838 which affected England, the United States, and France; 1848 which was circumvented to several European countries and the U.S.; and the Baring crisis of 1890 that shook England dramatically. Kindleberger (1978) mentions that liquidity shortage led to occasional bilateral transactions between central banks, some of which included the participation of merchant banks.

One major, illustrative crisis engendering this kind of collaboration is the Baring crisis of 1890. The main reason behind Baring's near failure was its overexposure to Argentinean and Uruguayan securities.[5] The bank was the main underwriter of the bonds issued by the two governments as well as by British and Argentinean companies operating in those countries (Flores, 2011). By 1890, and after a ten-year lending boom, both governments were on the brink of default (Ferns, 1992). The rescue of Baring involved a heightened cooperation under the auspices of the Bank of England. Its role was twofold. First, it provided liquidity through a short-term advance and the organization of a bailout committee in which a syndicate of banks guaranteed Baring's liabilities. Second, the Bank also supported debt negotiations between a group of commercial banks and Argentina's government. The objective was to avert a unilateral default by Buenos Aires, which would have had a major impact on Baring's solvency.[6]

The Bank of England's intervention was consistent with the action undertaken by the Bank of France one year before. The episode in Paris had required the central bank to intervene given the problems faced by one systemic institution: the Comptoir d'Escompte.[7] The policies implemented helped to prevent the bankruptcy of the Comptoir d'Escompte, and a generalized banking failure through the provision of liquidity to the market and the guarantee that depositors would suffer no losses. According to Hautcoeur et al. (2014), the French central bank eliminated moral hazard through the penalization of those banks which had contributed to the failure of the Comptoir d'Escompte, requiring them to participate in the guarantee syndicate in a larger proportion as compared to other banks.

However, contrary to the French crisis, the intervention of the Bank of England during the Baring crisis included an international dimension, given the potential strain on the Bank of England's gold reserves. The Bank was first obliged to secure the necessary means domestically to guarantee Baring's liabilities and liquidate the bank holding the "toxic" assets while creating a new one with the "good" assets. Additionally, it secured two loans from the Bank of France and the State Bank of Russia, through a swap of £3 million of gold for Treasury bills (White, 2016). The Bank of England also convinced the Russian government to refrain from withdrawing a deposit held by Baring until the liquidity problems could be solved.

Despite the ad hoc nature of this cooperation, the Baring crisis illustrates how central banks were obliged to cooperate in order to maintain certain stability in the international monetary system. According to Flandreau (1996), central banks developed the necessary tools to intervene in foreign markets more efficiently. This involves the diversification of assets in central bank's reserves, including sterling-denominated bills of exchange, but also the capacity to sell gold at varying prices, which avoided the use of the discount rate and its potential destabilizing effects. Flandreau (1996) stresses the efforts to institutionalize the cooperation between central banks – in particular after the crisis of 1907 – through the creation of an international network of financial assistance. These types of proposals were never implemented, however, given the fear that automatic credit lines might have reduced bankers' responsibility and led to more instability.[8]

1.2 Coping with debtor and creditor moral hazard in the sovereign debt market

During the late 19th century, central banks were increasingly committed to ensure stability to their banking sector and to the gold standard. While creditor moral hazard remained a major concern, governments and central banks managed to coordinate to prevent potential debtor moral hazard problems. During the Baring crisis, the Bank of England had also to cope with Argentina's own securities and thus, maintain a permanent communication with the government. On the other hand, the British government closely monitored the negotiations between bankers' committee and Buenos Aires. The resulting bailout agreement, signed in 1891, imposed certain macroeconomic conditions, mostly related to fiscal and monetary policies. This agreement had to be renegotiated two years later to alleviate the burden placed upon Argentina's public finances (Marichal, 1989).

Nevertheless, in most cases of sovereign defaults, governments maintained a hands-off attitude. Bondholder associations gained official recognition and were soon in charge of negotiating with borrowing governments (Mauro et al., 2006). The capacity of bondholders to enforce settlements stemmed from the General-Purpose Committee of the London Stock Exchange, which could exclude a government from having access to London's capital market (Flandreau, 2013). International cooperation between various bondholder associations served to expand this exclusion to other capital markets, if necessary (Flores Zendejas et al., 2021). Moreover, underwriting banks were also likely to cooperate with bondholders and supervise the negotiations with foreign governments. This could have engendered conflicts of interest among underwriting banks, given their interest in bringing defaulters back to the market and earning underwriting fees. However, as Flandreau and Flores (2012) show, top underwriting banks prevented unfavorable deals with bondholders, and conditioned bailout loans to specific economic policies. These conditional loans were frequent in the 1890s (e.g., in Greece and Brazil in 1893 and 1898, respectively; see Flores, 2012).

These market mechanisms worked relatively well to fight debtor moral hazard. The threat of foreign intervention was also a major deterrent to default. In the most extreme cases, a default might lead to a loss of sovereignty (e.g., the establishment of a colonial regime, as happened in Egypt). However, this procedure could also raise other questions regarding the capacity of bondholder associations to lobby their governments to assume a more proactive role. The risk of *creditor* moral hazard was key to understanding why the British government abstained from intervening on behalf of its bondholders. Lord Palmerston, the British Foreign Secretary in the 1840s, referred to a creditor moral hazard argument to defend this policy. While he could grant a diplomatic support to bondholders, such support remained discretionary. In addition, he considered that the losses stemming from defaulted bonds were the consequence of investors' imprudence. Furthermore, he stressed that the absence of governmental intervention was a "salutary warning" to creditors (Waibel, 2011). Platt (1968, p. 37) also emphasizes that the Foreign Office constantly refrained from resorting to force on the ground that it would have encouraged unwise speculations.

Section 2 1923–1939, the role of new international institutions to foster cooperation

World War I destroyed the economic and financial globalization that had been built so far. During the immediate postwar years, governments in Europe and in the U.S. attempted to restore a stable monetary system and boost international trade. In 1920, the Economic and Financial Organization of the League of Nations (EFO) was established to reactivate long-term credit for reconstruction and development. One decade later, the BIS was founded to act as a trustee of the German Dawes and Young loans, and to foster central bank cooperation.

During the 1920s, the League of Nations promoted stabilization loans to Central and Eastern European nations. The governments that solicited the League had generally been excluded from capital markets. The League's support involved two steps. The first one was the design and implementation of a stabilization program, based on a preliminary set of missions established by League representatives in the country. The macroeconomic policies that were requested by the League were related to the achievement of budgetary balances and the stabilization of the exchange rate through adherence to the gold standard. In countries where central banks were absent, the League favored their establishment with a certain degree of autonomy. Once the government accepted these goals, the League sent permanent representatives to monitor the progress of the programs and the use of the loans' proceeds.[9] The second step was the issuance of a foreign loan, for which the League acted as an intermediary between borrowing governments, underwriters, and creditor governments.

To some extent, this conditionality was designed to help the recovery of the economy, but also to provide investors with sufficient guarantees to finance the stabilization programs. In the case of Austria, the League lobbied and succeeded in obtaining an external guarantee for the loan granted by a group of European countries. When supported countries attempted to negotiate the initial terms as requested by the League, they systematically failed. The permanent presence of foreign advisors in central banks or in Finance Ministries was not always accepted.[10] The lack of flexibility observed in the League's interventions reflected the institution's risk aversion. Why? Because the League was not endowed with its own capital and was constrained as a lender of last resort. This feature similarly implied that the risk of either debtor or creditor moral hazard was also limited. Yet, when the financial and economic turmoil of the early 1930s erupted, the fragilities of the League's design became blatant.

In fact, borrowing countries needed urgent and massive assistance that the League was unable to provide. The League continued to support countries in financial distress through stabilization programs and long-term loans, such as Austria's second guarantee loan in 1933. There is a consensus among historians that countries such as Romania – which approached the League after its previous stabilization program failed – or Poland would have benefited from an earlier collaboration with the League. By the mid-1930s, the financial environment had deteriorated dramatically and worldwide defaults hindered new investments (see Gaillard, 2011, pp. 191–192).

The establishment of the BIS in 1930 complemented the League's work through its historical trademark, i.e., bridge loans which served as last-resort interventions.[11] So, foreign capital, therefore, continued to flow when it was urgently needed. The BIS was thus considered a top candidate to provide ILOLR services. Under a fixed exchange regime as the one established in the 1920s, Hawtrey (1932) regarded the BIS as the central bank of central banks, one which could contribute to stabilize world price levels and provide liquidity in times of financial stress. While Hawtrey contemplated several alternatives on how such an institution could work, one straightforward proposal was that an ILOLR could centralize the holdings of gold through the concentration of central banks' gold deposits. The ILOLR would then directly lend to national central banks when necessary. Hawtrey anticipated a potential problem of debtor moral hazard; such a facility would have required the BIS to distinguish between the borrowers suffering from temporary exogenous shocks to their balance of payments and those resorting to the BIS loans because of their "own imprudence" (p. 278). In fact, whereas the BIS had begun lending to countries facing liquidity shortage, it rapidly suspended these operations as it perceived that most borrowers were facing structural imbalances (Baer, 1999).

The wave of sovereign defaults of the early 1930s convinced policymakers to introduce certain changes to sovereign debt markets. An illustrative episode was the set of meetings organized by a committee hosted by the League of Nations. These meetings were driven by the excessive, uncoordinated lending of the 1920s. In this regard, the introduction of an international regulatory framework represented a significant challenge. To avert problems of over-indebtedness, the committee suggested to implement joint examination by underwriting banks in different domestic markets (League of Nations, 1939, p. 8). The committee further proposed to set up an international financial authority with the capacity to appoint financial experts to give their advice on each new loan. The purpose was to provide an objective and complete survey of the risks involved.

The committee also examined the design of debt contracts, which paralleled some of the more recent debates on a sovereign debt restructuring mechanism. The committee discussed the inclusion of clauses related to bondholders' representation. Such clauses were considered unproblematic when a bondholder association existed (i.e., in most European capital-exporting nations). An alternative was the creation of a bondholder representative, whose legal powers could vary (League of Nations, 1939, p. 20). His decisions would be binding to all bondholders, especially if all or a majority of bondholders endorsed him (in practice, a collective action clause). However, the report also enumerated a number of legal complications, including possible disagreements with the representative or the existence of holdout creditors.

Section 3 1944–1973, an international financial architecture without ILOLR

In 1944–1945, the main economic objectives of Western leaders and policymakers were to reconstruct Europe and restore multilateralism. This entailed a high degree of cooperation and a new international financial architecture.

3.1 Two new pillars: The World Bank and the International Monetary Fund

The Bretton Woods Conference of July 1944 established the International Bank for Reconstruction and Development (IBRD)[12] and the IMF.[13] Years after years, these two institutions managed to set and maintain high standards for their operations. In addition, they helped to reduce information asymmetry and debtor moral hazard problems.

The IBRD's primary mission was to reconstruct the war-damaged nations of Europe but, starting in the early 1950s, the Bank offered project loans mostly to low- and middle-income economies. The interest rates charged by the Bank were more favorable than those prevailing in member countries or charged by private creditors (see International Bank for Reconstruction and Development, 1950, p. 14). The profitability of the Bank was largely underpinned by its pioneering role in terms of credit risk assessment, debt reporting system, and project supervision (International Bank for Reconstruction and Development, 1960; Avramovic et al., 1964; International Bank for Reconstruction and Development, 1975).[14]

The IMF was responsible for maintaining the new international monetary system, which involved fixing a foreign par value for a currency by using gold (or a currency tied to gold) and then keeping the exchange rate within 1% of its par value. Exchange rates remained adjustable and the Fund facilitated loans to countries experiencing temporary balance-of-payments deficits.[15] In 1952, the IMF launched the so-called "stand-by arrangement." This credit line, limited to a period of six months but renewable, carried an interest rate of 0.25% per annum (International Monetary Fund, 1953, p. 95). Stand-by arrangements were granted in support of programs designed to correct external imbalance, such as the adoption of a sustainable exchange rate and inflation control (Polak, 1991).[16] The surveillance activity of the Fund was especially important to ensure that the applicant countries would be able to implement the necessary reforms and that the borrowing governments did respect their commitments.

Conditionality and monitoring practices enabled the two Bretton Woods institutions to preserve a high level of credibility and cemented their senior creditor status.

3.2 The tradeoff between restructuring and refinancing

In the aftermath of World War II, creditors had to struggle to reach debt restructuring agreements. In December 1952, the most recalcitrant debtors (those whose defaulting government bonds exceeded $30 million) were the Soviet Union, Romania, Yugoslavia, Greece, China, Hungary, Bolivia, East Germany, Austria, Poland, Bulgaria, and Czechoslovakia.[17] In the meantime, other traditional sovereign borrowers – whether they had remained solvent or renegotiated their debt in the 1930s and 1940s – started a new indebtedness cycle. Very soon, some governments faced difficulties in obtaining the foreign exchange needed to service their external debt. As a result, they requested debt rearrangements, which might include a moratorium, a debt cancellation, a rescheduling, and/or a refinancing.[18] These rearrangements could be settled on a bilateral or multilateral basis. Bilateral debt agreements were more opaque and thus might encourage debtor moral hazard. In contrast, multilateral deals – based on the most-favored nation clause – obliged creditors as well as debtors to calibrate their demands more reasonably.

A key step toward the multilateral approach was the establishment of the Paris Club in 1956. This informal organization brought together creditor countries in order to increase cooperation and deal with debtor problems.[19] During 1956–1972, twenty-two multilateral debt renegotiations involving nine countries[20] were reached (Klein, 1973). As these renegotiations were frequently part of a global economic stabilization plan, they could be accompanied by stand-by arrangements. The IMF was in no way an ILOLR since its financial assistance did not aim at preventing debt restructurings. In most agreements, the debts subject to consolidation were exclusively those resulting from Western export credit agencies' and/or the U.S. Exim Bank's loans (International Bank for Reconstruction and Development, 1969). The IBRD loans were exceptionally included in the India 1968 agreement. In fact, the World Bank was extremely reluctant to reschedule its long-term, low-interest rate loans on the ground that they financed complex projects. It is important to note that creditor governments (either directly or through an export credit scheme) were also prone to make new loans to distressed debtors.

Three lessons can be drawn from these debt renegotiation episodes. First, debt restructurings were not a taboo: official bilateral creditors consented to some haircuts in order to avert outright default or repudiation. Second, the World Bank and the IMF were considered senior creditors by the international financial community. Third, there was no de facto or de jure ILOLR likely to rescue distressed debtors.

3.3 The "World Central Bank" and the "ILOLR": two hot topics

The debate over a possible world central bank intensified in the 1960s, fed by the growing instability of the Bretton Woods system. Two prominent but opposing schools of thought emerged. On the one hand, in his famous dilemma, Triffin (1960) assessed that the United States could not simultaneously preserve the value of the dollar in terms of a fixed supply of gold and provide the international liquidity needed by the global economy. As a result, he advocated the conversion of the IMF into a bank of issue. The increase in IMF quota in 1959 and 1965, the General Arrangements to Borrow (GAB) concluded in 1962,[21] and the creation of Special Drawing Rights (SDRs) in 1969 seemed to be key steps toward this end.[22] On the other hand, Despres et al. (1966) downplayed the risk of payments imbalances, arguing that the system of international financial intermediation should be based on the dollar, which would sanctify the position of the Federal Reserve as de facto world central bank. This proposal was consistent with the establishment of currency swap lines by the Federal Reserve in 1962[23] and the development of Eurodollar markets in Europe.

The world central bank and the international liquidity issues were addressed in a fascinating manner by the speakers at the Annual Meeting convened by the Per Jacobsson Foundation in September 1970. In his lecture, William McChesney Martin, Jr. – who had just left the chairmanship of the Board of

Governors of the Federal Reserve – highlighted that the functions that might be performed by a world central bank were partly performed by existing institutions (e.g., the IMF, the BIS, and major monetary authorities). He also suggested that the world bank of the future could have a "federal-type organization" (Per Jacobsson Foundation, 1970, pp. 15–27). In his comments, economist Harry G. Johnson stated that, at the time, there was no threat of liquidity crisis because the potential lenders of last resort were ready for action. However, he warned against the inaccurate contra-cyclical management of reserves by the ILOLRs and the risk of "blackmail on the part of the less responsible countries" (Per Jacobsson Foundation, 1970, pp. 44–48). As we will see below, Johnson's fears proved prescient.

Section 4 1973–2006, a network of ad hoc ILOLRs

The collapse of the Bretton Woods system in 1971–1973 coincided with the oil crisis and it shook the world economy: GDP growth slowed dramatically while inflation and unemployment rates soared. This unstable economic environment led Western governments to take unprecedented measures to save jobs and bail out some distressed firms.[24] In the meantime, the resources of the IMF were expanded in order to support developing countries, especially oil-importing ones. Many of these measures, thought to be transitory, were perpetuated.

The new paradigm that arose in the second half of the 1970s entailed heightened cooperation between international institutions, creditor nations, and major banks. It did not result in the establishment of a full-fledged ILOLR but instead a *network of ad hoc ILOLRs*. This network was underpinned by three key principles: (i) the recourse to novel policies and tools aimed to provide massive liquidity to the world financial system; (ii) the imposition of stricter conditionality rules on the debtor governments borrowing from the IMF and a strong aversion to debt restructurings; and (iii) the implementation of new regulatory rules designed to strengthen the stability of the international banking system.

4.1 Liquidity: the sinew of the post-Bretton Woods world

Two complementary trends contributed to increase international liquidity. By far, the most important one is related to the structural, long-run shifts that occurred in the U.S. monetary, fiscal, and regulatory landscape. The other involves the new IMF credit arrangements launched to rescue distressed sovereign debtors.

4.1.1 The United States as the global liquidity provider

The central financial role played by the United States during 1973–2006 (and to a greater extent until today) was fundamentally driven by the capacity of

U.S. authorities to overcome the Triffin dilemma. To sum up, Washington managed to provide international liquidity without jeopardizing the credibility of the U.S. dollar. Several key factors can be identified.

Starting in the early 1970s, the Federal Reserve monetary policy swung between a *slightly* and *significantly* expansive course.[25] The best illustration was the so-called "Great Moderation" observed under Alan Greenspan's tenure (1987–2006): it consisted of setting an implicit inflation target of around 2% without taking into account the price rise of financial and nonfinancial assets.[26] This pattern, amplified by the credit channel, led to capital outflows that fed asset bubbles. Put it another way, the low level of the Fed Funds rates as well as the asymmetry of monetary policy reactions[27] during this period encouraged risk-taking and leverage strategies in the United States *and abroad* (see Cecchetti et al., 2017).

Liquidity provision was also spurred by the unsurpassable fiscal capacity of the U.S. administration. Despite a structural fiscal deficit and a rising public debt to GDP ratio (from 33% in 1973 to 61% in 2006), T-Bills and T-Bonds remained the most liquid and abundant *risk-free* assets in the world. Backed on the first economic and military power in the world, they were rated AAA by credit ratings agencies and had no rival.

Lastly, the wave of U.S. deregulation (from the Garn-St. Germain Depository Institutions Act of 1982 to the Gramm-Leach-Bliley Act of 1999 and the Commodity Futures Modernization Act of 2000) and the lenient practices of overwhelmed regulators (e.g., Rule 3a-7 and the "voluntary regulation" adopted by the Securities and Exchange Commission in 1992 and 2004, respectively)[28] were decisive in the context of international financial liberalization. It fostered financial innovation (e.g., derivatives and securitized debt instruments) and enabled globalized financial intermediaries and their foreign affiliates to trade *risk-free* and *speculative* dollar-denominated assets.

These factors strengthened the role of the dollar as top reserve currency[29] as well as "hot money" channel. Besides, they averted its sharp depreciation which the growing US current account deficit might have presaged.[30] More importantly, the dominance of the dollar in the post-Bretton Woods decades reinforced the global financial cycle among industrialized economies by synchronizing risk appetite across international capital markets (see Jordà et al., 2018). This trend exacerbated the likelihood of international financial crises and spillovers, which required the intervention of a lender of last resort at the domestic and international levels. In the latter case, this function was mostly fulfilled by the IMF.

4.1.2 The IMF as ILOLR-in-chief

The emergence of an ILOLR scheme in the immediate post-Bretton Woods years was a complex, empirical, and desultory process. The strains on the international financial system and the growing global public debts in less developed countries (LDCs) convinced policymakers to enhance cooperation and contemplate new forms of emergency liquidity provision and last-resort lending. Several institutions contributed to shaping this ad hoc ILOLR network: G10 central banks, the BIS, the IBRD, regional development banks, and the IMF.

In the wake of the generalized floating regime, risky foreign exchange operations intensified among Western commercial banks. Inevitably, some of them experienced huge losses and even collapsed, like Herstatt Bank in June 1974 (Schenk, 2014). Its closure by German authorities had international repercussions and led the central bank governors of the G10 to release a press communiqué in September in which they explained they had exchanged views on

> the problem of the lender of last resort in the Euro-markets. They recognized that it would not be practical to lay down in advance detailed rules and procedures for the provision of temporary liquidity. But they were satisfied that means are available for that purpose and will be used if and when necessary (see Altamura and Flores Zendejas, 2020).

This statement was a milestone in at least three regards. First, it showed that central banks accepted the principle of ILOLR if the stability of the international financial system was at risk. Second, they did not commit to intervene systematically, thus adopting a "constructive ambiguity" strategy. Third, they agreed to cooperate in the event of a severe crisis and thus established the Basel Committee on Banking Supervision in December 1974.[31]

At the same time, the IMF was on the front line to fight against macroeconomic imbalances caused by the oil crisis and the economic slowdown. Starting in 1974, the Fund expanded its "emergency lender" status by implementing new types of loans: the "oil facility" and the "extended fund facility" (EFF).[32] The former helped countries finance payments deficits caused by the surge in oil prices. The latter provided medium-term assistance to governments with balance of payments problems resulting from structural economic changes.[33]

Very soon, the financing of the IMF itself became a major issue. Two quota increases were approved in 1976 and 1978 but the most prominent move was certainly the establishment of a supplementary financing facility (also called "Witteveen facility") in 1977. Fourteen governments or national institutions expressed their readiness to make SDR8.65 billion available to the Witteveen facility.[34] This initiative was praised by economist Albert Fishlow who viewed it as an indispensable "bailout of the international financial system" but warned that it was "a first, and minimal, step" (United States Senate, 1978, pp. 61–63).[35] These additional resources enabled the Fund to expand its financial assistance in a context of heightened country risk (see Gaillard, 2020, pp. 46–47 and 50–52).

However, this financial truce was short-lived. As early as 1981, Poland rescheduled part of its debt to commercial banks (see Gaillard and Michalek, Chapter 7 of this volume).[36] Other major sovereign borrowers struggled to remain solvent but failed to do so. In August 1982, Mexico announced a 90-day moratorium on the repayment of its bank debt to 1,400 banks due in 1983. The United States provided $1 billion in prepayment for imports from Mexico and a $925 million loan. The BIS granted a facility for the same amount. Despite these fresh loans, the moratorium was extended. In December 1982, Jacques de Larosière, Managing Director of the IMF, stated that the Fund could not rescue the country unless Mexico's creditors agreed to provide a $5 billion complementary financing. Commercial banks surrendered and the Fund approved a $3.8 billion arrangement under Mexico's first credit tranche and an EFF (Mendelsohn, 1983, pp. 23–24).

This "cooperative scheme" was, to various degrees, applied to other distressed debtors. It marked a watershed in the history of international finance as the IMF acted as crisis manager and ILOLR-in-chief. Its prerogatives went well beyond what the Bretton Woods Agreement had established and what an international financial institution had ever been granted.

In the subsequent years, the ad hoc functions of the Fund were confirmed in two ways. On the one hand, the IMF set up new credit arrangements, such as the structural adjustment facility (SAF), the enhanced SAF (ESAF), the systemic transformation facility (STF), the emergency financing mechanism (EFM), the supplemental reserve facility (SRF), the contingent credit lines (CCL), and the exogenous shocks facility (ESF) established in 1986, 1988, 1993, 1995, 1997, 1999, and 2005, respectively.[37] Although these loans had different purposes, they were mostly designed to contain financial, economic, or political shocks driven by the growing interconnectedness of emerging economies.

On the other hand, the frequent financial shocks which materialized in the 1990s enabled the Fund to reinforce its role as crisis manager. During the Tequila and Asian crises that occurred in 1994–1995 and 1997–1998, respectively, the IMF lent not only a total of $52.8 billion to Mexico, Thailand, Indonesia, and South Korea but it was also instrumental in coordinating the financing commitments of the official sector. The IBRD, regional development banks, and bilateral creditors provided $18, $11, and $77 billion, respectively, to the four emerging countries (Bank for International Settlements, 1998, p. 134).

The crisis that hit South Korea was especially serious, partly because of Seoul's great reluctance to ask for assistance from the IMF (Camdessus, 2014, pp. 333–336).[38] In fact, the stand-by arrangement approved on December 4, 1997 fell short of stopping the financial panic. It was not until December 29, when the Federal Reserve rolled over short-term debts, that risk aversion declined (Sachs, 1999, p. 185).[39]

The rescue packages of the 1990s exposed several shortcomings of the ILOLR-in-chief function performed by the Fund. First, the financing of the Washington-based institution had become a key concern. The stand-by credit for Mexico (February 1995) was the largest financial commitment in the IMF history but it was soon surpassed by the facility for South Korea. The principle of quota increases seemed outdated. Even the New Arrangements to Borrow (NAB) – adopted in January 1997 as first and principal recourse to provide supplementary resources to the Fund and activated in December 1998 to finance a stand-by arrangement for Brazil – could be considered insufficient in the event of a major threat to the stability of the world financial system.[40]

Second, the ILOLR mechanism did not prevent massive sovereign defaults. Despite an EFF granted in 1996, Russia failed to repay its debt to official and private creditors the two following years. In 1999, the total Russian sovereign debt in default reached $96 billion. Argentina obtained multiple credit lines in 2000–2001 but went bankrupt in December 2001 and ended with debt arrears to the IBRD and the IMF in 2002–2003.[41] In these two cases, as confessed by IMF economists, it seems that *expectations* of and *effective* official financial support may have induced *debtor* moral hazard (Mussa, 1999, pp. 228–229; Jeanne and Zettelmeyer, 2005, pp. 79–80).

Third, contrary to the modus operandi enforced during the 1982–1983 debt crisis, the bailouts described above did not involve private creditors. One of the main reasons was that a growing proportion of them were bondholders with a lower capacity and willingness to coordinate with official creditor countries (Bank for International Settlements, 1998, p. 135). This new paradigm was likely to encourage *creditor* moral hazard and questioned the current international financial architecture.

During 1998–2005, there were feverish debates over the merits and pitfalls of the Fund performing the function of ILOLR and the subsequent risk of moral hazard. Several analyses deserve examination. For Calomiris (1998), the power of the IMF should be limited because its bailouts create creditor as well as debtor moral hazard. Only domestic central banks can be lenders of last resort. IMF First Deputy Managing Director Fischer (1999) claims that the international system needs a lender of last resort and the Fund can fulfill this mandate.[42] He also admits that "moral hazard is something to be lived with and controlled, rather than fully eliminated." Mishkin's (2001) view is consistent with Fischer's article but he makes some concrete proposals to address moral hazard issues, such as punishing the owners of insolvent institutions and making last-resort lending less frequent. Kamin (2002) finds that creditor moral hazard did not significantly distort international capital markets in the second half of the 1990s, which tends to support IMF-led financing packages. Such findings are partly refuted by Haldane and Scheibe (2004).

What arose from these diverging views was that debtor moral hazard had become a lesser concern than creditor moral hazard. This conclusion was in contradiction with the concomitant evolution of the IMF conditionality.

4.2 No credible ILOLR without conditionality

The conditions imposed on a distressed sovereign debtor applying for an emergency loan changed dramatically between 1973 and 2006. Several complementary reasons can be advanced, such as the increasing responsibilities of the IMF and the greater power of private creditors in the environment of globalized capitalism.

A remarkable feature of the 1970s was that the IMF credit lines and their joint programs aimed to correct payments imbalances were frequently a *condition* to the restructuring of official and commercial bank debts (see Brau et al., 1983, pp. 9–14; Gaillard, 2020, pp. 46–47). The interpenetration of debt restructuring, refinancing, and macroeconomic stabilization processes reached its climax during the resolution of the sovereign debt crisis in 1982–1983 (see Section 4.1.2). In the subsequent years, the "debt restructuring" dimension was abandoned, and the conditionality of the IMF remained the exclusive counterpart to its last resort lending.

The nature of the IMF conditionality started to evolve as early as the late 1970s. Once it appeared that commercial banks were unable to oversee their borrowers' economic policy (Lipson, 1981, pp. 622–623), there was a growing consensus that conditionality had become the prerogative of the Fund. The establishment of the supplementary financing facility in 1977 was logically accompanied by a set of new guidelines on the use of the IMF resources. For example, distressed countries were encouraged to come to the Fund as soon as possible and the prior adoption of certain measures could be regarded as indispensable. Next, stand-by arrangements were extended to up to three years and adjustment programs were likely to include a wider array of policy areas (from exchange rate and trade to fiscal and foreign borrowing issues). Performance criteria, benchmarks, and review clauses were also used more extensively to evaluate the implementation of the program and adapt it if necessary (Guitian, 1981, pp. 22–23; Polak, 1991, pp. 24–28; International Monetary Fund, 2001).

Within a few years, the IMF developed an ex-ante and ex-post conditionality with high monitoring performance and medium-term objectives. This "structural conditionality" diverged radically from the Bagehotian rules (see Ugolini, Chapter 3 of this volume) because IMF loans did not require collateral, carried below-market interest rates, and their amount were carefully calibrated to solve a country's external imbalance problems.[43] More importantly, structural conditionality was excessively intrusive and failed to boost implementation rates (International Monetary Fund, 2001, pp. 84–85; Goldstein, 2001, pp. 85–88). In the early 2000s, one could conclude that the IMF had succeeded in curbing *debtor* moral hazard. What about *creditor* moral hazard?

The IMF has traditionally limited creditor moral hazard by lending into arrears and requiring financing assurances.[44] As Bianco explains in Chapter 6 of this volume, the revision of these policies in the 1990s and 2000s benefited private creditors, who could exercise a de facto veto to IMF credit lines. As a result, it appears that the Fund placed much greater emphasis on preventing *debtor* moral hazard than *creditor* moral hazard. One may assume that the latter issue cannot be addressed unless private creditors are involved in debt restructuring programs, as had happened until the mid-1980s.

This option was explored when Anne Krueger, then IMF First Deputy Managing Director, advocated the establishment of a sovereign debt restructuring mechanism (SDRM). Although Krueger's (2002) proposal did not explicitly mention creditor moral hazard, it stated that "when there is no feasible set of policy adjustments to resolve [a] crisis unless accompanied by a restructuring, it is in the interests of neither the debtor nor the majority of its creditors to delay the inevitable." Krueger had undoubtedly identified a major flaw in the international financial architecture; unfortunately, her project failed. Why?

First, there was a legitimate fear that this new approach might resurrect debtor moral hazard. Next, reaching a consensus about what a *sustainable* public debt looked like was an arduous task. Third, the SDRM did not secure collective action from creditors – a major issue in the sovereign bond market era.[45] Fourth, the philosophy of the SDRM was questionable in the sense that private creditors would be more willing to restructure sovereign debts amid a serious financial turmoil than accept a haircut amid a relatively low-risk aversion period. Fifth, the new burden sharing promoted by Krueger could be considered unfair and untimely as financial institutions had to comply with an increasing number of international regulatory rules.

4.3 Capital adequacy rules as second-best options to fight against creditor moral hazard

The creditor moral hazard issue seems to have been indirectly and imperfectly addressed through the development of microprudential regulations. In this respect, the role of the BIS was central.

The series of banking crises that hit Western economies in 1974 (see Schenk, 2014) revealed the shortcomings in domestic and international financial regulatory rules. The establishment of the Basel Committee in December of that year strengthened and helped to coordinate prudential supervision. In 1975, it set out guidelines for cooperation between national authorities in the supervision of banks' foreign establishments: it encouraged direct transfers of information between regulatory authorities, direct inspections by parent authorities of their domestic banks' foreign establishments, and indirect inspections of foreign banking establishments by parent authorities through the agency of host authorities (Bank for International Settlements, 1975). In 1979, the Committee clarified its views and recommended that

> all parent supervisory authorities should [...] be required to give effect to the agreed principle that the capital adequacy and the risk exposure of all their banks be examined and assessed on the basis of the totality of their international activities. (Bank for International Settlements, 1979).

However, major disagreements persisted between central bankers and BIS officers in 1979–1980. They involved the regulation of Euro-markets, the control of international lending, and the scope of prudential supervision. Economic Adviser and Head of the Monetary and Economic Department at the BIS, Alexandre Lamfalussy was concerned about overlending risk and promoted a *macroprudential* approach to ensure financial stability. In contrast, the Federal Reserve and the Bank of England – primarily eager to preserve the dominant position of their commercial banks in the international sovereign lending and Euro-market areas, respectively – prioritized soft, *microprudential* supervision (Maes, 2011).

The lessons learnt from the debt crisis of 1982–1983 were partly inaccurate in the sense that they failed to set up macroprudential rules and supervise increasing capital mobility. Instead, the deterioration of international banks' capital ratios observed until the early 1980s convinced the Basel Committee to focus on capital regulation. In 1988, the G10 central banks approved an accord that called for a minimum ratio of capital to risk-weighted assets of 8%. This so-called Basel Accord was revised a decade later and resulted in Basel II rules in 2004. This new framework comprised three pillars: (i) updated minimum capital requirements based on external or internal credit ratings; (ii) supervisory review of an institution's capital adequacy and internal assessment process; and (iii) effective use of disclosure as a lever to encourage sound banking practices and strengthen market discipline.

The reinforcement of microprudential regulation contributed to enhance the solvency of Western banks but fell short of reducing creditor moral hazard. In fact, central bankers and regulators overlooked that a liquidity glut in an environment of high capital mobility increased the volatility of financial flows and thus made the intervention of a lender of last resort even more indispensable to eliminate systemic risk. This "moral hazard spiral" was aggravated by the growing size of international banks and their "too-big-to-fail" (TBTF) status. This new paradigm – active as early as 1984 (see Gaillard and Michalek, 2019; Gaillard and Michalek, Chapter 7 of this volume) – was magnified by the repeal of the Glass-Steagall Act in 1999.

Section 5 Concluding remarks

This chapter shows that there was no *official* ILOLR during the past two centuries. Yet, several institutions happened to play an *unofficial* role as last-resort lender: namely, the central banks of major capital-exporting nations, the League of Nations, the BIS, and the IMF. They all managed to contain systemic risk, except in the 1930s. Such success was primarily driven by the *cooperation* between these key institutions.

However, a significant drawback of last-resort facilities was the development of moral hazard. In the context of the 19th century, the Bank of England and the Bank of France were especially efficient to fight moral hazard. In the interwar years, the League loans were contingent on the implementation of certain macroeconomic policies designed to prevent debtor moral hazard. Such schemes foreshadowed the IMF conditionality, which expanded notably in the last quarter of the 20th century.

Following the globalization process starting in the 1980s and the growing importance of the financial sector, a new international financial architecture emerged: its main objective was to avert systemic risk by any means available. Since then, the main threat to the international financial system has consisted less in the default of a government than in the losses that TBTF banks would incur in the event of a sovereign default. In the present creditor moral hazard era, major investment funds and TBTF banks take advantage of the abundant liquidity created by the Federal Reserve as well as the bailouts announced by the IMF to increase their lending. One must lament that top policymakers have failed to understand that the future of market capitalism and the long-term credibility of any de facto ILOLR are contingent on the capacity to solve this creditor moral hazard problem.

Notes

1 K. Rogoff, "The sisters at 60," *The Economist*, 24 July 2004; available at https://www.economist.com/by-invitation/2004/07/22/the-sisters-at-60.
2 Fischer (1999) mentions in particular the work by Freixas (1999).
3 Our analysis ends in 2006 as the most recent aspects of moral hazard – driven by the excessive financialization of the U.S. economy – are tackled by Gaillard and Michalek, Chapter 10 of this volume.
4 On the globalization in the 19th century, see Bordo et al. (2003).
5 Baring's being a systemically important financial institution (SIFI) is found in Cassis (2011, p. 59).
6 See Marichal (1989) for details on these negotiations.
7 Giannini (2011) provides some parallels between both episodes.
8 Flandreau (1996, p. 759) quotes, in particular, Raffalovich, who opposed the creation of an international lender of last resort in the aftermath of the 1907 financial crisis.
9 Pauly (2003, p. 247) referred to the League's experience as more intrusive as compared to the IMF experience.
10 Specific episodes are provided in Flores Zendejas and Decorzant (2016).
11 The BIS was created at the Hague Conference of January 1930. In its statutes, it is explicitly stated that it aimed to promote the cooperation between central banks and "provide additional facilities for international financial operations" (Baer, 1999, p. 342).
12 Henceforth, the terms "IBRD," "World Bank", and "Bank" are used interchangeably.
13 The IMF traces its roots in the EFO of the League of Nations. Pauly (1996) highlights the influence of Jacques Polak in shaping the working methods of the Fund. Recall that Polak (1914–2010) spent seven years at the League before serving 40 years at the IMF.
14 The net income of the IBRD increased from $13.7 million in 1950 to $63 million in 1961 and $185.6 million in 1973 (International Bank for Reconstruction and Development 1950, 1961, and 1973).
15 Member countries can make use of IMF resources to address payment problems under credit tranche policies.
16 In 1963, the Fund established the compensatory financing facility (CFF) to compensate for shortfalls in export revenues.
17 Authors' calculations based on International Bank for Reconstruction and Development (1953, 1955).
18 For an overview of the different forms of sovereign defaults, see Gaillard (2014, pp. 3–9). On the debt negotiations with bondholders after 1945, see Flores Zendejas et al., 2021).

19 For a focus on the origins of the Paris Club and its first discussions with a distressed debtor (namely, Argentina), see García Heras (1996).
20 Argentina, Brazil, Chile, Ghana, India, Indonesia, Pakistan, Peru, and Turkey.
21 The GAB consisted of an agreement to provide the IMF with additional funds to increase its lending ability. The liquidity providers were Belgium, Canada, France, Germany, Italy, Japan, the Netherlands, Sweden, the United Kingdom, and the United States. These countries were referred to as the Group of Ten (or G10).
22 The SDRs were international reserve assets designed to supplement IMF member countries' official reserves.
23 The amount of these currency swaps increased from $2 billion in 1963 to $10 billion in 1969. These operations involved the Federal Reserve, major central banks, and the BIS; see Moessner and Allen, 2010, pp. 25–26.
24 For a focus on the bailouts announced in the United States, see Gaillard and Michalek, Chapter 7 of this volume.
25 A prominent exception was the monetary policy under the leadership of Paul Volcker. During 1979–1982, in particular, Volcker implemented monetarist measures which curbed inflation. He "normalized" monetary policy once it appeared that the 1982 sovereign debt crisis threatened the US banking system (see Gaillard and Michalek, Chapter 7 of this volume).
26 In fact, Greenspan's monetary policy was increasingly dovish. The average differential between the Fed Funds rates and the inflation rate declined from 2.1 percentage points during 1987–1996 to 1.2 percentage points during 1997–2006 (authors calculations). During 1987–2006, the annual inflation rate exceeded the 2% threshold 18 times out of 20.
27 Asymmetrical policy reactions mean that central bankers are reluctant to raise interest rates once recovery is confirmed (see Lamfalussy, 2004).
28 Rule 3a-7 permitted structured finance issuers to offer their securities publicly without registering under and complying with the Investment Company Act and its regulations. The "voluntary regulation" allowed big investment banks lacking a supervisor under the law to submit *voluntarily* to regulation. See Gaillard and Michalek (2019).
29 We consider that the role of the dollar as vehicle currency in commodity trade and funding currency by some non-US borrowers is a byproduct of its reserve currency status.
30 The U.S. current account was roughly balanced in the 1970s. Starting in the 1980s, the deficit widened and reached $806 billion in 2006.
31 Initially named "Committee on Banking Regulations and Supervisory Practices," the Basel Committee was designed to enhance cooperation between member countries and coordinate banking supervision and regulation.
32 The oil facility was discontinued in 1976 whereas the EFF was still an active scheme in 2020.
33 For an article examining the first case of assistance under the EFF, see Bhatia and Rothman (1975).
34 The participating countries and institutions were Abu Dhabi, Belgium, Canada, Iran, Japan, Kuwait, the Netherlands, Nigeria, Qatar, Saudi Arabia, Venezuela, West Germany, the United States, and the Swiss National Bank (see Zanzi, 1977, p. 4).
35 Fishlow advocated a global response to what was a few years later termed "systemic risk" (see Gaillard and Michalek, Chapter 7 of this volume).
36 Mourlon-Druol (2020) examines the painful experience of the French government as major creditor of Poland in the 1970s.
37 For an overview of these financial support schemes, see Polak 1991, Boughton (2001, pp. 705–756), and https://www.imf.org.
38 One may assume that the stigma problem had never been so acute since 1945.

39 This interpretation is supported by the evolution of South Korea's Emerging Markets Bond Index spread.

40 The NAB was in line with the Witteveen Facility adopted 20 years earlier. The participants in the NAB were Australia, Austria, Belgium, Canada, Denmark, the Deutsche Bundesbank, Finland, France, the Hong Kong Monetary Authority, Italy, Japan, Kuwait, Luxembourg, Malaysia, the Netherlands, Norway, Saudi Arabia, Singapore, South Korea, Spain, the Sveriges Riksbank, the Swiss National Bank, Thailand, the United Kingdom and the United States. See https://www.imf.org/en/News/Articles/2015/09/14/01/49/pr9705.

41 See Beers and de Leon-Manlagnit's (2019) database.

42 The *1998 IMF Annual Report* (p. 69) stated that its Directors had "expressed the view that ESAF financing for debt- and debt-service-reduction operations should be used in a subsidiary, or "last resort," role, only if other financing options were not available." It was the first time an IMF Annual Report suggested that the role of ILOLR could be played by the Fund.

43 It is important to highlight that the interest rates charged by the IMF were contingent on the facilities offered and thus could vary dramatically. For instance, the SAF and ESAF – replaced by the Poverty Reduction and Growth Facility in 1999 – were highly concessionary loans. In contrast, under the SRF, borrowers had to pay a surcharge of 300 basis points above the rate of charge on IMF loans during the first year from the date of approval of financing. See International Monetary Fund (2001, p. 15) and https://www.imf.org/en/News/Articles/2015/09/14/01/49/pr9759.

44 The "lending into arrears" policy describes the circumstances in which the IMF extends financial assistance to a government with arrears to other creditors. Financing assurances consist of refraining from granting a credit facility as long as private creditors do not guarantee that they continue to finance the debtor.

45 The problem of holdout creditors would materialize in the case of Argentina, which had just defaulted when Krueger presented her SDRM proposal.

References

Altamura, C. E. and Flores Zendejas, J. (2020) "Politics, International Banking, and the Debt Crisis of 1982," *Business History Review*, Vol. 94, No. 4, pp. 753–778.

Avramovic, D., et al. (1964) *Economic Growth and External Debt*. Baltimore: Johns Hopkins Press.

Baer, G. D. (1999) "Sixty-Five Years of Central Bank Cooperation at the Bank for International Settlements," in Holtfrerich, C-L., Reis, J. and Toniolo, G. (Eds), *The Emergence of Modern Central Banking from 1918 to the Present*. London: Routledge.

Bank for International Settlements (1975) *Report to the Governors on The Supervision of Banks' Foreign Establishments*. Basel: Committee on Banking Regulations and Supervisory Practices, 26 September.

Bank for International Settlements (1979) *Consolidated Supervision of Banks' International Activities*. Basel: Committee on Banking Regulations and Supervisory Practices, March.

Bank for International Settlements (1998) *68th Annual Report*, Basel: Bank for International Settlements.

Bank for International Settlements (2014) "Re-Thinking the Lender of Last Resort," *BIS Papers No. 79*.

Beers, D. and de Leon-Manlagnit, P. (2019) "The BoC-BoE Sovereign Default Database: What's New In 2019?," *Bank of Canada Staff Working Paper 2019-39*.

Bhatia, R. J. and Rothman, S. L. (1975) "Introducing the Extended Fund Facility: The Kenyan Case," *Finance & Development*, December, Vol. 12, No. 4, pp. 38–41.

Bignon, V., Flandreau, M. and Ugolini, S. (2012) "Bagehot for Beginners: The Making of Lending-of-Last-Resort Operations in the Mid-19th Century," *Economic History Review*, Vol. 65, No. 2, pp. 580–608.

Bordo, M. D., Taylor, A. M. and Williamson, J. G. (2003) *Globalization in Historical Perspective*. Chicago: University of Chicago Press.

Boughton, J. M. (2001) *Silent Revolution – The International Monetary Fund, 1979–1989*. Washington, DC: International Monetary Fund.

Brau, E., Williams, R. C., Keller, P. M. and Nowak, M. (1983) "Recent Multilateral Debt Restructurings with Official and Bank Creditors," *IMF Occasional Paper No. 25*.

Broz, L. (2015) "The Federal Reserve as Global Lender of Last Resort, 2007–2010," *SRC Discussion Paper No. 30, Systemic Risk Centre, London School of Economics and Political Science*.

Calomiris, C. W. (1998) "The IMF's Imprudent Role as Lender of Last Resort," *Cato Journal*, Vol. 17, No. 3, Winter, pp. 275–294.

Camdessus, M. (2014) *La scène de ce drame est le monde – Treize ans à la tête du FMI*. Paris: Editions des Arènes.

Cassis, Y. (2011) *Crises and Opportunities: the Shaping of Modern Finance*. Oxford: Oxford University Press.

Cecchetti, S., Mancini-Griffoli, T. and Narita, M. (2017) "Does Prolonged Monetary Policy Easing Increase Financial Vulnerability?", *IMF Working Paper WP/17/65*.

Despres, E., Kindleberger, C. P. and Salant, W. S. (1966) "The Dollar and World Liquidity: A Minority View," *The Economist*, 5 February, pp. 526–529.

Evanoff, D. D., Hoelscher, D. S. and Kaufman, G. G. (Eds) (2009) *Globalization and Systemic Risk*. Singapore: World Scientific.

Ferns, H. S. (1992) "The Baring Crisis Revisited," *Journal of Latin American Studies*, Vol. 24, No. 2, pp. 241–273.

Fischer, S. (1999) "On the Need for an International Lender of Last Resort," *Journal of Economic Perspectives*, Vol. 13, No. 4, pp. 85–104.

Flandreau, M. (1996) "The French Crime of 1873: An Essay on the Emergence of the International Gold Standard, 1870–1880," *Journal of Economic History*, Vol. 56, No. 4, pp. 862–897.

Flandreau, M. (2013) "Sovereign States, Bondholders Committees, and the London Stock Exchange in the Nineteenth Century (1827–68): New Facts and Old Fictions," *Oxford Review of Economic Policy*, Vol. 29, No. 4, pp. 668–696.

Flandreau, M. and Flores, J. (2012) "Bondholders versus Bond-Sellers? Investment Banks and Conditionality Lending in the London Market for Foreign Government Debt, 1815–1913," *European Review of Economic History*, Vol. 16, No. 4, pp. 356–383.

Flores, J. H. (2011) "Information Asymmetries and Conflict of Interest During the Baring Crisis, 1880–1890," *Financial History Review*, Vol. 18, No. 2, pp. 191–215.

Flores, J. H. (2012) "Crying on Lombard Street: Fixing Sovereign Defaults in the 1890s," *European Review of History: Revue européenne d'histoire*, Vol. 19, No. 6, pp. 979–997.

Flores Zendejas, J. H. and Decorzant, Y. (2016) "Going Multilateral? Financial Markets' Access and the League of Nations Loans, 1923–8," *Economic History Review*, Vol. 69, No. 2, pp. 653–678.

Flores Zendejas, J., Pénet, P. and Suter, C. (2021) "The Revenge of Defaulters: Sovereign Defaults and Interstate Negotiations in the Post-War Financial Order, 1940–65," in Pénet, P. and Flores Zendejas, J. (Eds), *Sovereign Debt Diplomacies – Rethinking Sovereign Debt from Colonial Empires to Hegemony*. Oxford: Oxford University Press.

Freixas, X. (1999) "Optimal Bail Out Policy, Conditionality and Creative Ambiguity," *IDEAS Working Paper Series from RePEc.* https://ideas.repec.org/p/fmg/fmgdps/dp327.html.

Gaillard, N. (2011) *A Century of Sovereign Ratings.* New York: Springer.

Gaillard, N. (2014) *When Sovereigns Go Bankrupt – A Study on Sovereign Risk.* Cham: Springer.

Gaillard, N. (2020) *Country Risk – The Bane of Foreign Investors.* Cham: Springer.

Gaillard, N. and Michalek, R. J. (2019) "How and Why Moral Hazard Has Distorted Financial Regulation," in Hira, A., Gaillard, N. and Cohn, T. H. (Eds), *The Failure of Financial Regulation – Why A Major Crisis Could Happen Again.* International Political Economy Series. Cham: Palgrave Macmillan.

García Heras, R. (1996) "La Argentina y el Club de París: Comercio y pagos multilaterales con la Europa Occidental, 1955–1958," *El trimestre económico*, Vol. 63, No. 4, pp. 1277–1308.

Giannini, C. (2011) *The Age of Central Banks.* Cheltenham: Edward Elgar Publishing.

Goldstein, M. (2001) "IMF Structural Conditionality: How Much Is Too Much?," *Revision of paper presented at NBER Conference on "Economic and Financial Crises in Emerging Market Economies" Woodstock, Vermont, October 19-21, 2000.*

Guitian, M. (1981) "Fund Conditionality – Evolution of Principles and Practices," *IMF Pamphlet Series No. 38.*

Haldane, A. G. and Scheibe, J. (2004) "IMF Lending and Creditor Moral Hazard," *Working Paper No. 216, Bank of England.*

Hautcoeur, P-C., Riva, A. and White, E. N. (2014) "Floating a 'Lifeboat': The Banque de France and the Crisis of 1889," *Journal of Monetary Economics*, Vol. 65, July, pp. 104–119.

Hawtrey, R. G. (1932) *The Art of Central Banking.* London: Longmans Greene.

International Bank for Reconstruction and Development (1950) *Fifth Annual Report 1949-1950.* Washington, DC: IBRD.

International Bank for Reconstruction and Development (1953) *Survey of Publicly-Held Foreign Bonds – Part I: Bonds Issued in the United States.* 15 December, Washington, DC: International Bank for Reconstruction and Development.

International Bank for Reconstruction and Development (1955) *Survey of Publicly-Held Foreign Government Bonds.* 28 January, Washington, DC: International Bank for Reconstruction and Development.

International Bank for Reconstruction and Development (1960) *Some Techniques of Development Lending.* Washington, DC: IBRD.

International Bank for Reconstruction and Development (1961) *Sixteenth Annual Report 1960-1961.* Washington, DC: IBRD.

International Bank for Reconstruction and Development (1969) *Multilateral Debt Renegotiations: 1956–1968.* 11 April, Washington, DC: International Bank for Reconstruction and Development.

International Bank for Reconstruction and Development (1973) *World Bank/IDA Annual Report 1973.* Washington, DC: World Bank.

International Bank for Reconstruction and Development (1975) *First Annual Review of Project Performance Audit Results.* Operations Evaluation Department, Washington, DC: IBRD.

International Monetary Fund (1953) *International Monetary Fund Annual Report 1953.* Washington, DC: International Monetary Fund.

International Monetary Fund (2001) "Structural Conditionality in Fund-Supported Programs," *Prepared by the Policy Development and Review Department*, February 16.

Jeanne, O. and Zettelmeyer, J. (2005) "The Mussa Theorem (and Other Results on IMF-Induced Moral Hazard), *IMF Staff Papers*, Vol. 52, IMF Conference in Honor of Michael Mussa.

Jordà, Ò., Schularick, M., Taylor, A. M. and Ward, F. (2018) "Global Financial Cycles and Risk Premiums," *NBER Working Paper No. 24677.*

Kamin, S. B. (2002) "Identifying the Role of Moral Hazard in International Financial Markets," *International Finance Discussion Papers No. 736*, Board of Governors of the Federal Reserve System, September.

Kindleberger, C. P. (1978) *Manias, Panics and Crashes: A History of Financial Crises.* Basingstoke: Macmillan.

Klein, T. M. (1973) "Economic Aid Through Debt Relief," *Finance & Development*, September, Vol. 10, No. 3, pp. 17–20 & 34–35.

Krueger, A. O. (2002) *A New Approach to Sovereign Debt Restructuring.* Washington, DC: International Monetary Fund.

Lamfalussy, A. (2004) "Central Banks and Financial Stability," Pierre Werner Lecture delivered at the Banque Centrale de Luxembourg, in Maes, I. (Ed), *Alexandre Lamfalussy – Selected Essays.* Budapest: Magyar Nemzeti Bank and National Bank of Belgium.

League of Nations (1939) *Report of the Committee for the Study of International Loan Contracts.* Geneva: League of Nations.

Lipson, C. (1981) "The International Organization of Third World Debt," *International Organization*, Vol. 35, No. 4, pp. 603–631.

Maes, I. (2011) "Alexandre Lamfalussy et les tentatives de la BRI pour éviter un endettement excessif en Amérique latine dans les années 1970," *Histoire, économie & société*, Vol. 30, décembre, pp.59–77.

Marichal, C. (1989) *A Century of Debt Crises in Latin America: From Independence to the Great Depression, 1820–1930.* Princeton: Princeton University Press.

Mauro, P., Sussman, N. and Yafeh, Y. (2006) *Sovereign Defaults and the Corporation of Foreign Bondholders. Emerging Markets and Financial Globalization.* Oxford: Oxford University Press.

Mendelsohn, M. S. (1983) *Commercial Banks and The Restructuring of Cross-Border Debt.* New York: Group of Thirty.

Mishkin, F. S. (2001) "The International Lender of Last Resort: What Are The Issues?," in Siebert, H. (Ed), *The World's New Financial Landscape: Challenges for Economic Policy.* Berlin and Heidelberg: Springer.

Moessner, R. and Allen, W. A. (2010) "Banking Crises and the International Monetary System in the Great Depression and Now," *BIS Working Papers No. 333.*

Mourlon-Druol, E. (2020) "The Role of a Creditor in the Making of a Debt Crisis: The French Government's Financial Support for Poland, Between Cold War Interests and Economic Constraints, 1958–1981," *Financial History Review*, Vol. 27, No. 1, pp. 73–94.

Mussa, M. (1999) "Reforming the International Financial Architecture: Limiting Moral Hazard and Containing Real Hazard," in Gruen, D. and Gower, L. (Eds), *Capital Flows and the International Financial System.* Sydney: Reserve Bank of Australia.

Pauly, L. W. (1996) "The League of Nations and the Foreshadowing of the International Monetary Fund," *Essays in International Finance No. 201. Princeton University.*

Pauly, L. W. (2003) "International Financial Institutions and National Economic Governance: Aspects of the New Adjustment Agenda in Historical Perspective," in Flandreau, M., Holtfrerich, C-L., and James, H. (Eds), *International Financial History in the Twentieth Century: System and Anarchy.* Cambridge: Cambridge University Press.

Per Jacobsson Foundation (1970) *Toward a World Central Bank?*. Washington, DC: Per Jacobsson Foundation.

Platt, D. C. M. (1968) *Finance, Trade, and Politics in British Foreign Policy: 1815–1914*. Oxford: Clarendon Press.

Polak, J. J. (1991) "The Changing Nature of IMF Conditionality," *Working Paper No. 41, OECD Development Centre*, pp. 13–81.

Sachs, J. (1999) "The International Lender of Last Resort: What are the Alternatives?," in Little, J. S. and Olivei, G. P. (Eds), *Rethinking the International Monetary System*. Boston: Federal Reserve Bank of Boston.

Schadler, S. (2014) "The IMF's Preferred Creditor Status: Does It Still Make Sense After the Euro Crisis?," *CIGI Policy Brief, No.* 7, pp. 1–8.

Schenk, C. R. (2014) "Summer in the City: Banking Failures of 1974 and the Development of International Banking Supervision," *English Historical Review*, Vol. 129, No. 540, pp. 1129–1156.

Triffin, R. (1960) *Gold and the Dollar Crisis*. New Haven: Yale University Press.

United States Senate (1978) *The Witteveen Facility and the OPEC Financial Surpluses*, Hearings before the subcommittee on foreign economic policy of the committee on foreign relations – September 21, and 23, and October 6, 7, and 10, 1977. Washington, DC: U.S. Government Printing Office.

Waibel, M. (2011) *Sovereign Defaults before International Courts and Tribunals*. Cambridge: Cambridge University Press.

White, E. N. (2016) "Rescuing a SIFI, Halting a Panic: The Barings Crisis of 1890," *Bank Underground*, 10 February, available at https://bankunderground.co.uk/2016/02/10/rescuing-a-sifi-halting-a-panic-the-barings-crisis-of-1890.

Zanzi, A. W. (1977) "Supplementary Financing Facility Established," *Finance & Development*, December, Vol. 14, No. 4, pp. 4–5 & 50.

6 Moral hazard at the IMF: an analysis of the Fund's policies and status

Giuseppe Bianco

This chapter studies how the International Monetary Fund (IMF) manages to fight moral hazard. Debt sustainability analysis and conditionality are two key policy tools that limit debtor moral hazard. When necessary, a country is required to restructure its debt before being allowed to receive assistance. Next, in exchange for the IMF assistance, a country must commit to economic reforms: this conditionality is intended to ensure that the government "does its homework." The policies of lending into arrears (while taking a senior creditor position) and requiring financing assurances are designed to contain creditor moral hazard. They push private creditors toward a negotiated agreement with their sovereign debtor to solve the debt crisis and facilitate the IMF's intervention. The preferred creditor status of the Fund mitigates both types of moral hazard. This chapter highlights the strengths and inconsistencies in the use and application of these policies.

The International Monetary Fund (IMF, or Fund) is one of the pillars of the post-World War II international system established at the Bretton Woods Conference in 1944. Its mandate includes three essential roles: the provision of financial assistance to its member countries, the provision of technical services, and the surveillance of the international monetary and financial system and of the exchange rate policies of its members (Cissé, 1995, p. 278). The first two roles come into play with respect to the Fund's interventions during sovereign debt crises.

When a country is in debt turmoil, i.e., it is unable to repay the money it owes to its official or private creditors, there is no pre-defined international mechanism for resolution. Instead, it is the IMF that is almost inevitably called upon to act, by virtue of its unique expertise and resources (Hagan, 2020). The Fund can assess the sustainability of the debt, incentivize an agreement between the debtor government and its creditors, and provide financing to overcome the crisis. The IMF has been called "the ultimate judge of the appropriate mix between the magnitude of a heavily indebted developing country's adjustment effort and the commitment to it of new external finance for its remaining balance of payments deficit" (Robichek, 1984–1985, p. 146).

In recent decades, several other organizations of a regional character have come to light which could potentially threaten the exclusive role of the IMF.

DOI: 10.4324/9781003139249-6

For instance, the European Commission possesses the technical expertise to assess a country's debt sustainability. It provides such analysis in the framework of its role as the guardian of fiscal discipline, especially in the euro area.[1]

Sometimes the founders of regional organizations have explicitly sought to create an alternative to the Fund. Therefore, there is a concern that regional financial arrangements might undermine the agreements reached by the Fund with respect to private-sector involvement and sovereign debt restructurings (Henning, 2006, p. 179). A competition could develop between the Fund and a regional arrangement which might offer a more relaxed and therefore more appealing conditionality to the borrower. Yet, the IMF resources and expertise make it quite unlikely that such alternatives will fully displace it.

With respect to IMF action in sovereign debt crises, moral hazard can take mainly two forms (Jeanne and Zettelmeyer, 2005). First, and more manifestly, moral hazard could involve the debtor country. The latter could be tempted to obtain financial assistance at the low interest rate that the Fund offers, but then increase its debt burden, and ultimately default on the IMF loans.

Against this first instance of moral hazard, the Fund assesses the sustainability of the member country's debt burden in the medium term. If it is deemed unsustainable, the country undertakes restructuring (part or all of) its debt before receiving assistance. Moreover, in exchange for the IMF loans, the country must commit to economic reforms: this conditionality ensures that the government "does its homework" to stop the crisis. Furthermore, the preferred creditor status of the Fund requires the member country to reimburse the IMF before repaying any other creditor.[2]

A second form of moral hazard is harder to identify at a first glance. It concerns private creditors, whose proportion within countries' creditor community has grown over time. These creditors have an incentive to demand full repayment from the debtor country (also to the detriment of other creditors), and to refuse to be involved in debt restructurings.

Against this second strand of moral hazard, the preferred creditor status of the Fund is again intended to displace private creditors' repayment expectations. In addition, as explained further in Section 2 below, the IMF policies on lending into arrears (LIA) and requiring financing assurances were established to ensure that the debtor did not have outstanding arrears toward its creditors and that banks would be ready to continue providing funding to the debtor. These two conditions had to be fulfilled for the Fund to act. Thus, private creditors were incentivized to find an agreement with their official debtor in order to enable the Fund's intervention and thereby reach a solution to the crisis.

This chapter examines the extent to which the IMF policies are effective in tackling the two aspects of moral hazard. It explores the evolution of these policies, especially in recent years with respect to the Eurozone sovereign debt crisis. It brings to light some strengths and highlights several inconsistencies, which show how moral hazard within sovereign debt restructuring remains an open issue.

Section 1 addresses the debtor country's moral hazard. First, it investigates the IMF assessment of debt sustainability. When the Fund considers the debt to be unsustainable, a restructuring is usually in order. The IMF decision to grant financial assistance is subject to several conditions, each of which was tested in the Eurozone crisis from 2009 onward. In the case of Greece, the Fund included the risk of systemic spillover amongst its conditions, via a special procedure. This is analyzed as an example of the difficulties of using the assessment of debt sustainability to tackle moral hazard.

Next, Section 1 examines conditionality, which is intended to reduce debtor moral hazard through the need to implement reforms. It investigates the evolution of conditionality over time, in light of the changing IMF legal and policy framework. The high number of conditions in the 1980s and 1990s seemingly went too far in addressing moral hazard and arguably made debt crises more severe, as it discouraged countries from approaching the Fund at an early stage of their external imbalances (the so-called "stigma problem"). Subsequently, the role of conditionality has been defined more precisely, but its relationship with moral hazard still represents an open issue.

Third, Section 1 enquires into the seniority of IMF claims. This is intended to address the moral hazard of the government's failing to repay the Fund in order to reimburse other creditors. Practical – rather than legal – arguments are usually put forward for the IMF preferred creditor status. While the consistent *practice* of private and state creditors is respectful of such seniority, the prevention of moral hazard by the assertion of the Fund's preferred creditor status is not based on an unassailable legal provision.

Section 2 explores creditor moral hazard. Creditors may lend to states without due consideration of the debtor country's prevailing economic conditions, but still expect full repayment thanks to financial assistance from the Fund. In addition to its preferred creditor status, two other IMF policies can mitigate creditor moral hazard: lending into arrears and requiring forward financing assurances.

The section then explains that lending into arrears was originally conceived as an exception. However, in partial recognition of the risk of moral hazard, the Fund later adopted a softer approach. The criteria for the IMF to decide on this question have been amended over time and our analysis illustrates how they continue to be challenging.

Section 2 also examines the policy on financing assurances and highlights the obstacles the Fund has faced in its relationships with creditors. Given the challenges debtor states face in effecting a successful negotiation, banks have the ability to veto the IMF's assistance, or significantly delay it. Thus, we illustrate the Fund's struggle to ensure the protection of its own financial interests on the one hand and the power to assist a country in need without being at the mercy of private creditors on the other.

Section 3 offers concluding remarks. The Appendix provides an example of a letter of intent and of a memorandum of understanding as a practical illustration of the topics discussed in the chapter.

Section 1 Coping with debtor moral hazard

1.1 Assessment of debt sustainability

For a debtor country, knowing that the IMF is potentially available as a source of funding may give rise to moral hazard.[3] The provision of financial assistance at below-market rates could incentivize national policymakers to increase the state's debt burdens indefinitely.

The first barrier to this form of moral hazard is that the IMF assesses the debt sustainability to determine if it can grant "exceptional access" to its resources beyond the normal limits. If the Fund deems the debt is not sustainable with high probability, this constitutes "the trigger for many debt restructurings" (Leckow and Ams, 2017, p. 15). Restructuring for a country implies a difficult process, from a political, economic, and social point of view.

The IMF decision on exceptional access is subject to both procedural and substantive conditions. The procedural requirements are:

> a process for early and regular consultation with the Executive Board on the progress in reaching agreement on a program; the presumption that staff reports for exceptional access arrangements would be published; an assessment of the risks to the Fund of high and/or concentrated exposure; and an ex post evaluation one year after the completion of exceptional access arrangements (Schadler, 2016, p. 3).

The substantive criteria, agreed in March 2009, are the following:

- a "The member is experiencing or has the potential to experience exceptional balance of payments pressures on the current account or the capital account, resulting in a need for Fund financing that cannot be met within the normal limits.
- b A rigorous and systematic analysis indicates that there is a high probability that the member's public debt is sustainable in the medium term. Debt sustainability for these purposes will be evaluated on a forward-looking basis and may take into account, inter alia, the intended restructuring of debt to restore sustainability. This criterion applies only to public (domestic and external) debt. However, the analysis of such public debt sustainability will incorporate any potential contingent liabilities of the government, including those potentially arising from private external indebtedness.
- c The member has prospects of gaining or regaining access to private capital markets within the timeframe when Fund resources are outstanding.
- d The policy program of the member provides a reasonably strong prospect of success, including not only the member's adjustment plans but also its institutional and political capacity to deliver that adjustment" (International Monetary Fund, 2009b, p. 31).

In particular, deciding whether a country's debt is sustainable is extremely sensitive. The Fund has to assess "whether a country's debt can be serviced without an unrealistically large future correction in the balance of income and expenditure" (International Monetary Fund, 2002, p. 3). This judgment is of paramount importance as it strikes a balance between the burden that the government can continue to bear and the portion of the debt which has to be renegotiated with the creditors.

To counter debtors' potential moral hazard, the assessment of debt sustainability has long aimed at "discipline and transparency."[4] In particular, the criteria were intended to guarantee uniformity of treatment of IMF members (Sorel, 1996, p. 56), shape members' expectations, set benchmarks for decision-making, and safeguard Fund resources.[5]

If a country's crisis can provoke a contagion or give rise to systemic effects, this risk could be factored into the substantive requirements.[6] However, this may incentivize moral hazard in the bigger economies and endanger uniformity of treatment. Consequently, in 2003 the Executive Board rejected the inclusion of such a criterion. Giving special consideration to the potential for systemic effects was deemed incompatible with the objectives of the framework.

However, the Eurozone crisis of 2009–2011 tested this state of affairs.[7] Fund members which were part of a monetary union necessitated financial assistance, given the potential for systemic spillovers. This increased contagion risk and represented an unprecedented issue for the IMF.

The Fund's involvement in the euro area crisis entailed several difficulties.[8] In May 2010, when the IMF Executive Board discussed the financial assistance to be granted to Greece, it included an exception to one of the substantive criteria. The second requirement thus became that:

> A rigorous and systematic analysis indicates that there is a high probability that the member's public debt is sustainable in the medium term. *However, in instances where there are significant uncertainties that make it difficult to state categorically that there is a high probability that the debt is sustainable over this period, exceptional access would be justified if there is a high risk of international systemic spillovers.* Debt sustainability for these purposes will be evaluated on a forward-looking basis and may take into account, inter alia, the intended restructuring of debt to restore sustainability. This criterion applies only to public (domestic and external) debt. However, the analysis of such public debt sustainability will incorporate any potential contingent liabilities of the government, including those potentially arising from private external indebtedness (International Monetary Fund, 2011, p. 426, emphasis added).

The decision to introduce such a modification into the official policy rather than as a one-off exception was justified on the grounds of transparency and even-handedness, i.e., uniformity of treatment for other members that could have benefited from the same exception in the future. This was the case for Ireland and Portugal, two members of the Eurozone which required financial assistance and whose debt sustainability assessment was characterized by potential systemic spillovers (Schadler, 2016, pp. 7–9).

Thus, the Fund allowed for an exception in case of systemic spillovers and treated differently those (presumably small) countries whose crises could not have such effects. In other words, the Fund freed itself from the previously established framework (Bismuth, 2012, p. 753). Moral hazard from sovereign debtors was countered less effectively, like the "too-big-to-fail" financial institutions benefiting from an implicit bailout guarantee from their states of incorporation.

In that instance, the inclusion of the contagion exception was used to disregard the possibility of restructuring the Greek sovereign debt. The systemic importance of Greek debt was the justification for rejecting the idea of reducing the debt burden by renegotiating with creditors. The option of an early debt restructuring, voiced by practitioners and academics outside the IMF, was not seriously taken into account (Schadler, 2016, pp. 16 –17). As the restructuring actually took place two years later, in hindsight the introduction of the systemic spillovers exception appears to have significantly postponed a necessary step, making it all the more complicated and burdensome. As the Fund (2013b, p. 28) acknowledged later, "[a]n upfront debt restructuring would have been better for Greece."

The major opposition to an early restructuring came from the EU institutions and several governments of the Eurozone (Independent Evaluation Office, 2016, p. 15).[9] The influence exerted by such actors was enough to rule the option completely off the table. Although the subsequent reports did not evidence an outright interference by country authorities, it can safely be argued that the choice to adopt the systemic exception and assist Greece without requiring a restructuring was heavily determined by such external pressure. Consequently, neutrality (i.e., independence from political pressure) was not upheld by the IMF. As it has been argued, "by not following an open, transparent process, the Fund created the perception that a decision made in Europe had been imposed on it" (Independent Evaluation Office, 2016, p. 17).

In addition, the breach of neutrality was two-fold: the systemic exception was actually deleted after being used for Eurozone countries. In January 2016, the Executive Board decided to eliminate the amendment of 2010[10] Consequently, countries other than Greece, Ireland, and Portugal could not benefit from the exception. Arguably, the practical effect was similar to allowing one-off exceptions for each of them rather than formally changing the Fund policy.

The thorough study carried out by the Independent Evaluation Office (2016) highlighted a further contentious aspect. The procedure followed to amend the debt sustainability criterion was new. Instead of carefully debating the advantages and potential drawbacks stemming from a change in the policy, the

Executive Board was presented with the amendment almost without notice. The "permanent" modification of the substantive requirements for the exceptional access policy was embedded and, as it were, hidden, within the approval of the Stand-By Agreement with Greece (Schadler, 2016, p. 8). This curtailed the discussion and did not allow for a careful examination of the proposal.

Thus, the Eurozone sovereign debt crisis opened a breach in the IMF framework. It introduced an exception to the uniformity of treatment of member states by allowing systemic spillovers to be taken into account. This highlights the difficulties of using the assessment of debt sustainability to tackle moral hazard, especially for bigger economies or those which are members of a monetary union.[11]

1.2 Conditionality

At the IMF, conditionality can be concisely defined as "the link between the approval or continuation of the Fund's financing and the implementation of specified elements of economic policy by the country receiving this financing."[12] If a country has to implement (often politically unpalatable) reforms, the moral hazard of seeking IMF financial assistance is reduced.

Conditionality accompanies the country for one or more years in its path to economic recovery. The IMF Executive Board takes a unilateral decision to grant financial assistance (Leckow, 2005, p. 58) and the debtor government presents a letter of intent, a memorandum of economic-financial policies, and a technical memorandum of understanding with the reforms demanded by the Fund.[13] There is no formal agreement between the IMF and the government spelling out conditionality.

This subsection analyzes the evolution of conditionality over time, in light of the changing IMF legal and policy framework. The inquiry seeks to explore the interests and objectives shaping this extremely important aspect of sovereign debt crises, which has been the subject of considerable academic controversy.[14] Such controversy is at least in part due to the intractable problem of moral hazard embedded within the challenge of assisting sovereign debtors. However, this is not to overlook other, broader factors that have shaped conditionality, such as the evolution of economic ideas or the changing *clientele* of the IMF (see Chwieroth (2010) and Polak (1991) respectively).

Whereas "conditionality" did not feature in the IMF Articles of Agreement, Article V, Section 3 mentioned *Conditions governing use of the Fund's resources.* However, such "conditions" applied to both conditional and unconditional uses of the Fund's resources (Gold, 1979, p. 1). Over the first years of its existence, the Fund asserted its powers of assessing the use of resources by the government before or after agreeing to a request for financial assistance.

Article V, Section 3(a)(i) stipulated that a member seeking to draw from the Fund must represent that it needed the desired currency for the purpose of making in that currency payments "which are consistent with the provisions of this Agreement." The Fund related this to the purposes of the organization, one of which is to give "confidence to members by making the general resources of the Fund temporarily available to them under adequate safeguards, thus providing them with opportunity to correct maladjustments in their balance of payments without resorting to measures destructive of national or international prosperity" (Article I(v)). Thus, the IMF decided that it could proportion the safeguards to the number of its resources that a member sought to use (Gold, 1971, p. 6).

Consequently, the Fund asserted both its right to challenge the country's request and the need for the use of resources to comply with the Fund's purposes. As a result, this legal basis provided the Fund with the authority to determine the conditions of access to its resources (Gianviti, 1989, p. 249). This can be deemed as giving the IMF the means to prevent debtor moral hazard.

Originally, the Fund's quite liberal approach was to allow drawings up to a member's "gold tranche" – which was deemed to represent the member's contribution to the Fund's activities (Gold, 1979, p. 3). For example, the IMF assured each of its members that they could expect to receive "the overwhelming benefit of any doubt respecting drawings which would raise the Fund's holdings of its currency to not more than its quota."[15] Conversely, requests beyond the first credit tranche needed substantial justification. Such requests would be accepted where they intended to "support a sound program aimed at establishing or maintaining the enduring stability of the member's currency at a realistic rate of exchange" (International Monetary Fund, 1959, p. 22).

The Annual Reports from the 1960s testify to the incipient use of conditionality terminology. In 1964, drawings beyond the gold tranche were deemed to be conditional on the adoption of policies "designed to ensure the temporary character of their payments problem and designed also to eliminate or reduce the member's reliance on exchange restrictions or certain other exchange practices" (International Monetary Fund, 1964, p. 34). The following year, the Report stated that "the credit tranches…, which are made available on condition that the drawing country maintains or adopts policies calculated to correct in due time the payments deficit in question, constitute 'conditional' liquidity." The use of quotation marks belies the novelty of such wording (Gold, 1979, p. 2).

Moreover, by 1960 performance criteria had become a feature of almost all stand-by arrangements in the upper credit tranche (International Monetary Fund, 2009a, p. 21). Conditionality also featured in different facilities that the Fund established to tackle specific problems (Sorel, 1996, p. 54).

On May 31, 1968, the Board of Governors approved the First Amendment. It introduced provisions that required the Fund to adopt policies on the use of its resources by members. Furthermore, it prohibited the establishment of new facilities without conditionality. Conditionality – and thus a further tool to address moral hazard – was embedded in the Articles of Agreement.

The newly added provision[16] obliged members to maintain or introduce measures which the Fund considered relevant both to solve their balance of payments problems and to ensure that their use of IMF resources would be temporary. However, it did not spell out what the Fund's or the member's policies should be. Another provision[17] ensured that where the Fund did not deem the country's measures consistent with the provisions and policies of the IMF, then it had to challenge the government's representation under Article V (Gold, 1971, p. 21).

Stand-by arrangements have proven particularly significant in the development of conditionality by the Fund. The content of a letter of intent by a member country could include both current and future policies. Some of the measures could involve objective data whose observance would become a criterion to determine whether the government would be allowed to make a request under the stand-by arrangement. If the criterion were not satisfied, the member would have to negotiate with the Fund and agree on implementing the same or a new policy (Gold, 1971, p. 21). This experience of deciding on each occasion whether to grant resources led the Fund to gradually develop general principles for the use of its resources and subsequently formulate them as policies (Gold, 1979, p. 5).

The gradual process of formalization of conditionality policies increased in the 1970s. Structural conditionality was inaugurated. Next, the Second Amendment introduced and updated several key provisions in the Articles of Agreement. Third, the Executive Board in 1979 adopted for the first time a decision that established guidelines on conditionality.[18] However, the plethora of special mechanisms and facilities continued to represent a resort to derogations from the "*droit commun del'Organisation*" (Sorel, 1996, p. 56).

The new Guidelines on conditionality suggested the adoption of corrective measures at an early stage of balance of payments problems. Moreover, the envisaged duration of programs was defined as one year, with the option of a longer period (up to three years) upon the government's request. The short timeframe reflects the concern that a longer period would be perceived as a dilution of the rigor of conditionality (Gold, 1979, p. 18).

Between the 1970s and the 1990s, the Fund had to face the debt crisis of developing countries, the transition of socialist countries to market economies, and the increased influence of global capital markets, which all had implications for conditionality (Allegret and Dulbecco, 2007, p. 310). The experience with conditionality policies in those decades was characterized by several excesses, as highlighted by academics and acknowledged by the Fund itself.

The Fund dealt with the unprecedented magnitude of the problems by increasing the number of conditions attached to programs. The mean value of the average number of binding conditions for arrangements initiated between 1952 and 1973 was 4.23; between 1974 and 1982 7.13; between 1983 and 1990 12.07; and between 1991 and 1995–2000 12.42 (Allegret and Dulbecco, 2007, p. 310).

Another problematic change was the resort to procedural rather than target conditionality. The former dictates both ends and means and reduces the country's margin of action to a higher extent. With its focus on institutional and analytical conditions, it can delay the start of disbursements. The new conditionality adopted by the Fund also embraced more governance-related issues. This led to a heightened impact on institutional change, with a less clear link with balance of payments issues (Allegret and Dulbecco, 2007, p. 310). Furthermore, it was acknowledged that several structural conditions included in IMF arrangements lay outside the Fund's core mandate and should have been addressed by the World Bank.

In the wake of the Asian financial crisis, IMF conditionality came again under international scrutiny. In the period 1996 to 1999, the typical number of structural policy conditions for an Extended Fund Facility (EFF) program was eighteen measures per annum and for a one-year stand-by arrangement it was between nine and fifteen, whereas they should have been included only in exceptional cases according to the 1979 guidelines (Goldstein, 2001; Independent Evaluation Office, 2007, p. 34). Furthermore, the average number of structural performance criteria in the programs with the three Asian crisis economies in 1997 (i.e., Indonesia, South Korea, and Thailand) was approximately four times higher than the average for all 37 Fund programs over the 1993–1999 period (Goldstein, 2001, p. 36).

Moreover, the high number of conditions seemingly went too far in addressing moral hazard and arguably made the debt crisis more severe, as it dissuaded countries from approaching the Fund at an early stage of their balance of payments problems. This was the case with Thailand in 1997. In addition, some countries would turn to other financial assistance providers as Malaysia did with the low-conditionality Miyazawa Initiative funds in 1998 (Goldstein, 2001, p. 6). Thus, this effort to constrain post-funding moral hazard may have actually induced moral hazard by incentivizing debtors to embrace low-conditionality sources, with reduced exclusivity for the Fund.

In the early 2000s, the Fund assessed its experience with conditionality in the previous decades. Confronted with significant criticisms from academic and non-governmental commentators, the organization attempted to implement a profound reform of its policies.

The IMF strived to strengthen member countries' sense of ownership, in particular by reducing the number of conditions and giving the authorities greater choice in deciding how to reach particular objectives. Ownership requires the Fund to be flexible and responsive to the real circumstances of the debtor country. Furthermore, to the same end, it was recommended that the program be shared with society as a whole, for example, by publishing the memorandum of economic policies (Leckow, 2005, p. 60).

In addition, the Fund's conditionality was refocused to cover monetary, exchange rate and fiscal policy, leaving other areas to other international organizations, for instance, social safety nets and privatization to the World Bank. However, conditions in such areas might still be introduced where considered to be particularly important for the success of the program.

The Guidelines on Conditionality were revised in 2002[19] and 2006.[20] Their first paragraph now clearly spells out the two complementary purposes of conditionality: to ensure that the resources are used to assist countries to resolve their balance of payments problems in a manner consistent with the Articles of Agreement; and to establish adequate safeguards for the temporary use of the Fund's resources. The language on the approval of requests is tougher: a request can be approved "only if" the Fund believes that the program is consistent with IMF provisions and policies, that it will be implemented, and that the member is sufficiently committed. In the conditions, performance criteria must refer to policies so critical for the program or its monitoring that purchases or disbursements should be interrupted in cases of non-observance. They should refer to clearly specified variables or measures that can be objectively monitored by the staff.

Despite the considerable efforts, commentators have underscored substantial differences between the aspirations of the Fund's management and the actual changes eventually achieved (Killick, 2002, p. 2). The Independent Evaluation Office (2007, p. 8) reviewed programs approved between 1995 and 2004 and found that structural conditions were not always critical and were often too detailed. In addition, compliance was considerably lower with *structural* conditionality than with *macroeconomic* conditionality,[21] and this represented a reputational risk for the Fund. Compliance did not lead to further reforms in the sectors concerned, which was deemed to be a sign of the ineffectiveness of structural conditionality (Independent Evaluation Office, 2007, p. 19).

The 2011 Review by the IMF (largely confirmed subsequently, see International Monetary Fund, 2019a) found an overall level of good compliance with the conditionality guidelines. It also underscored, however, the challenges that the global financial crisis posed; in particular, structural conditionality had become more extensive. The number and depth of structural conditions slightly increased in 2011 (International Monetary Fund, 2012, p. 27). In high-debt countries, the magnitude of the policy adjustment was considerable and output losses resulted (International Monetary Fund, 2012, p. 4). Substantial conditionality is not prohibited under the Guidelines when it is necessary for the success of the program. However, structural conditionality needs to be parsimonious and macro-critical (International Monetary Fund, 2012, p. 9).

The 2011 Review underscored several positive results achieved according to the Fund. Programs have given more attention to social aspects, with the objective of protecting the most vulnerable segments of the population. Furthermore, social spending has been maintained or even increased. On the other hand, in some cases cuts in expenditures, including in social spending, have been considerable, highlighting difficulties in achieving consistency across programs and in the political ownership of programs. In addition, social impact analysis had not been conducted in all cases (International Monetary Fund, 2012, pp. 16–18).

Furthermore, the experience with the aftermath of the Global Financial Crisis showed that the assumptions about the effects of measures recommended in the framework of conditionality often proved overoptimistic.

Specifically, so-called "austerity" worsened the growth prospects of advanced economies more than the IMF had predicted (Blanchard and Leigh, 2013).

In 2014, the Fund adopted the Revised Operational Guidance on the 2002 Conditionality Guidelines. It recommends that staff accommodate country authorities' preferences with respect to growth, job market, and distributional targets to the extent permitted by the need to resolve balance of payments problems. Furthermore, the relations between program goals, strategies, and conditionality need to be carefully examined. Early contingency planning and contacts with country authorities and other institutions can improve the quality of programs, which would not have to be drawn up in the time-constrained context of crises. The conditionality of regional financing arrangements should not be inconsistent with the Fund's nor should Fund conditionality aim to imitate the regional one (International Monetary Fund, 2014, pp. 6–9).

The equal treatment of countries is another recurring criticism. Commentators have held that the Fund is ready to demand of developing countries structural reforms that it would not have asked of industrialized countries (Goldstein 2001, p. 7). The famous quote that is often repeated is that: "When the Fund consults with a poor and weak country, the country gets in line. When it consults with a big and strong country, the Fund gets in line" (Volcker and Gyohten, 1992, p. 143).

An underlying time inconsistency permeates IMF conditionality. Whereas programs must have a short time span, the reforms needed by a country often require a much longer period (Sorel, 1996, p. 52). In addition, some commentators have argued that the Fund's dual role as advisor and financial backer creates the potential for conflicts of interest and should be disentangled (Allegret and Dulbecco, 2007, p. 324). The suggestion would be to have the Fund provide advice to countries, without also offering financial assistance. However, the opposite would not be allowed under the current legal regime, i.e., providing resources without the advice embodied in conditions.

There is a clear difficulty in the relationship between the provision of IMF assistance and the flow of official and private funds to the country concerned. During the 1970s and 1980s, the IMF moved from a focus on the provision of resources "from its own coffers" to facilitating the flow of balance-of-payments financing from private creditors (Cohen, 1983, pp. 315–336; Lipson, 1981, pp. 603–631). Thanks to the "seal of approval" obtained from the Fund, the government has access to more private resources (Sorel, 1996, p. 49). On the one hand, the Fund is proud of its resulting catalytic role (Gianviti, 2005, p. 15), albeit with mixed empirical evidence.[22] However, on the other hand, supplementary financiers are seen as having the potential to influence the terms of Fund conditionality, as the Fund considers their financing important for the success of programs (Gould, 2003, p. 552).[23] For example, during the 1982 Mexican debt crisis, the IMF Managing Director held meetings with major foreign commercial banks. To accommodate the latter's demands, original conditions were extended to include the settlement of arrears on interest payments due by Mexican private borrowers to foreign private financial institutions (Gould, 2003, pp. 575–577). Furthermore, an intrinsic difficulty of conditionality concerns the need to manage institutional change. The Fund does not necessarily have the ability to introduce reforms to develop market processes and maintain the institutional order in member countries (Allegret and Dulbecco, 2007, p. 311).

The evolution of conditionality shows that debtor moral hazard remains an ongoing concern. Over time, the role of conditionality has been defined more precisely. However, where conditionality covers too many aspects, not tightly linked with the IMF areas of focus, its effects can be excessive and countries are deterred from approaching the IMF.

1.3 The Fund's preferred creditor status

The hierarchy of a debtor country's creditors is not firmly established. Against this background, the government could be tempted not to repay the IMF and rather reimburse other creditors. This would represent an aspect of moral hazard at the expense of the Fund. To counter this strand of moral hazard, the IMF can rely on its preferred creditor status.[24]

The claims of intergovernmental organizations as the Fund, but also the International Bank for Reconstruction and Development, regional development banks, and the Bank for International Settlements have been preferred over those of any other creditor. The reasons given to justify this treatment are essentially that non-reimbursement of these claims would have affected the very existence of such institutions, and that access to financial markets would have become much costlier if the debtor country defaulted with regard to these international institutions.

Although some scholars have affirmed that the preferred status of international organizations stems from a customary rule (Carreau, 1985, p. 15), general international law does not seem to recognize a preferred status for such creditors (Martha, 1990, p. 810). Even the international organizations themselves offer practical rather than legal arguments for their alleged preferred creditor status. For example, the IMF Interim Committee urged all members to treat the Fund as a preferred creditor (Boughton, 2001, pp. 820–821). The reasons given were

> the unique position of the Fund as an international cooperative institution, its role in the international monetary system, the revolving nature of its resources, and the consequent need for all members, creditors and debtors alike, *in practice*, to treat the Fund as a preferred creditor.[25]

Thus, the higher status was to be provided as a matter of practice rather than law.

Paris Club creditors have consistently exempted both the IMF and the World Bank from the restructuring processes (Martha, 1990, p. 809).

However, it is difficult to gauge whether such conduct is based on a legal rule or simply on pragmatic solutions for the situations at hand. As a matter of fact, the seniority of the IMF is widely accepted by private market participants (see Steinkamp and Westerman, 2013).

With regard to regional financial arrangements, the European Financial Stability Facility (EFSF) does not claim to enjoy a preferred status.[26] The Preamble of the Treaty establishing the European Stability Mechanism (ESM) recognizes the seniority status of its own loans, as well as the super-seniority of the IMF:

> In the event of ESM financial assistance in the form of ESM loans following a European financial assistance program existing at the time of the signature of this Treaty, the ESM will enjoy the same seniority as all other loans and obligations of the beneficiary ESM Member, with the exception of the IMF loans.[27]

Thus far, this is the only example of a legal provision specifically designating the seniority of regional and international financial institutions. The provision implements one of the Principles envisaged by the G20 for cooperation between the IMF and regional financing arrangements.[28]

The development of regional arrangements might be characterized by a need for more precise legal provisions with respect to the *status quo*, and this might have implications for the broader legal context.[29] For the rest, the practice of sovereign debt restructurings has recognized the preferred status of international financial institutions without a clearly established legal basis.

Consequently, the prevention of moral hazard by the means of the Fund's preferred creditor status is not based on an unassailable legal provision. However, the consistent practice of private and state creditors provides sufficient evidence for its effectiveness.

Section 2 Coping with creditor moral hazard

2.1 Lending into arrears

The creditor of a government could rely on the availability of IMF financial assistance to indulge in moral hazard. It could lend without adequate consideration of the country's economic conditions, and then expect full repayment. As illustrated above, the Fund's preferred creditor status addresses this strand of moral hazard, as creditors would have to accept the higher ranking of the Fund's claims.

Two other IMF policies can mitigate moral hazard in this respect: lending into arrears and financing assurances. Lending into arrears concerns both official and private creditors; the focus here will be on the latter.

With regard to official creditors, the Fund had long maintained that it would not provide financing to a debtor which had arrears toward them unless a rescheduling was agreed with the Paris Club or such official creditors agreed to the IMF financing despite the arrears. The Executive Board had decided not to codify its practice on such delicate matters, which essentially relied on the Paris Club.[30] However, over time the share of debt held by Paris Club members shrank relatively to other creditors (i.e., official creditors outside of the Paris Club, and private bondholders) and there were instances of small official creditors blocking negotiations (Leckow and Ams, 2017, p. 18). After the 2015 reform, the IMF now takes into account a Paris Club agreement only where it involves the majority of financing required by the debtor and allows the IMF to provide financing even despite arrears to a non-cooperating official bilateral creditor under certain circumstances – e.g., if the debtor is making an effort in good faith to reach agreement with the creditor (see International Monetary Fund, 2015). As will be seen, this recent development mirrors the evolution of the policy with respect to private creditors.[31]

With regard to the policy on lending into arrears to private creditors, this was originally conceived as an exception. The IMF would not lend to a country that had arrears in payments toward private creditors because such arrears risked aggravating the balance of payment difficulties and ran against the logic of international monetary cooperation (Simpson, 2006, p. 10). The use of lending into arrears gradually materialized as a tool against creditors' moral hazard. As will be seen, "creditor moral hazard is… likely to be stimulated if LIA policy is too lax" (Simpson, 2006, p. 20).

The possibility of lending into arrears was formally stipulated in decision 3153-(70/95) of 26 October 1970. The financial assistance granted was subjected to the conditions that arrears had to be eliminated within the duration of the program and that, in its letter of intent, the member state had to commit not to incur such arrears (International Monetary Fund, 1976, pp. 142–143).

The ground for this was found in Article V(3)(a) of the IMF Articles of Agreement: "The Fund shall adopt policies on the use of its general resources, … that will establish adequate safeguards for the temporary use of the general resources of the Fund." The other guiding principle for IMF action, found in Article I(v), was to avoid "resorting to measures destructive of national or international prosperity." The Fund considered that arrears toward private creditors endangered the prosperity of the debtor state and of the international payments and financial system (International Monetary Fund, 2013a, p. 45). The consequence was the imposition of conditions for assisting a country that was unable to reimburse its private creditors.

The lending into arrears policy has since gone through a significant evolution. In a 1980 decision it was remarked that it would sometimes be impossible to eliminate the payment arrears during the adjustment program and acknowledged that "[s]pecial arrangements may be needed for the renegotiation of outstanding debt obligations when debt problems are particularly severe."[32] Notwithstanding such flexibility, during the Latin American crisis of the 1980s the Fund was rather rigid. It did not grant assistance if the government had not first erased its arrears by rescheduling or by new loans meant to reimburse the previous ones. Consequently, this allowed for private creditors' moral hazard: their contractual position in restructuring negotiations was stronger, as the country needed to reach an agreement with them before approaching the IMF (Buchheit and Lastra, 2007, p. 943).

In a partial recognition of this risk of moral hazard, the Fund reacted by adopting a softer approach in 1989, in connection with the launch of the Brady bonds. The IMF could, "on a case-by case basis, approve an arrangement outright before the conclusion of such negotiations, provided that prompt Fund support is judged essential for program implementation, that negotiations between the member and its bank creditors have begun, and that it can be expected that a financing package consistent with external viability will be agreed within a reasonable period of time."[33] It also decided that "an accumulation of arrears to banks may have to be tolerated where negotiations continue and the country's financing situation does not allow them to be avoided."[34] This change had a profound effect on sovereign debt restructuring processes: it has provided a "critical backstop to the negotiations," as it "gives the debtor greater leverage in the debt restructuring process" (Hagan, 2020, p. 7).

In 1998, the importance of bonds in sovereign debt, and the delays and difficulties that this could entail for restructuring talks, led the Fund to amend its criteria. Besides the need for loans for the adjustment program and to have begun negotiations, the third requirement demanded that negotiations for debt restructuring be conducted in good faith (Buchheit and Lastra, 2007, p. 945). This good faith criterion was slightly modified the following year to: "the member is… making a good faith effort to reach a collaborative agreement with its creditors."[35] This amendment concerns the result of negotiations, which had to be of a "collaborative" character, i.e., private parties should not just be offered a take-it-or-leave-it proposal, but rather they should be invited to negotiations and participate in them in an active manner (Buchheit and Lastra, 2007, p. 946).

In a 2002 decision, the Fund developed (in a more exhaustive way) the good-faith requirement and drew up a list of principles.[36] Such principles aim to guide the assessment, which continues to be on a case-by-case basis, and recommend a rapid initiation of negotiations, the exchange of non-confidential information, and the possibility for creditors to give their opinion on the program for restructuring and the instruments to be used. These principles have often been criticized because of the qualitative nature of the assessment required, which leaves a considerable margin for varying interpretations and an inconsistent application (Bedford and Irwin, 2008, p. 6).

The inclusion of the good-faith criterion marked an important step in the IMF lending into arrears policy. It went beyond what was necessary to protect the financial interests of the Fund (mandated by the Articles of Agreement) and signaled its will to play a quasi-arbiter role in sovereign debt restructuring. This manifested another instance of the Fund's ability to "*étendre son domaine d'intervention*" (Bismuth, 2011, p. 73).

However, this does not fall within the explicit competencies of the organization and also opens up the possibility for private creditors to lobby the IMF to revisit whether the government's behavior is or is not in good faith and therefore should not be provided assistance. Thus, moral hazard could not be effectively prevented, as bondholders could blackmail the debtor state (Buchheit and Lastra, 2007). If one considers that the IMF's objective since the 1980s has been to keep private creditors from preventing the Fund's support to a country, one must notice that the framework currently in place frustrates that objective. The Fund appears to be aware of such risks and plans to reconsider its policy: "although the collaborative, good-faith approach to resolving external private arrears embedded in the lending into arrears (LIA) policy remains the most promising way to regain market access post-default, a review of the effectiveness of the LIA policy is in order in light of recent experience and the increased complexity of the creditor base" (International Monetary Fund, 2013a, p. 7).

2.2 Financing assurances

Financing assurances represent the complementary aspect of the IMF lending into arrears policy and their evolution matches the latter. Initially, in early 1980s, the IMF declared to commercial bank creditors that it would not adopt a stand-by agreement until banks had guaranteed that they would continue to finance the debtor. The practice was for the Executive Board to approve the agreement in principle under the condition that banks representing a critical mass of the debt (assessed case-by-case, but always 90% or more) provided financing (see International Monetary Fund, 2013a, p. 43 and Cissé, 1995, p. 284).

In the 1980s, this practice came upon a substantial roadblock and creditor moral hazard was exposed. Since it was ever more difficult for debtors to successfully complete negotiations, banks could effect a *de facto* veto (or a considerable delay) to the IMF's assistance. This situation led to a change in the IMF guidelines in 1989, as discussed above, which allowed for the adoption of a program even before the conclusion of a financing agreement with the banks. However, it also left open the possibility to continue the previous practice: "[w]hen circumstances warrant, the practice of seeking a critical mass, as well as the possibility of approving an arrangement in principle, will continue to be followed" (International Monetary Fund, 1989, p. 26).

This remains the official policy of the Fund. It assesses whether the financing needs for the first 12 months of the program are covered by firm commitments and whether for the next 12 months there are good prospects for adequate funds. In cases involving a debt restructuring, the Fund deems sufficient an assurance by Paris Club members that they will draw up Agreed Minutes immediately after the adoption of the arrangement by the IMF. By virtue of the comparability of treatment principle respected by the Club, the other state creditors are expected to follow the same terms of the restructuring (International Monetary Fund, 2013a, p. 44).

With regard to private creditors, the Fund must be satisfied that a credible process leading to restructuring is in place with sufficient participation by creditors. The factors taken into account include: the state's appointment of legal and financial advisors; the launching of consultations with creditors; and the consideration of a debt restructuring strategy with provisions for new bonds and the incentives for creditors to participate (International Monetary Fund, 2013a, p. 45).

Thus, the lending into arrears and financing assurances policies are tightly interconnected and have undergone parallel evolutions. Their current state testifies to the difficulties encountered by the Fund to ensure the protection of its own financial interests on the one hand and the power to assist a country in need without being at the mercy of private creditors on the other. In 2007, there was a hope that a revision of the policies on lending into arrears would eventually materialize but this was ultimately postponed indefinitely, with revisions now being adopted "as needed."[37]

By the means of its lending into arrears and financing assurances policies, the IMF strives to achieve two conflicting objectives: the protection of its resources and the assistance to countries with balance of payments problems. Creditors' moral hazard materializes in their ability to use their veto, de facto blocking the Fund's action in a sovereign debt crisis. A further calibration of these policies could address this risk more effectively.[38]

Section 3 Conclusions

This chapter has investigated several aspects of moral hazard affecting the IMF involvement in sovereign debt crises. Two angles have been considered: that of the debtor government and that of the country's creditors, which interact with the potential moral hazard of the Fund itself.

With respect to the sovereign debtor, the prospect of restructuring the portion of its debt deemed unsustainable can mitigate moral hazard. The IMF expertise in its assessment can be effective in this respect. However, the systemic exception temporarily adopted in the context of the euro area crisis shows the potential for suboptimal tweaks to the process in the case of bigger – or more integrated – economies.

Conditionality linked to the Fund's financial assistance is arguably the most effective tool against debtor moral hazard. Over time, its role has become more established in IMF practice, and has at times grown to cover a host of areas. This has produced excessive results, as it curtailed countries' margin of action in a significant manner and eventually dissuaded them from requesting the Fund's intervention at an early stage of their balance of payments problems. Consequently, this has had a negative impact on solving sovereign debt crises.

The IMF preferred creditor status addresses the moral hazard of both the debtor and the creditors, as they both must accept that the Fund's claims stand senior. The practice in the markets provides a strong indication of the effectiveness of such a principle. However, the absence of a clear legal basis may still give rise to difficulties if brought before a court.

Finally, lending into arrears and financing assurances have gradually "matured" from quasi-exceptions to fully fledged policies. Their evolution is probably the most apparent illustration of the IMF struggle with creditor moral hazard. Further fine-tuning of these policies could improve the Fund's ability to intervene efficiently in sovereign debt crises and reduce moral hazard.

Moral hazard presents a complex challenge, and it is hard to assess its magnitude and respective role vis-à-vis other factors that can shape an institution's behavior over time. However, its relevance for efficient IMF interventions on sovereign debt warrants further research in this area.

Notes

1 Pursuant to Article 126 of the Treaty on the Functioning of the European Union, the European Commission is tasked with examining member states' compliance with budgetary discipline, inter alia by monitoring "whether the ratio of government debt to gross domestic product exceeds a reference value" indicated in a Protocol annexed to the Treaty. For a concrete example, see European Commission (2020, p. 15).

2 Darbellay and Gaillard, Chapter 4 of this volume, investigate how a creditor with a junior status is likely to encourage debtor moral hazard.

3 It has been argued that, prior to the Latin-American crises of the 1980s, factors other than debtor moral hazard were key to the occurrence of sovereign debt problems; see Díaz-Alejandro (1984). However, the availability of IMF financial assistance, without requirements, would have the potential to give rise to moral hazard even when exogenous shocks are the immediate cause of a crisis.

4 International Monetary Fund, "IMF Discusses Assessments of Sustainability," *Public Information Notice No. 02/69*, 11 July 2002; available at https://www.imf.org/external/np/sec/pn/2002/pn0269.htm.

5 International Monetary Fund, "IMF Concludes Discussion on Access Policy in the Context of Capital Account Crises; and Review of Access Policies in the Credit Tranches and the Extended Fund Facility," *Public Information Notice No. 03/37*, 21 March 2003, available at http://www.imf.org/en/news/articles/2015/09/28/04/53/pn0337.

6 See Flores and Gaillard, Chapter 5, and Gaillard and Michalek, Chapter 7 of this volume, for the implications of "systemic risk."

7 On the specific financial concerns of the Eurozone, see Andenas and Chiu (2013, p. 348).

8 The IMF had to cooperate with the European Commission and the European Central Bank as well as with the countries directly concerned. See Viterbo and Cisotta (2012).

9 The IEO is a body established in 2001 to assess the Fund's policies and activities.

10 The current provision now reads (emphasis on the revised language): "A rigorous and systematic analysis indicates that there is a high probability that the member's public debt is sustainable in the medium term. *Where the member's debt is assessed to be unsustainable ex ante, exceptional access will only be made available where the financing being provided from sources other than the Fund restores debt sustainability with a high probability. Where the member's debt is considered sustainable but not with a high probability, exceptional access would be justified if financing provided from sources other than the Fund, although it may not restore sustainability with high probability, improves debt sustainability and sufficiently enhances the safeguards for Fund resources. For purposes of this criterion, financing provided from sources other than the Fund may include, inter alia, financing obtained through any intended debt*

restructuring. This criterion applies only to public (domestic and external) debt. However, the analysis of such public debt sustainability will incorporate any relevant contingent liabilities, including those potentially arising from private external indebtedness" (International Monetary Fund, 2019b, p. 405).

11 See also U.S. House of Representatives (2016).

12 International Monetary Fund, "Conditionality in Fund-Supported Programs – Overview," para. 2, 20 February 2001; see http://www.imf.org/external/np/pdr/cond/2001/eng/overview.

13 See the Appendix for an example of a letter of intent, memorandum of economic policies, technical memorandum of understanding.

14 See, among others, Calomiris (1998), Goldstein (2001), Jeanne and Zettelmeyer (2005), Wahi (2006), and De Sena (2010).

15 International Monetary Fund, "Executive Board Decision No. 102–(52/11)." See International Monetary Fund (1976, p. 40).

16 Article V, Section 3, letter (c).

17 Article V, Section 3, letter (d).

18 International Monetary Fund, "Executive Board Decision No. 6056-(79/38)." See IMF (1979, pp. 136–138).

19 International Monetary Fund, "Executive Board Decision No. 12864-(02/102)," 25 September 2002.

20 International Monetary Fund, "Executive Board Decision No. 13814-(06/98)," 15 November 2006.

21 *Macroeconomic* conditionality includes the choice of exchange rate regime, monetary policy and fiscal policy. *Structural* conditionality measures can be identified by their primary economic objectives: underpinning stabilization efforts, increasing economic flexibility and efficiency, and addressing vulnerabilities. See International Monetary Fund (2004, pp. 4 and 56).

22 Improved access to international capital markets is not uniform across all IMF-supported programs. See Saravia and Mody (2003).

23 See also the evolution of the lending into arrears and the financing assurances policies below.

24 The Fund's preferred creditor status, without credible rules on the assessment of debt sustainability (as it occurred with the change in criteria for the aid to Greece), could give rise to moral hazard. In fact, the IMF could decide to provide financial assistance without serious committments by the recipient country, knowing that its resources are guaranteed. See https://voxeu.org/article/imf-preferred-creditor-status-and-eurozone-crisis. However, as discussed before, the subsequent deletion of the systemic spillover exception has rectified this issue.

25 Emphasis added. See International Monetary Fund (1988) and Boughton (2001, p. 832).

26 It is remarkable to note that the EFSF itself acknowledges the seniority of the IMF, see p. 3 at: https://www.esm.europa.eu/sites/default/files/2016_02_01_efsf_faq_archived.pdf.

27 Recital 13, signed on 2 February 2012 – consolidated version following Lithuania's accession to the ESM, T/ESM 2012-LT/en, p. 7, available at: https://www.esm.europa.eu/sites/default/files/20150203_-_esm_treaty_-_en.pdf.

28 G20 Finance Ministers and Central Bank Governors, "G20 Principles for Cooperation between the IMF and Regional Financing Arrangements," 15 October 2011, principle No. 6 at: http://www.g20.utoronto.ca/2011/2011-finance-principles-111015-en.pdf.

29 On regional financial arrangements, see the discussion above.

30 International Monetary Fund, "Summing Up by the Acting Chairman – Settlement of Disputes Between Members Relating to External Financial Obligations – Role of the Fund," IMF (2013c, pp. 119–122).

31 With some differences: "the LIOA [lending into official arrears] policy does not result in official bilateral creditors being treated exactly like private creditors: official bilateral creditors enjoy greater leverage (although not the degree that they enjoyed prior to the introduction of the policy). The rationale for this asymmetry is that, unlike private creditors, official bilateral creditors provide critical financing for Fund-supported programs in the context of a crisis; when the new policy was being considered, there was a concern that any decision to lend into the arrears of official bilateral creditors could undermine their willingness to provide such financing in the future". See Hagan (2020, p. 8).
32 International Monetary Fund, "Review of Fund Policies and Procedure on Payments Arrears – Executive Board Meeting 80/154," 17 October 1980. See IMF (2008, p. 344).
33 International Monetary Fund, "Summing Up by the Chairman – Fund Involvement in the Debt Strategy – Executive Board Meeting 89/61," 23 May 1989. See IMF (1996, pp. 151–152).
34 International Monetary Fund, "Summing Up by the Chairman – Fund Involvement in the Debt Strategy – Executive Board Meeting 89/61," 23 May 1989. See IMF (1996, p. 152).
35 International Monetary Fund, "Summing Up by the Acting Chairman – Fund Policy on Arrears to Private Creditors – Further Considerations – Executive Board Meeting 99/64," 14 June 1999. See IMF (2019b, p. 397).
36 International Monetary Fund, "The Acting Chair's Summing Up – Fund Policy on Lending into Arrears to Private Creditors – Further Consideration of the Good Faith Criterion – Executive Board Meeting 02/92," 4 September 2002. See IMF (2019b, pp. 399–400).
37 See International Monetary Fund, "Decision No. 14036-(08/01)," 27 December 2007; International Monetary Fund, "Decision No. 14235-(09/1)," 31 December 2008. See IMF (2019b, p. 402).
38 See Flores and Gaillard, Chapter 5 of this volume, for a discussion on sovereign debt restructuring.
39 Abridged version from IMF website: https://www.imf.org/External/NP/LOI/2001/arg/02/index.htm.

References

Allegret, J-P. and Dulbecco, P. (2007) "The Institutional Failures of International Monetary Fund Conditionality," *Review of International Organizations*, Vol. 2, No. 4, pp. 309–327.

Andenas, M. and Chiu, I. H-Y. (2013) "Financial Stability and Legal Integration in Financial Regulation," *European Law Review*, Vol. 38, No. 3, pp. 335–359.

Bedford, P. and Irwin, G. (2008) "Reforming the IMF's Lending-into-Arrears Framework," *Bank of England, Financial Stability Paper No. 4*, pp. 1–13.

Bismuth, R. (2011) "Le droit international économique: entre libéralisation et régulation," *Questions internationales*, No. 49, pp. 68–74.

Bismuth, R. (2012) "L'assistance financière du FMI aux États membres de la zone euro: de l'inconcevable au conventionnel (ou comment "conventionnaliser" l'inconcevable)," *Revue des Affaires Européennes – Law & European Affairs*, Vol. 19, No. 4, pp. 747–757.

Blanchard, O. and Leigh, D. (2013) "Growth Forecast Errors and Fiscal Multipliers," *IMF Working Paper No. 13/1.*

Boughton, J. M. (2001) *Silent Revolution – The International Monetary Fund, 1979–1989.* Washington, DC: IMF.

Buchheit, L. C. and Lastra, R. M. (2007) "Lending into Arrears – A Policy Adrift," *The International Lawyer*, Vol. 41, No. 3, pp. 939–954.

Calomiris, C. W. (1998) "The IMF's Imprudent Role as Lender of Last Resort," *Cato Journal*, Vol. 17, No. 3, pp. 275–294.

Carreau, D. (1985) "Le rééchelonnement de la dette extérieure des Etats," *Journal du droit international*, Vol. 112, No. 1, pp. 5–48.

Chwieroth, J. M. (2010) *Capital Ideas: The IMF and The Rise of Financial Liberalization*. Princeton: Princeton University Press.

Cissé, H. (1995) "Le fonds monétaire international et l'endettement extérieur des Etats," in Shaw, M. N. and Carreau, D. (Eds), *La dette extérieure / The External Debt*. The Hague Academy of International Law. Leiden: Brill Nijhoff.

Cohen, B. J. (1983) "Balance-of-Payments Financing: Evolution of a Regime," in Krasner, S. D. (Ed), *International Regimes*. Ithaca: Cornell University Press.

De Sena, P. (2010) "International Monetary Fund, World Bank and Respect for Human Rights: A Critical Point of View," *Italian Yearbook of International Law*, Vol. 20, pp. 247–274.

Díaz-Alejandro, C. F. (1984) "Latin American Debt: I Don't Think We Are in Kansas Anymore," *Brookings Papers on Economic Activity*, Vol. 1984, No. 2, pp. 335–389.

European Commission (2020) *Debt Sustainability Monitor 2019*. Brussels: European Commission.

Gianviti, F. (1989) "The International Monetary Fund and External Debt (Volume 215)," in *Collected Courses of the Hague Academy of International Law*. Leiden: Brill Nijhoff.

Gianviti, F. (2005) "Economic, Social and Cultural Rights and the International Monetary Fund," in International Monetary Fund, *Current Developments in Monetary and Financial Law*, Vol. 3. Washington, DC: IMF.

Gold, J. (1971) "Use of the International Monetary Fund's Resources: 'Conditionality' and 'Unconditionality' as Legal Categories'," *George Washington Journal of International Law and Economics.*, Vol. 6, No. 1, pp. 1–26.

Gold, J. (1979) "Conditionality," *IMF Pamphlet Series No. 31*.

Goldstein, M. (2001) "IMF Structural Conditionality: How Much Is Too Much?," *Revision of paper presented at NBER Conference on "Economic and Financial Crises in Emerging Market Economies" Woodstock, Vermont*, October 19–21, 2000.

Gould, E. R. (2003) "Money Talks: Supplementary Financiers and International Monetary Fund Conditionality," *International Organization*, Vol. 57, No. 3, pp. 551–586.

Hagan, S. (2020) "Sovereign Debt Restructuring: The Centrality of the IMF's Role," *Peterson Institute for International Economics, Working Paper 20–13*.

Henning, C. R. (2006) "Regional Arrangements and the International Monetary Fund," in Truman, E. M. (Ed), *Reforming the IMF for the 21st Century*. Special Report 19. Washington, DC: Institute for International Economics.

Independent Evaluation Office (2007) *Structural Conditionality in IMF-Supported Programs*. Evaluation Report. Washington, DC: IMF.

Independent Evaluation Office (2016) *The IMF and the Crises in Greece, Ireland, and Portugal*. Evaluation Report. Washington, DC: IMF.

International Monetary Fund (1959) *Annual Report 1959*. Washington, DC: IMF.

International Monetary Fund (1964) *Annual Report 1964*. Washington, DC: IMF.

International Monetary Fund (1976) *Selected Decisions of the International Monetary Fund and Selected Documents*. Washington, DC: IMF.

International Monetary Fund (1979) *Annual Report 1979*. Washington, DC: IMF.

International Monetary Fund (1988) *Report of the Executive Board to the Interim Committee of the Board of Governors on Overdue Financial Obligations to the Fund*. 9 September. Washington, DC: IMF.

International Monetary Fund (1989) *Annual Report 1989*. Washington, DC: IMF.

International Monetary Fund (1996) *Selected Decisions and Selected Documents of the International Monetary Fund – Twenty-First Issue, Washington, DC – June 30, 1996*. Washington, DC: IMF.

International Monetary Fund (2002) *Assessing Sustainability*. 28 May. Washington, DC: IMF.

International Monetary Fund (2004) *Macroeconomic and Structural Policies in Fund-Supported Programs: Review of Experience*. 24 November. Washington, DC: IMF.

International Monetary Fund (2008) *Selected Decisions and Selected Documents of the International Monetary Fund – Thirty-Second Issue, Washington, DC – December 31, 2007*. Washington, DC: IMF.

International Monetary Fund (2009a) *Conditionality in Fund-Supported Programs – Purposes, Modalities, and Options for Reform*. 29 January. Washington, DC: IMF.

International Monetary Fund (2009b) *GRA Lending Toolkit and Conditionality: Reform Proposals*. 13 March. Washington, DC: IMF.

International Monetary Fund (2011) *Selected Decisions and Selected Documents of the International Monetary Fund*. Washington, DC: IMF.

International Monetary Fund (2012) "2011 Review of Conditionality," *Overview Paper*, 19 June.

International Monetary Fund (2013a) *Sovereign Debt Restructuring – Recent Developments and Implications for the Fund's Legal and Policy Framework*. 26 April. Washington, DC: IMF.

International Monetary Fund (2013b) "Greece: Ex Post Evaluation of Exceptional Access under the 2010 Stand-By Arrangement," *IMF Country Report No. 13/156*. Washington, DC: IMF.

International Monetary Fund (2013c) *Selected Decisions and Selected Documents of the International Monetary Fund, Thirty-Seventh Issue, 31 December*. Washington, DC: IMF.

International Monetary Fund (2014) "Revised Operational Guidance to IMF Staff on the 2002 Conditionality Guidelines," *Policy Paper*, 23 July.

International Monetary Fund (2015) "Reforming the Fund's Policy on Non-Toleration of Arrears to Official Creditors," *Policy Paper*, December.

International Monetary Fund (2019a) "2018 Review of Program Design and Conditionality," *Policy Paper*, 20 May.

International Monetary Fund (2019b) *Selected Decisions and Selected Documents of the International Monetary Fund – 40th Issue*. Washington, DC: IMF.

Jeanne, O. and Zettelmeyer, J. (2005) "The Mussa Theorem (and Other Results on IMF-Induced Moral Hazard)," *IMF Staff Papers*, Vol. 52, pp. 64–84. IMF Conference in Honor of Michael Mussa.

Killick, T. (2002) "The 'Streamlining' of IMF Conditionality: Aspirations, Reality and Repercussions," *Report for U.K. Department for International Development*. London: Overseas Development Institute.

Leckow, R. (2005) "Conditionality in the International Monetary Fund," in International Monetary Fund, *Current Developments in Monetary and Financial Law, Vol. 3*. Washington, DC: IMF.

Leckow, R. and Ams, J. (2017) "Sovereign Debt Restructuring in the IMF Experience," in *ESCB Legal Conference 2016*. Frankfurt am Main: European Central Bank.

Lipson, C. (1981) "The International Organization of Third World Debt," *International Organization*, Vol. 35, No. 4, pp. 603–631.

Martha, R. S. J. (1990) "Preferred Creditor Status under International Law: The Case of the International Monetary Fund," *International and Comparative Law Quarterly*, Vol. 39, No. 4, pp. 801–826.

Polak, J. J. (1991) "The Changing Nature of IMF Conditionality," *Working Paper No. 41, OECD Development Centre.*

Robichek, E. W. (1984–1985) "The International Monetary Fund: An Arbiter in the Debt Restructuring Process," *Columbia Journal of Transnational Law*, Vol. 23, No. 1, pp. 143–154.

Saravia, D. and Mody, A. (2003) "Catalyzing Capital Flows: Do IMF-Supported Programs Work As Commitment Devices?," *IMF Working Paper No. 03/100.*

Schadler, S. (2016) "Living with Rules: The IMF's Exceptional Access Framework and the 2010 Stand-By Arrangement with Greece," *IEO Background Paper, No. BP/16-02/08.*

Simpson, L. (2006) "The Role of the IMF in Debt Restructurings: Lending into Arrears, Moral Hazard and Sustainability Concerns," *G–24 Discussion Papers 40, United Nations Conference on Trade and Development.*

Sorel, J-M. (1996) "Sur quelques aspects juridiques de la conditionnalité du F.M.I. et leurs conséquences," *European Journal of International Law*, Vol. 7, No. 1, pp. 42–66.

Steinkamp, S. and Westerman, F. (2013) "The Role of Creditor Seniority in Europe's Sovereign Debt Crisis," mimeo, *Osnabrück University & CESifo.*

U.S. House of Representatives (2016) *The Impact of the International Monetary Fund: Economic Stability or Moral Hazard? – Hearing before the Subcommittee on Monetary Policy and Trade of the Committee on Financial Services, 17 June 2015.* Washington, DC: Government Printing Office.

Viterbo, A. and Cisotta, R. (2012) "La crisi del debito sovrano e gli interventi dell'UE: dai primi strumenti finanziari al Fiscal Compact," *Il diritto dell'Unione europea*, Vol. 17, No. 2, pp. 323–366.

Volcker, P. and Gyohten, T. (1992) *Changing Fortunes*. New York: Crown.

Wahi, N. (2006) "Human Rights Accountability of the IMF and the World Bank: A Critique of Existing Mechanisms and Articulation of a Theory of Horizontal Accountability," *UC Davis Journal of International Law Policy*, Vol. 12, No. 2, pp. 331–407.

Appendix 6.1: Example of Letter of Intent, Memorandum of Economic Policies, Technical Memorandum of Understanding

Argentina – Letter of Intent, Memorandum of Economic Policies, Technical Memorandum of Understanding, Buenos Aires, August 30, 2001[39]

Mr. Horst Köhler
Managing Director
International Monetary Fund
700 19th Street, N.W.
Washington, DC 20431

Dear Mr. Köhler,

1 The economic policy framework of the government of Argentina for the period 2000-02, in support of which we requested a three-year Stand-By Arrangement from the Fund, was outlined in our memorandum of economic policies dated February 14, 2000. These policies center on fiscal

consolidation and wide-ranging structural reforms aimed at promoting a sustained recovery of output and employment, with price stability and a continuing improvement in the external accounts.

2 Substantial progress has been made in the implementation of these policies, as described in the policy memoranda accompanying the previous reviews under this program. Nevertheless, adverse domestic and external developments have continued to impede a sustained recovery of confidence and have led to a sharp tightening of financing constraints for both public and private Argentine borrowers, making it more difficult to restart growth and affecting adversely the fiscal performance. [...]

3 We trust that the determined implementation of the government's strengthened economic strategy, in conjunction with this enhanced financial support package, will bolster market confidence in Argentina, facilitating a progressive return of borrowing costs to more normal levels, and a sustained recovery of domestic activity and investment. We will maintain a close policy dialogue with the Fund, and take any further steps that may be needed to promote the achievement of the government's economic policy objectives, in the light of evolving circumstances. Reviews of the program will be carried out before December 15, 2001 and March 15, 2002.

Sincerely yours,
Roque Maccarone – President, Central Bank of the Republic of Argentina
Domingo Cavallo – Minister of Economy

Memorandum of Economic Policies

[...]
III. The Government's Revised Program for 2001...
[...]

Technical Memorandum of Understanding

1 Cumulative balance of the Federal Government.
2 Cumulative ceiling on primary expenditure of the Federal Government.
3 Cumulative balance of the provincial governments.
4 Cumulative change in the debt of the Federal Government.
5 Cumulative change in short term debt of the Federal Government.
6 Cumulative change in the debt of the Consolidated Public Sector (CPS).
7 The net domestic assets (NDA) of the BCRA.

Structural Benchmarks
[...]

Part III

Moral hazard in the financial and corporate areas

7 The institutionalization of bailouts, 1970–1984

Norbert Gaillard and Rick Michalek

This chapter argues that the frequent bailouts observed during 1970–1984 paved the way to the present moral hazard era. In 1971, the bailout of Lockheed was passed by the Congress by a narrow margin, reflecting policymakers' concerns over state interventionism. Yet, during 1974–1981, bailouts became a common policy tool. The size of the entity was clearly a key factor when public authorities had to decide whether to rescue or not (e.g., Chrysler in 1979). The institutionalization of the "too big to fail" (TBTF) policy was completed during 1982–1984. In 1982, the Reagan administration asked for additional IMF quotas to support U.S. banks affected by the sovereign debt turmoil. In 1984, the Comptroller of the Currency established that major banks were now TBTF. This new paradigm encouraged risk-taking and gave birth to an insidious form of "big government."

The years covering 1970–1984 (also called here the "turmoil years") undoubtedly constitute the missing link in the history of moral hazard and, more surprisingly, a key period in the history of state interventionism. This chapter tackles these two issues and advocates that many economic decisions taken during these 15 years contributed to "institutionalize" bailouts, paved the way to the moral hazard era, and gave birth to a new, insidious form of "big government."

Despite its idiosyncratic features, the institutionalization of bailouts was the outcome of a long trend of growing interventionism. In fact, it is possible to identify three such periods until the shift to the moral hazard era in 1984: the Roosevelt-Truman years, the Kennedy-Johnson era, and the turmoil years. Although the economic policies implemented by the different administrations had different purposes and were designed to satisfy their own respective groups of voters and lobbies, they all share four fundamental characteristics. First, these policies were aimed at preserving or improving social welfare, either by maximizing GDP growth or averting a sharp recession. Second, they were driven by an imprimatur of *necessity*, mainly because policymakers invariably dramatized debates and considered alternatives to their options hazardous. Third, they were inspired by *pragmatism* and not ideological motives. Fourth, they were promoted, launched, and implemented at least as much by lawyers as by actual *experts* (e.g., the "Brain Trust", the technostructure, or more prosaically, regulators and central bankers). We now look at these three periods in turn.

DOI: 10.4324/9781003139249-7

The New Deal enabled the reversal of the economic depression and virtually halted runaway unemployment. This unprecedented program consisted of boosting federal expenditures to the detriment of local government expenditures (see Wallis, 1984), exploiting and then enhancing the role of executive power. A new set of regulatory bodies, including the Securities and Exchange Commission (SEC) and the Federal Deposit Insurance Corporation (FDIC) came into being. This move toward the increasing role and power of the federal government (what would later be called "Big Government"), was subsequently challenged by the Supreme Court. In *Schechter Poultry Corp. v. United States* (1935), the Court abolished the National Industrial Recovery Act and held that Congress had exceeded its authority by delegating too much legislative power to the White House and industrial groups. Despite this setback, President Roosevelt was re-elected three times and the Democrats managed to hold the majority in Congress until his death in 1945. After World War II (which saw another spectacular increase in federal expenditures), the role of the federal government did not wane. Largely influenced by Keynesian principles, the Employment Act was passed in 1946. This Act stated that all the powers of the federal government should be used to maintain "maximum employment, production, and purchasing power" and established the Council of Economic Advisers to help the President carry out such responsibility. We discuss how the increasing global intervention in the foreign policy sphere following World War II may have engendered a parallel culture of intervention in the management of the U.S. domestic economy.

The "New Frontier" and "Great Society" programs launched by Presidents Kennedy and Johnson, respectively, addressed urban and health care problems, education inequality, and racial discrimination during the 1960s. These measures led to a structural budget deficit but enabled the U.S. economy to reach an average GDP growth of 5%.[1] The contrast with the preceding fiscal orthodoxy observed under the Eisenhower administration is striking, particularly when noting the three recessions endured during the Republican presidency. (For a comparison between the Republican and Democratic administrations' fiscal policies, see Saulnier, 1963). In addition, the Democratic administrations sought to expand the use and prerogatives of the executive power and increase economic interventionism. Here are two illustrations. The *1962 Economic Report of the President* (p. 22) advocated for the revision of the terms of the officers and members of the Board of Governors of the Federal Reserve System "so that a new President will be able to nominate a Chairman of his choice for a term of four years coterminous with his own." This reform did not materialize. Next, in order to stop the fall in the current account surplus and preserve the central role of the dollar in the Bretton Woods system, President Johnson imposed in 1968 a partial moratorium on U.S. direct investment and the repatriation of some financial assets held abroad

(International Monetary Fund 1968, p. 58). In furtherance of global economic intervention, the Congress allowed the Exim Bank to grant riskier loans with the explicit objective of increasing U.S. exports (see Darbellay and Gaillard, Chapter 4 of this volume).

Less than a year after Richard Nixon entered the White House, the U.S. economy slipped into recession. Starting in 1970, a succession of economic and financial shocks convinced the White House as well as legislators and regulators to rescue a series of failing banks and companies. This shift from *expansive fiscal* to *emergency* policies could be regarded as a new paradigm. This is not our view. We argue that the bailouts of the 1970s are the perpetuation and the predictable application of so-called Keynesian measures. These bailouts may have taken a novel form due to an unstable international economy, but they were primarily designed to ensure a high, if not the maximum, level of GDP growth.

These bailouts were more frequent, more costly, and increasingly took the form of discretionary programs. In fact, what evolved most significantly were the interest groups that took advantage of these ad hoc measures. At the very beginning of this third period under consideration, industrial firms absorbed the benefit of these rescue packages. Later, the bailouts were driven by a concern for systemic risk to the banking system, a pillar of the U.S. hegemony in the international economy. The apparent success of the financial bailouts accelerated the financialization of the economy and encouraged neoliberal policies.

The conclusion we can draw is that the institutionalization of bailouts is "ideology-free": it is fundamentally disconnected from either the Keynesian or neoliberal dogma. Rather, it quickly became a pure policy tool that tends to favor the most established and influential pressure groups at a given time (Lowi, 1979). Considering the evolution of the U.S. economic and financial landscape in the early 1980s, it is not surprising that such institutionalization paved the way for the creation and emergence of mega-banks exploiting morally hazardous strategies. The remainder of this chapter follows both a chronological and analytical order.

During 1970–1973, the Nixon administration intervened extensively to support economic activity. It pressured the Federal Reserve to lower interest rates while the FDIC rescued several distressed banks. Despite that overt pressure, the bailout of defense giant Lockheed in 1971 was passed in the Congress by a very narrow margin, reflecting the growing concern from many policymakers and economists reluctant to use taxpayer funds to bail out private entities (Section 1).

During 1974–1981, in the context of the oil crisis, rising unemployment and international competition, bailouts became a common policy tool. The size of the entity was clearly a key factor when the FDIC, the Federal Reserve, and/or the U.S. administration had to decide whether to bail out or not (Nurisso and Prescott, 2017). It is interesting to note that in contrast to the hesitancy in the Lockheed case, a growing number of politicians came to accept the "bailout" principle, as evidenced by the rescue of Chrysler in 1979 (Section 2).

The institutionalization of the "too big to fail" (TBTF) policy at the international and domestic levels was completed during 1982–1984.[2] In 1982, the Reagan administration and the Federal Reserve asked for additional IMF quotas to support U.S. banks affected by the default of developing countries and thereby avert global systemic risk (Gaillard, 2020). And, in 1984, the General Accounting Office developed guidelines for rescuing large failing entities even as the Comptroller of the Currency established that major banks were now TBTF. This new paradigm facilitated, if not encouraged, moral hazard but it also furthered the increasing collusion between Washington and Wall Street (Section 3).

Section 1 From policy to practice, the birth of institutional bailouts

The administrative state that has steadily grown post World War II can be considered an inevitable consequence if not response to the governance challenge presented by the combination of accelerated growth of the U.S. population and the reinvigoration of the domestic focus of its economy. The continued creation of, and delegation to, specialized bureaus, agencies, and departments continued the rationalization of the duties of the increasingly sprawling federal government.

Underlying this response is something akin to a wishful faith in a potentially "automatic society"; one in which properly harnessed capitalism and market forces can be relied upon to automatically correct for excesses and, to the extent there are or remain negative effects therefrom, institutions (i.e., bureaus, agencies, and regulatory departments) can and must be established to address such effects (Lowi, 1979, Chapter 1 et seq.) The historically developed confidence in responding to society's needs and goals by delegating and assigning governmental functions and large scale public projects to a professionalized bureaucracy accelerated the divergence between traditional lawmaking functions of the highest elected officials and the technical and detailed implementation of those laws as carried out by *appointed* delegees within the administrative state.[3] This creation of, and delegation to, a professionalized bureaucracy often relieved (and avoided) the burden of legislative drafting, and allowed, *and allows*, Congressional Representatives and Senators to promulgate law "by assignment", as in the Dodd-Frank Act:[4] "(8) RULES. – Not later than 18 months after the date of enactment of this Act, the Board of Governors [of the Federal Reserve] and the [Federal Deposit Insurance] Corporation shall jointly issue final rules implementing this subsection."[5]

It is a combination of these two tendencies – the increasing reliance on the expertise and experience of specialized agencies and bureaus (which are often "captured" if not merely sponsored by special interest groups), and the politician's natural preference to focus on the end goal rather than the details of attainment – that perfectly prepares the ground for the use and employment of bailouts as an important tool for the protection and propagation of policy.

1.1 Penn Central and Lockheed – original debate without a foregone conclusion or merely hesitancy on the precipice of the slippery slope?

The generalized confidence in delegating authority and control to increasingly decentralized departments and agencies has waxed since the Roosevelt administrations and its installation of the precursors of the modern administrative state. Whether subsequent administrations have tempered the growth and/or degree of public intervention and involvement in the nation's economy and private activity – as might be said for the Eisenhower presidency – or have encouraged and fostered it, the existence and need for *some* intrusion is assumed (Saulnier, 1963). Nevertheless, confidence in the delegation of the power to intervene was tested and proven questionable in two groundbreaking events from 1970 and 1971. The collapse, bankruptcy, and subsequent nationalization of the Penn Central Railroad and the emergency loans made to save the Lockheed Corporation from insolvency (and from the predicted collateral damage resulting therefrom) generated honest presidential and congressional debate over whether the government (read: taxpayers) and not the shareholders and private lenders to the affected entities should bear the costs of corporate mismanagement.[6] The Department of Defense, and more accurately, the Defense Production Act, served as one conduit for funding in both cases.[7] The cases of Lockheed and Penn Central were not lacking in drama or significance.

Penn Central was the merged entity made of the Pennsylvania and New York Central railroads, once the "nation's two premier freight and passenger railroads." After years of struggling with fundamental and structural post-war changes, including the effects and competitive consequences of the national highway network and the emergence of highly subsidized nationwide trucking and passenger airline industries, the 1962 announcement of the merger of the "100,000-worker, 100,000-shareholder, 100,000-creditor behemoth" involved six years and multiple levels of public approval and negotiations.[8] The concessions made to gain political support for the merger included "no-layoff pledges" and an agreement to government-set rates, both of which contributed to the economic failure of the combined entity. The merger was finalized in February of 1968, but, on June 21, 1970, the entity filed for what was at the time the largest U.S. bankruptcy in history (see Daughen and Binzen, 1971).

The bankruptcy filing roiled the capital markets, as Penn Central was hugely indebted to numerous banks via the commercial paper issuance upon which it had been increasingly relying.[9] The filing was unexpected as public announcements had been made only two days prior signaling the imminent grant of government loan guarantee through the Department of Defense and pursuant to the Defense Production Act. News of the Nixon administration's withdrawal of support for the loan guarantee came as a shock and reduced Penn Central's options to filing for bankruptcy protection.[10] Congressional opposition to the issuance of the guarantee forced the president's hand, and despite previous assurances given by the administration in support of the critical importance of the nation's railroads, the political tides had changed.[11]

Turn now to Lockheed. The Burbank-based firm was the number one defense contractor in the U.S. However, after underbidding competitors to claim a $1.9 billion fixed-price contract for the C-5A cargo fleet for the U.S. Air Force, it experienced cost overruns of $1.8 billion. "Senior defense officials" reportedly decided to spare Lockheed from insolvency, and Deputy Defense Secretary David Packard engineered an agreement whereby the U.S. Pentagon would cover the cost overrun while Lockheed would be required to pay $200 million in installments.[12] Immediately following the cost overrun debacle on the C-5A, Lockheed was blindsided by the pending insolvency of Rolls-Royce, the main engine supplier for the pending completion of its fleet of commercial airplanes, the L-1011. After a consortium of lenders declined to fund the cashflow emergency created by its supplier's possible repudiation of its existing contract, the U.S. Congress passed the Emergency Loan Guarantee Act of 1971, which authorized a newly created Emergency Loan Guarantee Board to guarantee up to $250 million in private loans to major businesses.[13] The drafting of the law reinforces the principle of delegated subjective authority:

> §1843. Limitations and conditions of loan guarantees
>
> a Necessary findings
>
> A guarantee of a loan may be made under this chapter only if:
>
> 1 *the Board finds* that (A) the loan is needed to enable the borrower to continue to furnish goods or services and *failure* to meet this need *would adversely and seriously* affect the economy of or employment in the Nation *or any region thereof,* (B) credit is not otherwise available to the borrower under reasonable terms or conditions, and (C) the prospective earning power of the borrower, together with the character and value of the security pledged, furnish *reasonable* assurance that it will be able to repay the loan within the time fixed, and afford *reasonable* protection to the United States; and
>
> 2 the lender certifies that it would not make the loan without such guarantee.[14]

The foregoing two cases describe the continuing relaxation of the congressional resistance to using taxpayer funds as a source of relief for private enterprise. Given the widespread and well-documented mismanagement, and the observable risk identified by the increased financing costs the market was requiring, congressional resistance in the Penn Central case to the "socialization of risk" that would attend a bankruptcy-avoiding bailout of the railroad is not surprising. Similarly, political will favoring a bailout of the nation's number one defense contractor – despite its obvious mismanagement of cost projections and of critical overexposure to financially struggling suppliers, was easier to find in Lockheed's case. But *political will*, and not mere economics, was the ultimate determinant of both the decisions taken. The railroads were clearly disadvantaged by the subsidies provided to their main competitors. The National Highway System represented an enormous cost saving to the trucking industry and greatly increased the public's use and reliance on autos. Airlines avoided the costs of airport construction even as business and personal travel increasingly took to the skies.[15]

It is within that context of the progression of increased and politically motivated governmental intervention and involvement in the nation's economic affairs that we now turn our focus to the evolution of the reasoning employed.

1.2 "Essentiality" and the FDIC

The institutionalization of direct financial support *aka* bailouts[16] as a policy tool proceeded from opportunistic reactionary rationalization to the systematic and steady acceptance of the government as the *anticipated* lender of last resort. This progression is most clearly seen in the management of failing banks.

The FDIC traditionally relied upon three pathways for rescuing depositors of a failing bank: a) arranging and assisting in the merger of the failing bank with an existing acquiring bank, b) where no acquiring bank could be contracted, forming and funding a new Deposit Insurance National Bank chartered for the purpose of accepting the liabilities and assets of the failing bank, and c) closing and liquidating the failing bank while paying off depositors up to the insured amount (Federal Deposit Insurance Corporation, 1984).[17] The FDIC's options were extended when Congress amended Section 13(c) of the Federal Deposit Insurance Act of 1950. The amendment extended the authority of the FDIC to provide direct support to a failing bank "when in the opinion of the Board of Directors [of the FDIC] the continued operation of such bank is essential to provide adequate banking services in the community."[18] Nevertheless, justification for the exercise of bailout was a critical part of the process, and the FDIC's reliance on the nine words of the 1951 amendment, i.e., "*essential to provide adequate banking service in the community*" became to be known as the Essentiality Doctrine.

In 1971, the first use of the Essentiality Doctrine was employed in the rescue of Unity Bank of Boston. Importantly, Unity Bank was *not* too big to fail, as it only had approximately $11 million in assets, but the justification of its rescue as a continuing operation was in question (Nurisso and Prescott, 2017, p. 6). Because it was a minority-owned bank opened in a predominantly black neighborhood during a period of significant racial unrest (i.e., 1968), its potential failure raised concerns for renewed unrest (Sprague, 1986, p. 38).[19] The FDIC board believed the act as amended provided the ability to both set the terms of assistance and to define what was the relevant community. As the only minority-owned bank nearby, the board concluded that Unity Bank was *essential* to the African American community of Boston (Sprague, 1986, p. 43). This exercise of subjective authority by unelected administrators exemplifies the principle of "policy without law", representing an additional step toward "a state of permanent receivership" through the attenuation of democratic governance (Lowi, 1979, p. 232).

The bailout of Unity Bank set an important precedent for the employment of "essentiality" going forward. In 1972, the FDIC again turned to the essentiality provision in bailing out the Bank of the Commonwealth in Detroit (Michigan). With approximately $1.2 billion in assets, and with one of the country's largest banks as one of its largest shareholders, the Commonwealth bailout was arguably the first true test of the implicit "too big to fail" policy.[20] Having said yes to Unity Bank, saying no to the much larger Bank of the Commonwealth – which partially served a minority community – would test the consistency of the reasoning and utility of essentiality as justification (Sprague, 1986, p. 46).

First, an "arranged" merger was not available. In 1972, Michigan state law prevented out-of-state banks from acquiring Michigan banks, but the potential in-state acquirers already controlled 77% of the deposits in the Detroit region, and combining with Commonwealth would result in overconcentration (Sprague, 1986, p. 60). The FDIC explained its essentiality decision by pointing to the bank's "service to the black community in Detroit, its contribution to commercial bank competition in Detroit and the upper Great Lakes region, and the effect its closing might have had on public confidence in the nation's banking system" (FDIC, 1972, p. 5). Clearly, the boundaries of "the community," like the definition of essential, are elastic.

Section 2 Managing crisis without hesitation

In 1974, Franklin National Bank joined the ranks of "too big to fail" banks that required governmental intervention. After the dissolution of the Bretton Woods monetary system and the conversion by many countries to floating rates of exchange, Franklin lost a large amount of money by speculating in a rise in the relative value of the U.S. dollar (Spero, 1980, p. 79). Those losses were exacerbated by a bank run precipitated by the publication of the Federal Reserve's rejection of a proposed acquisition by Franklin of the Talcott National Corporation. The published decision of the Board of Governors pointed to the inadequacy of managerial and financial resources necessary to successfully manage the proposed acquisition when such resources should be instead used to address the bank's existing problems. In the three months following the publication of the decision, the bank's money market certificates of deposit were reduced by over $300 million, and its London branch saw foreign deposits reduced by over $500 million (Nurisso and Prescott, 2017, p. 12). Given its large foreign exchange portfolio, and the continuing uncertainty in the still novel foreign exchange market, regulators were concerned about the *international* consequences of an abrupt failure of Franklin. However, the Federal Reserve Bank of New York (FRBNY) permitted Franklin to remain liquid by serving as its *lender of last resort*, with Franklin borrowing through the discount window while waiting for an arranged merger to be organized by the FDIC.[21] The size of the debt to the FRBNY quickly grew to $1.7 billion, making it difficult to find a willing acquirer (Federal Deposit Insurance Corporation, 1984, p. 92). After the FDIC agreed to pay off the debt to FRBNY through periodic payments made from liquidating Franklin's assets, and the FRBNY agreed to assume, for compensation, Franklin's foreign exchange portfolio, the FDIC was able to sell Franklin.

The beneficiaries of bailouts need not be the direct recipients of the rescue funding, nor does the rescued bank necessarily need to be "too big to fail." When the FDIC moved to rescue the relatively small Farmers' Bank of the State of Delaware in 1975 (having merely $493 million in assets), the true beneficiary was its largest shareholder: the State of Delaware. By state law, Farmers' Bank was the sole depository for state funds. The finding of essentiality went not to the bank but to the State of Delaware.[22] As a part of the Farmers' rescue, the FDIC for the first time in its history bought stock in a member bank that it was *not* liquidating, furthering its reputation as a lender of last resort and, with the direct participation of what was – except in the most extreme circumstances – intended to be only the facilitating governmental agency, opening the door to institutionalizing moral hazard.

2.1 *"How else do you maintain discipline?"*[23]

The internal tension between those at the FDIC who favored market orthodoxy and those who were embracing the emergent real politic perspective that included the government's glove on Adam Smith's hand continued to resolve in the latter's favor with the First Penn bailout in 1980. First Penn's rescue was the third-largest bailout in the nation's history, and the first to depend on the assistance from the private sector.[24] First Penn is said to have begun its decline in 1976 with the ill-advised decision to use short-term loans to finance long-term investments. With the dramatic rise in rates from 1977 to 1979, the bank was unable to keep pace and quickly fell behind. Director Isaac expressed his, and what he claimed was also most of the senior staff's, view that a bailout would set a dangerous precedent (Sprague, 1986, p. 91). However, perhaps in anticipation of further tightening and the potential damage to confidence in the U.S. banking system that would result if the nation's oldest bank was allowed to fail – especially if such failure could be seen to have resulted from the Fed's decisions to raise rates – Federal Reserve Board of Governors' vice-chairman Fred Schultz favored a bailout, as did then chair of the FDIC, Irving Sprague. Chairman Sprague reinforced the reliance on the essentiality doctrine – albeit with starkly expanded boundaries as to the affected community – by stating that the bailout was necessary to "provid[e] general confidence in the banking system of our country", even while reassuring that "First Pennsylvania [is] an isolated incident… we don't project additional significant problems."[25]

The decision to rescue First Penn highlighted some of the repeated challenges and concerns the FDIC and the regulators were facing. State laws restricting out of state acquisition and federal and state concerns regarding concentration and its affect on competition increasingly interfered with merger proposals. This was especially true when the distressed bank was large, and with over $8 billion in assets in 1980; First Penn presented both issues.[26] We would argue that the combination of anti-trust concerns and the restriction on interstate banking, was, when combined with the hypothesized increased likelihood of a domino-effect from allowing a bank to fail, all that was needed to set the foundation for institutionalized bailouts.

The concern for bank failure contagion was not completely hypothetical. After Penn First started to falter, two other large banks also ran into trouble: Penn Square Bank of Oklahoma City (Penn Square) and Seattle First National Bank (Seafirst). Penn Square was overleveraged and overextended in the energy sector, making "high risk loans to oil drillers" and selling off participations to banks around the country (Sprague, 1986, p. 111). It then redeployed the revenue from the sold participations into even more loans and more participations. With the rising price of oil, the number of drillers increased dramatically, but number of profitable drilling locations did not. As more drillers missed payments, Penn Square felt the downside of its excess leverage. Regulators were concerned for vulnerable banks that were holding Penn Square participations, should Penn Square be allowed to fail. However, investigations revealed that Penn Square was also involved in fraudulent activities, presenting the FDIC with the risk of lawsuits from defrauded creditors should Penn Square's liabilities be absorbed by the FDIC (Isaac and Meyer, 2010, p. 30). The same fears were held by other banks, precluding the possibility of a merger. Given that there were 36 other banks in Oklahoma City, the argument that Penn Square was essential to the community would have strained even the elastic precedent of First Penn. Instead, the FDIC created a "payoff" bank, a Deposit Insurance National Bank, into which Penn Square depositors insured accounts were transferred.

The failure of Penn Square indeed did create problems for other banks. Seafirst Corporation, the bank holding company for Seattle First National Bank, was a $9.6 billion holding company and Seafirst was the largest bank in the Northwest. Holding $400 million in Penn Square participations and having originated another $800 million of its own energy loans, Seafirst reported an operating loss of $91.4 million in 1982 and was said to report even larger losses in the first quarter of 1983 (Nurisso and Prescott, 2017, p. 19). With a bank run beginning in 1983, the Federal Reserve Bank of New York, leading a consortium of 15 banks, stepped in with liquidity support, while the FDIC worked to find an acquiring bank. The State of Washington restriction on out-of-state mergers once again combined with the problem of no suitable in-state acquirer (given concerns for concentration), leaving the FDIC with no options other than a direct payoff.[27] At the last minute, the state legislature amended the state's banking laws to allow the California-based Bank of

America to acquire Seafirst. Although the consolidation of assets of these two large banking institutions would suggest an anti-trust constraint, the fear of the possible shock to domestic and international money markets that could result from Seafirst's bankruptcy determined the regulatory outcome.

2.2 Corporate bailout and the time consistency problem

The U.S. government's assistance to the private sector, as expressed through its various agencies and departments, has generally – but not uniformly – avoided direct aid to specific firms. Bailing out a specific failing firm is vulnerable to political critique from both the right and the left. It is considered presumptive, as it subsidizes that which the market has considered uneconomic, but also unfair as it provides a benefit to a privileged group of creditors, managers, and investors (Freeman and Mendelowitz, 1982, p. 444). Following a series of poor corporate decisions and fundamental changes in consumer demand (itself responding to the oil shocks of the decade), the Chrysler Corporation brought its precarious financial situation to the attention of the government. Inquiries were made to the Economic Development Administration (Department of Commerce), the Farmers Home Administration (Department of Agriculture), the Department of Defense and the Treasury Department. Possibly in protection of their jurisdictional boundaries, or because Chrysler struggled to identify how its problem properly fit within the ambit of each agency approached, little support was forthcoming. In late 1979, after failing to convince the Treasury to accelerate anticipated tax refunds, the company produced a proposal for private financing that would, subject to a $750 million government loan guarantee, close a projected $2.1 billion cash flow shortfall (Freeman and Mendelowitz, 1982, pp. 447–448).

Chrysler's plan was *prospective*: it was ramping into small car production (K car). While it shared all the problems of failing companies (its failure would generate all the same, or greater, negative consequences of lost jobs, broken contracts with suppliers, diminished and discounted asset values), the distinguishing feature – at the time of its appeal for assistance – was the promise and appeal of anticipated benefits ex post. If Chrysler survived, it would not only save hundreds of thousands of jobs by the expected (promised) expansion of production capacity to deliver one million modern small cars in a year's time, it would bring back automaking primacy to the U.S., reversing its steady decline in the face of the global shift in demand toward smaller fuel-efficient vehicles.[28] Without the government assistance, the production capacity of the company was insufficiently appealing to a merger partner (particularly in light of its existing debt structure and its pension obligations). With the assistance – effectively a government bridge loan – completion of the expanded production capacity gave the company, even if ultimately it fell into bankruptcy, a far more attractive asset base to offer acquirers.

While the negative consequences of Chrysler's failure would have been widespread, with suppliers, national dealers, the concentrated labor force in

Detroit, and its international partners all suffering severe economic disruption, this is simply the destruction side of the Schumpeter "creative-destruction" paradigm. However, by *underwriting* the "one-product" company, governmental policy took a further step toward Lowi's "second republic" and its state of permanent receivership.[29] Lee Iacocca's successful lobbying (i.e., aggressive threatening) cemented the implicit rule that begging for forgiveness – especially if conjoined to a plan to do better – will, if granted, allow you to have your cake and eat it, too.

Finally, the Chrysler case demonstrates the time-consistency problem: regulators analyzing a bailout must decide whether the immediate benefits of rescuing the failing firm justify the future loss of market discipline and increased moral hazard.[30] In the bank cases, there is relative certainty of direct and immediate losses to depositors and creditors, plus – where the institution is sufficiently large – the reasonably expected risk of a contagion affecting the payment system. Bailing out the failing private firm requires an analysis of when and why supplanting the market's decision for otherwise sending the company into the legally prescribed liquidation or reorganization process of bankruptcy is justified.[31]

Before turning to the signature case heralding the true arrival of the TBTF doctrine, i.e., the failure and subsequent bailout of Continental Illinois, it is appropriate to consider the broader global context.

Section 3 Systemic risk and TBTF banks, 1982–1984

3.1 When Warsaw blackmails Washington

The bailout of Chrysler in December 1979 took place in the midst of two major events that upset the world economy in the short and medium terms. First, the Federal Reserve's monetary policy changed dramatically under the tenure of Paul Volcker. In October 1979, a few weeks after he became Fed Chairman, Paul Volcker announced monetarist measures aimed at reining in inflation. The primary emphasis was "put on the supply of reserves which ultimately controls the money supply" (Volcker, 1979). This new policy drove up interest rates in the United States and abroad. Second, the Iranian revolution, the Saudi decision to cut oil production, and the price increases by the OPEC led to the second oil crisis. The landed costs of crude oil imports surged from \$14 in 1978 to \$21 in 1979, \$34 in 1980, and \$37 in 1981 (U.S. Energy Information Administration, 2012, p. 163).

These two economic shocks combined to depress world GDP growth and weaken the credit position of many LDCs, especially oil-importing ones. The average interest rate from all creditors and the ratio of interest payments to exports of goods and services of middle-income oil importers increased from 8.4% and 4.9% in 1978 to 12.2% and 7.4% (resp.) in 1981 (World Bank, 1985, pp. 14–15). Such evolution stirred growing concern in the United States as the outstanding claims of American banks on non-OPEC developing countries reached $90 billion in December 1981 (U.S. Senate, 1983, p. 533).

Fears mounted dramatically during the first days of 1982 and resulted in the institutionalization of bailouts and the legitimation of moral hazard. Everything started with Poland. In 1981, Warsaw managed to reschedule its official debt but postponed the payment of its debt to foreign private banks (Brau and Williams, 1983, pp. 16 and 23). In January 1982, the U.S. administration unexpectedly paid $70 million to American banks unable to collect loans to Poland, despite the rule established by the Commodity Credit Corporation (CCC) requiring that the debtor be first declared in default.[32] In fact, U.S. bankers and the U.S. administration wanted to avert Poland's default for several reasons. First, this would shed doubt on the credit position of other Eastern European borrowers. Second, this would oblige banks to write off these loans. Third, the recovery prospects would be low as Poland was experiencing hard political and economic times and owned very few assets in Western countries.

The U.S. intervention sparked controversy as it was considered a bailout of Poland as well as of American bankers. In February 1982, Senators Kasten and Moynihan promoted an amendment aimed to declare Poland in default. The same month, the U.S. Senate held hearings dealing with the Polish debt. Shortly after completing reschedulings on 1981 maturities in April 1982, tensions escalated when Warsaw threatened to default if it did not get fresh loans from the West.[33] As a matter of fact, Poland won the psychological battle against Washington and Wall Street and obtained additional reschedulings in 1982 and 1983 (Brau and Williams, 1983, p. 32).

Due to its specific geopolitical dimension, the Polish episode could be considered atypical. Despite all, it showed how feverish the U.S. administration was when a major sovereign debtor to American banks was on verge of default. More importantly, this foreshadowed what would happen during the world debt crisis that erupted in the summer of 1982.

3.2 Sounding the alarm

During the four months preceding the start of the debt crisis (August 1982), three fresh entities sounded the alarm against a possible international economic turmoil: the Ditchley Group, the Group of Thirty, and the Institute for International Economics.

The Ditchley Group first congregated in May 1982 at Ditchley Park (England). This meeting brought together representatives from major commercial banks, Jacques de Larosière (Managing Director of the IMF), C.T. Conover (Comptroller of the Currency of the United States), and other top officials working at the IMF, the World Bank, and in central banks (Surrey and Nash, 1984). The participants discussed their role in responding to the smoldering global financial crisis. They concluded that banks needed more accurate information regarding the credit position of sovereign debtors, thus implicitly admitting the poor performance of their internal country risk methodologies (for an overview, see Gaillard, 2020, pp. 50–51). The objective of the Ditchley Group was also to tighten relations between lenders and debtors and improve the process of international lending.[34]

The Group of Thirty (or G30) – established in 1978 as an "independent global body comprised of economic and financial leaders from the public and private sectors and academia"[35] – published in May 1982 two joint reports dealing with sovereign debt. In one of them, several relevant questions were asked: "Has growing integration brought with it a loss of control?" "How far-reaching would be the implications of a default by a major borrowing country, or a collapse of a large bank?" "Are existing arrangements for 'risk containment' adequate?" (Group of Thirty, 1982b, p. 1). These concerns were driven by a survey the G30 had just conducted. Around 62% of bankers considered that the international financial system was vulnerable to a "chain collapse" in the event of a crisis affecting a significant bank or group of banks. In connection with such concerns, 74% of bankers considered there was a need for clearer understanding about lender of last resort facilities for distressed banks (Group of Thirty, 1982a, p. 42). In response to these issues, the G30 insisted that the conditions under which a lender of last resort might intervene should remain ambiguous in order not to encourage some banks to take excessive risks. The G30 also considered that the IMF should play a key role in a case of massive debt rescheduling.

The Institute for International Economics (IIE) – a non-partisan, non-profit think tank founded by Fred Bergsten in 1981 – released another important contribution. In its first ever study published in August 1982, the IIE urged that the financial resources of the IMF be increased by at least two-thirds to serve the borrowing needs of developing countries. The study also lamented that Western banks and the IMF had recently cut their lending to LDCs and forced deflationary policies (Williamson, 1982).

It is remarkable that the three institutions understood the ins and outs of the ballooning public debt in LDCs before the world financial turmoil erupted in August 1982. The most penetrating analysis came undoubtedly from the G30 which not only highlighted the central role of the IMF in the event of a sovereign debt crisis but also warned against the risk of *creditor* moral hazard.

3.3 Coping with the international debt crisis

On August 20, 1982, the Mexican authorities invited a dozen of international banks to form an advisory committee and meet representatives of those banks to propose a three-month moratorium on the repayment of almost $20 billion of principal of public sector debt. Two days later, the U.S. administration provided $1 billion in prepayment for imports from Mexico plus a bridging facility of $925 million. In addition, the Bank for International Settlements (BIS) granted a $925 million bridge loan. The following day, the debt moratorium went into effect. On September 1st, 1982, Mexico announced bank nationalization and foreign exchange controls (see Mendelsohn, 1983, pp. 23–26, for a chronology of Mexico's debt restructuring).

Mexico's default shook American bankers and policymakers.[36] Concerns heightened in the first half of September after Argentina called for a rescheduling of its debt and the Reagan administration opposed a significant increase in IMF resources, arguing that such move would have inflationary effects.[37] However, the mindset of U.S. authorities evolved substantially during the following weeks. Several key ideas gained tremendous influence and contributed to shape the emergency policies that were set up by creditor nations, bankers, and international organizations in late 1982 and in 1983.

The fundamental issue was the widespread belief that the international debt crisis raised "the risk of financial disruption either within the U.S. banking system or elsewhere around the world", as Fred Bergsten said in a testimony delivered to the U.S. Senate on September 27 (U.S. Senate, 1982, p. 2). These fears were also expressed in October by Jeffrey Garten, Vice President of Lehman Brothers Kuhn Loeb,[38] and Federal Chairman Paul Volcker (U.S. Senate, 1982, p. 16, and Board of Governors of the Federal Reserve System, 1982, pp. 15–17, respectively). The risks stemming from the growing interdependence between industrial countries, LDCs, and financial institutions were encapsulated in the famous concept of "systemic risk" by economist William Cline (1983, p. 44; 1984).

Several policy tools were mobilized to fight against systemic risk. During the October meeting of the Federal Open Market Committee, Paul Volcker considered that the strains on the financial system required a much laxer monetary policy (Board of Governors of the Federal Reserve System, 1982, pp. 31–33) in order to support economic recovery in the United States and abroad.[39] A few days later, Paul Volcker convinced the White House to increase its IMF contribution,[40] thus enhancing the pivotal role of the IMF.[41]

This move came within the growing consensus over a possible new international financial architecture whose main features were well described by Fred Bergsten (U.S. Senate, 1982, p. 4). First, debtor countries in financial distress should implement a stabilization program to improve their external balance and restore confidence. Next, the IMF should bail out these countries and supervise their adjustment policy. Lastly, private banks should maintain their lending and, whenever necessary, consent to debt restructurings. This third point was challenged by U.S. bankers until Paul Volcker stated, on November 16, that "where new loans facilitate the adjustment process and enable a country to strengthen its economy and service its international debt in an orderly manner, new credits should not be subject to supervisory criticism" (Kraft, 1984, p. 49).[42]

This new paradigm, which involved coordinated efforts by debtor countries, international financial institutions, and official and bank creditors, shaped the rescue of several LDCs between the end-1982 and 1984. A major international debt and banking crisis was averted, and world GDP growth rebounded from 0.5% in 1982 to 4.5% in 1984. On narrow formal grounds, sovereign debtors were *bailed out* by the international institutions and *bailed in* by commercial banks, once pressured by the IMF and the U.S. administration. Although the "bail-in option" entailed that private creditors bore part of the cost of the debt restructurings, this episode reveals a clear dichotomy in the way debtors and creditors were treated.

First, the Reagan administration did not move ahead to rescue LDCs until October 1982 when economists (especially Fred Bergsten and Paul Volcker) warned against a contagion risk and a major disruption of the U.S. banking system. This suggests that Washington had not grasped what was at stake and had completely underestimated the country risk exposure of its banks as well as the growing world financial integration.

Second, the bailouts granted by the IMF enabled creditors to limit their losses in two manners. In the short term, they lessened the haircut they would have otherwise faced in the event of a "no bailout" scenario, a default, or a repudiation. In the longer term, the bailouts enhanced the sustainability of sovereign debts and thus increased the probability that creditors get repaid. It is also interesting that the role played by the IMF was more than that of a "crisis manager." The Washington-based institution was the "bad guy" – as Fred Bergsten said (U.S. Senate, 1982, p. 26) – in lieu of commercial banks.

Third, and more importantly, the conditionality imposed on debtors and creditors was clearly asymmetrical. LDCs had to accept IMF austerity programs that were costly in terms of unemployment and led to the "lost decade" in Latin America. In contrast, there was no conditionality on commercial banks: instead, the Federal Reserve committed to *relax*, not tighten, the banking regulatory rules provided banks continued to lend to distressed LDCs. Not only did this decision run counter to any elementary form of conditionality but it also implied that U.S. regulators assumed part of the credit risk.[43] According to economist Allan Meltzer, this was a step in "socializing the loss."[44]

In this novel, implicit "insurance contract" between the U.S. authorities and their banks, the "insurer" proved very reluctant to supervise the activities of the "insured" (see Claassen, Chapter 2 of this volume, for a conceptual analysis). Such views are consistent with Cohen (1985) who highlighted the "close connections between high finance and high politics."

In conclusion, the new functions devolved to the IMF and the U.S. regulatory and political forbearance enabled the bankers to escape the consequences of their poor country risk assessment. More dramatically, they encouraged riskier international lending practices and paved the way to some form of *creditor* moral hazard (see Flores and Gaillard, Chapter 5 of this volume).

3.4 The Continental Illinois turmoil and the "too big to fail" concept

The rescue of the Continental Illinois National Bank (CINB) in 1984 was the final step toward the institutionalization of bailouts. As the fall of the Chicago-based bank is well documented (see U.S. House of Representatives, 1984; Federal Deposit Insurance Corporation, 1997), it is briefly summarized here.

The credit position of the CINB declined dramatically in the context of the U.S. recession and the LDC debt crisis of 1981–1982. At the close of 1982, its nonperforming loans totaled $1.9 billion (5.6% of total loans and leases receivables), up from $653 million (1.9% of 1981 loan and lease receivables). The tight relationship with the defunct Penn Square Bank tarnished the reputation of the CINB, which obliged the institution to shift its funding sources to offshore markets. At the close of 1983, nonperforming loans exceeded 6.2% of total loans and leases receivables.

In May 1984, rumors of the bank's insolvency triggered a massive run by depositors. Despite a $3.6 billion loan from the Federal Reserve Bank of Chicago and a $4.5 billion line of credit from 16 of the nation's largest banks, the run continued. Regulators feared that the insolvency of the CINB would spill over to other banks. After a $1.5 billion capital infusion into the bank and the statement that it would extend support to the bank's creditors and the depositors with funds greater than $100,000, the FDIC announced that it would prevent the bank's failure by providing "permanent" assistance and committed to purchasing up to $4.5 billion in bad loans.

The House of Representatives inquired about the bailouts of the CINB in September and October 1984. The key moment of the hearings was certainly the testimony by C. T. Conover, Comptroller of the Currency. He explained that the CINB situation and how he dealt with it was influenced by his "judgment as to the impact of failure on the Nation's, if not the world's, financial system" (U.S. House of Representatives, 1984, p. 299). He also admitted that the Office of the Comptroller of the Currency would not let the top 11 multinational money center banks fail. In response, Congressman Stewart McKinney exclaimed: "We have created a new kind of bank. It is called too big to fail, TBTF, and it is a wonderful bank" (U.S. House of Representatives, 1984, p. 300).

This TBTF doctrine had incommensurable consequences. The day following the Comptroller of the Currency's statement, banks' stock prices reacted very idiosyncratically. The 11 banks considered TBTF by investors had a significant positive return. It is interesting to note that the bigger the bank and the greater its insolvency level, the higher the return. Conversely, for "non-TBTF" institutions, solvency had no effect on returns whereas size was a negative factor (O'Hara and Shaw, 1990). These findings are essential as they suggest that investors primarily took in account the *status* of the banks and not its credit position. In fact, the TBTF doctrine undermined fundamental market rules, led investors to disregard credit risk assessment, and gave birth to a "top caste" of financial institutions based on size. One understands better why the race to bigness became so crucial in the subsequent years (see Wilmarth, 2002). The key factor for a U.S. bank to survive and thrive in an increasing deregulated and competitive environment was now its capacity to remain or become a systemic (i.e., a TBTF) entity.

Section 4 Conclusion

The TBTF policy was the outcome of a 15-year process during which bailouts mushroomed and the predominant role of financial institutions was largely recognized. During 1970–1984, the amounts of the bailouts increased dramatically but an even more striking issue was observed. In the cases of the indirect rescue of major commercial banks threatened by the default of LDCs and of the bailout of the CINB, financial institutions obtained a support from public authorities and got taxpayers' money after a consensus emerged among top officials and regulators only. The Senate and the House of Representatives were left aside. At the very end, the institutionalization of bailouts appears to run counter to economic as well as political liberalism.

Notes

1 Authors' calculations based on Federal Reserve data; see https://fred.stlouisfed.org/series/A191RL1A225NBEA.
2 The coinage of the most emblematic phrase of bailouts, i.e., "too big to fail," can be traced to the comments of Congressional representative Stewart B. McKinney during the hearings investigating the failure of the Continental Illinois National Bank and Trust Company in 1984. "We have a new kind of bank. It is called too big to fail." U.S. House of Representatives (1984, p. 300). See discussion in Section 3.
3 One need only give cursory examination to the history of the Federal Register to understand the scope of the problem facing elected officials. In 1935, in the context of the New Deal, "[there was the] fundamental problem facing a democratic government that was exploding with new agencies and new regulations. Amidst the ferment of orders and codes issuing from agencies, even individuals working at the highest levels of government found it "difficult or impossible to keep track of all of them" (Office of the Federal Register, 2011, p. 2). See also *A.L.A. Schechter Poultry Corp. v. United States 295 U.S. 495* (1935) for the holding that the National Industrial Recovery Act was an unconstitutional delegation of legislative power to the executive branch.
4 Dodd-Frank Wall Street Reform and Consumer Protection Act 12 USC 5301 ("Dodd-Frank Act") Public Law 111-203 – July 21, 2010, 125 STAT.1427, Section 165(d)(8).
5 With 1601 sections, the Dodd-Frank Act exemplifies both the exigent need for delegation and the distance between the elected representatives and the detailed regulations ultimately promulgated by unelected officials.
6 While the Lockheed and Penn Central affairs are remarkable as landmark events in the history of governmental bailouts of private failing businesses, they are hardly isolated or initial examples thereof. The Reconstruction Finance Corporation (RFC), itself a governmental creation from 1932 until its termination and ultimate liquidation in 1957, had – according to the then chairman of the Committee on the Judiciary representative Emanuel Celler – "rescued from the teetering brink of bankruptcy many, many thousands of business entities" (Congressional Record – House, July 30, 1971, p. 28336, available at https://www.govinfo.gov/content/pkg/GPO-CRECB-1971-pt21/pdf/GPO-CRECB-1971-pt21-5-2.pdf). The Keynesian influence is revealed in the final report on the RFC that explicitly acknowledged that "there were many RFC activities in which funds were disbursed with no expectation that any recoveries could be made." See U.S. Secretary of the Treasury (1959, pp. vi–vii).
7 Reportedly, Lockheed received $200 million in Defense Department grants and Penn Central received $200 million "under a clause in the Defense Production Act enacted

[in 1959] to encourage companies to meet Defense Department needs." See D. Duggan, "Proxmire Hits U.S. 'Bail-Out' Loans," *Newsday*, 16 June 1970.

8 N. Gelinas, "Train Wreck: The Penn Central's Failure Resonates Today," *City Journal*, 22 January 2021; available at: https://www.city-journal.org/penn-central-railroad-failure-resonates-today.

9 Reportedly, the default by Penn Central on $87 million of commercial paper obligations so roiled the market that Goldman Sachs, the market leader in commercial paper issuance, faced potential losses that would have exceeded the firm's capital; see https://www.goldmansachs.com/our-firm/history/moments/1970-penn-central-bankruptcy.html.

10 "[W]ithdrawal of the Government's promised guarantee of the Penn Central's credit was a complete surprise to railroad observers." See R. E. Bedingfield, "U.S. Withdraws Backing of Loan to Penn Central," *New York Times*, 20 June 1970.

11 Consider Special Subcommittee on Investigation's Chairman Harley Staggers' subsequent recommendations for the improved (and increased) regulation of entities subject to the Interstate Commerce Commission (ICC) and of the SEC in his "Foreword" (pp. iii–vi) for the SEC report on the collapse of the Penn Central Company (see Securities and Exchange Commission, 1972).

12 S. Trimble, "Nearly 50 Years Apart, Lockheed Bailout Resonates During Boeing Crisis," *Aviation Week Network*, 24 March 2020; available at: https://aviationweek.com/defense-space/supply-chain/nearly-50-years-apart-lockheed-bailout-resonates-during-boeing-crisis.

13 The Lockheed Corporation – the sole applicant to the Board – successfully applied for the guarantee, thereby enabling the funding by the lending consortium.

14 Emergency Loan Guarantee Act of 1971. Emphasis added.

15 The argument for comparable economic assistance to the railroads as was received by the auto, trucking, and airline industries predates even the creation by the merger of the Penn Central Railroad. The Federal government was spending nearly $500 million annually to support airlines and airports with states contributing half again as much. National highway expenditures saw nearly $250 million from the Federal government, while private railroads were spending between $1 billion and $1.25 billion for maintenance and construction. "Had the automobile and airplane developed and functioned under the same ground rules as those for railroads, Penn Central not only would have survived but also could have become one of the most profitable of all American companies." See R. Sobel, "Railroads: How Free Enterprise Failed", *New York Times*, 20 November 1977.

16 Consider Casey and Posner's (2015, p. 481) definition "[A] bailout occurs when the government makes payments (including loans, loan guarantees, cash, and other types of consideration) to a liquidity-constrained private agent in order to enable that agent to pay its creditors and counterparties, when the agent is not entitled to those payments under a statutory scheme."

17 For a discussion of earlier bank bailouts, see Gorton and Tallman (2016).

18 Federal Deposit Insurance Act (1950), Pub. L. 797, 81st Congress, Ch. 957-23 2d Session; https://fraser.stlouisfed.org/files/docs/historical/congressional/federal-deposit-insurance-act.pdf. Prior to the amendment, the FDIC was authorized only to provide assistance to closed banks.

19 Irvine Sprague, a director of the FDIC at the time, explained that the FDI Act and its legislative history provide scant guidance as to the use and meaning of the essentiality provision, concluding that it was "ultimately a discretionary decision that depends on the judgment of the FDIC board."

20 Chase Manhattan Bank, then one of the nation's largest banks, was also one of the Bank of Commonwealth's largest shareholders. In addition to concerns for the possible failure of the Bank of Commonwealth, which held 10% of the deposits in the State of

Michigan, there was a concern for a contagion or "domino theory" of failures if one large bank was to fail (Sprague, 1986, p. 68). The Bank of Commonwealth bailout might have been politically motivated because Michigan was an important state in the 1972 national elections; see https://www.minneapolisfed.org/article/1998/interview-with-carter-h-golembe.

21 For a discussion of the steady shift of the Federal Reserve and FDIC toward a role as "lender of last resort", see Humphrey (1975) and Mayer (2001).

22 The Farmers' Bank rescue drew critical attention to the underlying motivations of the intervention for several reasons. The FDIC had already allowed larger banks to fail, including the similarly sized Hamilton Bank in the very same year as Farmers. Questionable loans to "politically connected" individuals together with the selection by the state's general assembly of several bank directors added to the scrutiny. See J. Gutman, "When a State Rescues a Bank", *New York Times*, 24 July 1977.

23 FDIC director William Isaac, explaining his overruled belief that a depositor payoff, and not a rescue, was the correct decision in the resolution of the failing First Pennsylvania Bank of Philadelphia, Pennsylvania (First Penn); see Isaac and Meyer (2010, p. 14).

24 The rescue package of approximately $500 million included a $325 million five-year loan from the FDIC plus $175 million in five-year loans and $1 billion line of credit from a consortium of 22 major U.S. banks. See N. L. Ross, "Third Largest Bailout Set up for Pa. Bank," *Washington Post*, 29 April 1980.

25 N. L. Ross, "Third Largest Bailout Set up for Pa. Bank," *Washington Post*, 29 April 1980.

26 The Mellon Bank of Pittsburgh was thought to be the only Pennsylvania bank large enough to absorb First Penn, and the combined bank would have affected competition in the state (Federal Deposit Insurance Corporation, 1998, p. 518).

27 In the event a bailout was required, the FDIC no longer had to strain to find room in the Essentiality Doctrine, thanks to a 1982 addition to Section 13(c) of the Federal Depository Insurance Act. This 1982 amendment expressly permitted the FDIC to provide temporary assistance to "arrange in an orderly fashion the merger, consolidation or sale of the Bank's assets and assumption of the Bank's liabilities." The FDIC, in anticipation of a bailout of Seafirst, prepared and documented a $250 million loan that would be immediately disbursed upon the decision to bailout the bank, should it come to that (Nurisso and Prescott, 2017, p. 20).

28 P. Behr, "Panel Says Chrysler Must Sell All K-Cars in 1981 to Survive," *Washington Post*, 13 May 1980.

29 Both Lockheed (a multiproduct company with important defense contracts) and Penn Central (effectively a public utility essential to maintaining existing regional if not national rail service) are distinguishable from the Chrysler bailout (Freeman and Mendelowitz, 1982, pp. 451–452).

30 William Proxmire, Democratic Senator of Wisconsin and then chair of the Senate Banking Committee argued in vain against the Chrysler bailout. "Who is going to say that to bail out Chrysler would be a precedent that could haunt our system for many years to come as our businesses lose the courage to accept the consequences of their mistakes." W. Proxmire, "The Case Against Bailing Out Chrysler", *New York Times*, 21 October 1979. For a general discussion, see Kyland and Prescott (1977).

31 Strong economic arguments favoring bailing out large failing banks and firms point to the difficulty in relying on market-sourced insurance. Casey and Posner (2015, p. 482) argue that "bailouts are socially desirable because Congress cannot anticipate the contingencies that would make possible an ex-ante insurance system that regulates behavior and charges firms in advance for liquidity support or other transfers." See also Prescott (2002).

32 The loans from U.S. banks to Poland were guaranteed by the CCC. See W. Safire, "Essay; Payoff for Repression," *New York Times*, 1 February 1982.

33 P. Lewis, "Poland Said to Threaten Default if Aid is Denied," *New York Times*, 8 June 1982.
34 The Ditchley Group led to the establishment of the Institute of International Finance (IIF) in 1983.
35 https://group30.org/about
36 L. Rout and J. Salamon, "Mexico's Leader Nationalizes Domestic Banks," *Wall Street Journal*, 2 September 1982.
37 H. Rowen, "Lost Opportunity at Toronto," *Washington Post*, 9 September 1982.
38 J. Garten's point of view was especially valuable as Lehman Brothers Kuhn Loeb was an *investment* bank, thus not directly involved in international lending.
39 As Minsky (1985, p. 15) wrote: "it should be clear that the Federal Reserve became monetarist in 1979 to protect the dollar-denominated system and abandoned monetarism three years later for the same reason."
40 R. Evans and R. Novak, "Bailing Out the Bankers," *Washington Post*, 8 December 1982.
41 The resolution on quota increase was officially adopted by the IMF Board of Governors in March 1983.
42 This decision involved that fresh loans would be treated as "performing" on the books of banks.
43 Such lenience among U.S. regulators increased in the following years; see Gaillard and Michalek (2019).
44 E. Heinemann, "A Fed Push on Foreign Loans Seen," *New York Times*, 15 January 1983.

References

Board of Governors of the Federal Reserve System (1982) *Meeting of the Federal Open Market Committee*. 5 October. Washington, DC: Federal Reserve System.

Brau, E. and Williams, R. C. (1983) "Recent Multilateral Debt Restructurings with Official and Bank Creditors," *IMF Occasional Paper No. 25*.

Casey, A. J. and Posner, E. (2015) "A Framework for Bailout Regulation," *Notre Dame Law Review*, Vol. 91, No. 2, pp. 479–536.

Cline, W. R. (1983) *International Debt and the Stability of the World Economy*. Washington, DC: Institute for International Economics.

Cline, W. R. (1984) *International Debt: Systemic Risk and Policy Response*. Washington, DC: Institute for International Economics.

Cohen, B. J. (1985) "International Debt and Linkage Strategies: Some Foreign-Policy Implications for the United States," *International Organization*, Vol. 39, No. 4, pp. 699–727.

Daughen, J. R. and Binzen, P. (1971) *The Wreck of the Penn Central*. Boston: Little Brown & Company.

Federal Deposit Insurance Corporation (1972) *Annual Report*. Washington, DC: FDIC.

Federal Deposit Insurance Corporation (1984) *The First Fifty Years – A History of the FDIC 1933-1983*. Washington, DC: FDIC.

Federal Deposit Insurance Corporation (1997) *History of the Eighties, Lessons for the Future, Volume 1*. Washington, DC: FDIC.

Federal Deposit Insurance Corporation (1998) *Managing the Crisis: The FDIC and RTC Experience 1980-1994*. Washington, DC: FDIC.

Freeman, B. M. and Mendelowitz, A. I. (1982) "Program in Search of a Policy: The Chrysler Loan Guarantee," *Journal of Policy and Management*, Vol. 1, No. 4, Summer, pp. 443–453.

Gaillard, N. (2020) *Country Risk: The Bane of Foreign Investors.* Cham: Springer.

Gaillard, N. and Michalek, R. J. (2019) "How and Why Moral Hazard Has Distorted Financial Regulation," in Hira, A., Gaillard, N. and Cohn, T. H. (Eds), *The Failure of Financial Regulation – Why A Major Crisis Could Happen Again.* International Political Economy Series. Cham: Palgrave Macmillan.

Gorton, G. and Tallman, E. W. (2016) "Too Big to Fail Before the Fed," *American Economic Review*, Vol. 106, No. 5, pp. 528–532.

Group of Thirty (1982a) *How Bankers See the World Financial Market.* New York: G30.

Group of Thirty (1982b) *Risk in International Bank Lending.* New York: G30.

Humphrey, T. (1975) "The Classical Concept of the Lender of Last Resort," *Federal Reserve Bank of Richmond, Economic Review*, Vol. 61, No. 1, pp. 2–9.

International Monetary Fund (1968) *Annual Report.* Washington, DC: IMF.

Isaac, W. M. and Meyer, P. C. (2010) *Senseless Panic: How Washington Failed America.* Hoboken: John Wiley & Sons.

Kraft, J. (1984) *The Mexican Rescue.* New York: G30.

Kyland, F. and Prescott, E. C. (1977) "Rules Rather than Discretion: The Inconsistency of Optimal Plans," *Journal of Political Economy*, Vol. 85, No. 3, pp. 473–492.

Lowi, T. J. (1979) *The End of Liberalism: The Second Republic of the United States.* New York and London: W. W. Norton & Company.

Mayer, M. (2001) *The Fed: The Inside Story of How the World's Most Powerful Financial Institution Drives the Market.* New York: Free Press.

Mendelsohn, M. S. (1983) *Commercial Banks and the Restructuring of Cross-Border Debt.* New York: G30.

Minsky, H. P. (1985) "Money and the Lender of Last Resort," *Challenge*, Vol. 28, No. 1, pp. 12–18.

Nurisso, G. C. and Prescott, E. S. (2017) "Origins of Too-Big-to-Fail Policy," *Federal Reserve Bank of Cleveland, Working Paper 17-10.*

Office of the Federal Register (2011) *A Brief History Commemorating the 70th Anniversary of the Publication of the First Issue of the Federal Register – March 14, 1936.* Washington, DC: Office of the Federal Register.

O'Hara, M. and Shaw, W. (1990) "Deposit Insurance and Wealth Effects: The Value of Being 'Too Big to Fail'," *Journal of Finance*, Vol. 45, No. 5, pp. 1587–1600.

Prescott, E. S. (2002) "Can Risk Based Deposit Insurance Premiums Control Moral Hazard?," *Federal Reserve Bank of Richmond, Economic Quarterly*, Vol. 88, No. 2, pp. 87–100.

Saulnier, R. J. (1963) "Economic Policy: Kennedy vs. Eisenhower," *Challenge*, Vol. 11, No. 10, July, pp. 18–21.

Securities and Exchange Commission (1972) *The Financial Collapse of the Penn Central Company.* Staff Report to the Special Subcommittee on Investigations, Washington, DC: Government Printing Office.

Spero, J. E. (1980) *The Failure of the Franklin National Bank: Challenge to the International Banking System.* New York: Columbia University Press.

Sprague, I. (1986) *Bailout: An Insider's Account of Bank Failures and Rescues.* New York: Basic Books.

Surrey, W. S. and Nash, P. N. (1984) "Bankers Look Beyond the Debt Crisis: The Institute of International Finance, Inc.," *Columbia Journal of Transnational Law*, Vol. 23, No. 1, pp. 111–130.

U.S. Energy Information Administration (2012) *Annual Energy Review 2011*. Washington, DC: U.S. Department of Energy.

U.S. House of Representatives (1984) *Inquiry into Continental Illinois Corp. and Continental Illinois National Bank – Hearings before the Subcommittee on Financial Institutions, Supervision, Regulation and Insurance of the Committee on Banking, Finance and Urban Affairs*. Washington, DC: Government Printing Office.

U.S. Secretary of the Treasury (1959) *Final Report on the Reconstruction Finance Corporation: Pursuant to Section 6(c) Reorganization Plan No.1 of 1957*. Washington, DC: Government Printing Office.

U.S. Senate (1982) *World Debt Situation – Hearings before the Subcommittee on International Economic Policy of the Committee on Foreign Relations*. Washington, DC: Government Printing Office.

U.S. Senate (1983) *Global Economic Outlook – Hearings before the Subcommittee on International Economic Policy and the Committee on Foreign Relations*. Washington, DC: Government Printing Office.

Volcker, P. (1979) *Transcript of Press Conference – Board of Governors of the Federal Reserve System*. 6 October. Washington, DC: Federal Reserve System.

Wallis, J. J. (1984) "The Birth of the Old Federalism: Financing the New Deal, 1932–1940," *Journal of Economic History*, Vol. 44, No. 1, pp. 139–159.

Williamson, J. (1982) *The Lending Policies of the International Monetary Fund*. Washington, DC: Institute for International Economics.

Wilmarth Jr., A. E. (2002) "The Transformation of the U.S. Financial Services Industry, 1975–2000: Competition, Consolidation, and Increased Risks," *University of Illinois Law Review*, Vol. 2002, No. 2, pp. 215–476.

World Bank (1985) *World Debt Tables – External Debt of Developing Countries*. Washington, DC: World Bank.

8 Varieties of moral hazard in the global automobile industry

Fumihito Gotoh and Timothy J. Sinclair

The automobile industry has witnessed various examples of moral hazard because of its highly politicized nature. This chapter highlights two contrasting types of moral hazard: the liberal critique of state interventionism and the critical view of short-termist financial capitalism. The former type of moral hazard is seen mainly in coordinated market economies, where the government intervenes through industrial policy and bailouts. A striking illustration is the Nissan and Renault cases subject to intervention by the Japanese and French governments. The latter type of moral hazard is observed primarily in liberal market economies, which emphasize short-term shareholder value and financial returns. The most telling example was the General Motors case where insufficient R&D investment and dependence on captive finance served to maintain large dividends and retiree benefits.

The global automobile industry is highly politicized because of the enormous scale of its market, employment, capital investment, and trade in the global economy, its extensive influence on other industries and national economies, and its multinational nature. Charles Erwin Wilson, CEO of General Motors (GM, 1946–1953) and U.S. Secretary of Defense (1953–1957), famously stated that:

> for years I thought that what was good for our country was good for General Motors, and vice versa. The difference did not exist. Our company is too big. It goes with the welfare of the country. Our contribution to the nation is considerable. (Safire, 1978, p. 803).

Due to the political nature of the industry, governments and creditor banks have provided financial support for automakers that have faced financial crisis. Examples include the U.K. government's partial nationalization of British Leyland in 1975, Sumitomo Bank's rescue of Mazda Motor Corporation in 1975, the U.S. government bailout of Chrysler in 1979, and the U.S. government bailouts of GM and Chrysler in 2008. Although these stand as incentives to and examples of moral hazard in the global automobile industry, in this chapter, we broaden the scope of the concept of moral hazard and discuss

DOI: 10.4324/9781003139249-8

two of its variants relevant to the global auto industry. Leaver (2015, p. 92) offers the following two comments about the global financial crisis to explain the contrasting types of moral hazard.

> If anything is obvious about the current crisis, it is that the system of managed state intervention into the financial system has failed dismally: it is not "free" – that is, unregulated – markets that have failed, but the statist system within which financial markets and institutions have been forced to operate… Measures that rein in moral hazard are to be welcomed and will help to reduce excessive risk-taking; measures that create or exacerbate moral hazard (such as massive bailouts?) will lead to even more excessive risk-taking and should be avoided. (Dowd, 2009, p. 163).

> Saving the world's financial system was unquestionably the right thing to do. But in the process of saving it, we protected those very market fundamentalists whose actions caused the crisis. The risk is now that their confidence has not been sufficiently dented; that they have not truly learned their lesson. And the danger with this moral hazard is that they could put us all at risk again. This is why a central part of restoring true market discipline to the world financial system must be major reform globally to the way banks and financial firms are governed and regulated. … We are serious about removing the safety net that has allowed those with blind faith in market efficiency to ignore the consequences of their lack of discipline.[1]

The first of these two quotes on moral hazard demonstrates a neoliberal critique of state interventionism (government failure). Harvey (2005, p. 66) argues that neoliberalism advocates for free capital mobility between sectors, regions, and countries, which suggests capitalist dominance (Harvey, 2005, p. 38). Neoliberals criticize state interventionism for leading the recipient of government support to excessive risk-taking, and eventually government failure. In contrast, the latter quote reveals the left's critique of financial/shareholder capitalism (market failure). Financial capitalism pursues short-term financial profit at the expense of the rest of society. The left criticizes financial capitalism for paying little attention to product quality and technology improvement through long-term trust relations with broad stakeholders (including employees, suppliers, and customers) and ultimately resulting in market failure. In the context of financial globalization, the former is a typical moral hazard, but we believe the latter type of moral hazard must also be examined. Attitudes and behavior with regard to economic efficiency, stability, and equality vary by region and country. The prevailing norms of all countries fall between the contrasting objectives of market efficiency and social stability and welfare. Coordinated market economies (CMEs), such as Germany and Japan, that rely on non-market-based coordination mechanisms (including state intervention through industrial policy and corporate bailouts) emphasize social stability and welfare, while liberal market economies (LMEs), including the United States and the United Kingdom, are primarily based on market mechanisms and short-term contractual relations (Hall and Soskice, 2001; Clift, 2014; Vogel, 2018).

Examples of the liberal critique of state interventionism as a source of moral hazard are witnessed mainly in CMEs, whereas examples of the left's critique of financial/shareholder capitalism are observed primarily in LMEs. In this chapter, we examine the cases of Nissan Motor and Renault, which were subject to interventions by the Japanese and French governments respectively, as examples of the former moral hazard, while we review the GM case – which involved insufficient R&D investment and excessive dependence on captive finance to maintain large dividends and retiree benefits – as an example of the latter. France is often categorized as a CME due to its *dirigiste* tradition, but through domestic financial deregulation (1984–1990), open capital flows (1990), and corporate governance reforms including the introduction of shareholder-focused management (1990–2002), it has become a hybrid of CME and LME that is characterized by state interventionism and shareholder capitalism (Clift, 2014; Tiberghien, 2007).

We argue that moral hazard associated with either government failure or market failure must ultimately be rectified by opposite measures – either restructuring or state intervention – which is true of both the Renault/Nissan and the GM cases. Furthermore, we contend the Renault-Nissan alliance experienced moral hazard related not only to government failure, but also to market failure. Furthermore, we hold that the clash of divergent social norms on shareholder capitalism between France and Japan contributed to tensions within the Renault-Nissan alliance, ultimately leading to the ousting of Carlos Ghosn, chairman of both Renault and Nissan, from the latter in November 2018.

We begin by investigating the moral hazard of Renault and Nissan, which stemmed from excessive state intervention, and the ensuing capitalist restructuring led by Carlos Ghosn. Subsequently, we will discuss the clash of the French and Japanese models of capitalism. Finally, we examine examples of the problems induced by moral hazard in GM derived from financial/shareholder capitalism. Unlike the dominant conception of moral hazard, "market-based moral hazard" has to do with the scale of the enterprise and a long history of competitive success. The complacency and poor performance this induces in the enterprise or parts of it, and thus increasing exposure to risk over time, is compensated or "insured" by the long experience of dominance which becomes a feature of the corporate culture. At some point, of course, as evident in the case of GM, market-based moral hazard can be transformed into moral hazard associated with government. In this sense, market-based moral hazard – where political and bureaucratic leadership deems it to be of strategic value – should be thought of as a pathway to moral hazard as typically conceived.

Section 1 Renault under *dirigisme* and shareholder capitalism

Fukuyama (1995) identifies three broad paths to sociability, holding that it is either based on family and kinship, intermediary organizations outside kinship, or the state. He also claims that the French rely heavily on the third path and to a lesser extent on the first path, while the Japanese depend on the second path. According to Tocqueville (1955), large class divisions and status hierarchies within classes pervaded France on the eve of its revolution, and this hampered people from working with one another. Due to its class-ridden nature, French society dislikes direct, face-to-face relationships, which can reduce or even prevent innovation and entrepreneurialism in its private sector (Fukuyama, 1995, pp. 113–119). It does, however, have a strong preference for centralized authority (bureaucracy), which attracts the best and the brightest from the *grandes écoles*. Most French family businesses are reluctant to dilute their control for the sake of expansion, and the gap between management and labor in large French firms is wider than in Japan. Fukuyama (1995, p. 123) claims that "French *dirigisme*, or the involvement of the state in economic life, was thus both the cause and the effect of the weakness of the French private sector and of its inability to create competitive large-scale enterprises on its own." There were many cases of the French government providing financial assistance for its national champions which faced financial crisis – e.g., Credit Lyonnais (commercial bank), Bull (computer company), France Telecom, Alstom (rail transport), and Areva (nuclear power).

Renault, which was nationalized in 1945 as a punishment for its cooperation with the German occupation, fell into financial crisis during the first half of the 1980s due to a sales slump triggered by the second oil shock, industrial action, excess workforce numbers, and debt. France's Commissariat Général du Plan (General Plan Commission) obtained a comparative analysis of the French and Japanese automotive industries from French and Japanese economists (Commissariat Général du Plan, 1990). Meanwhile, French automakers introduced Japanese-style production, consisting of the "just-in-time system" (which minimizes times within the production system, response times from suppliers and to customers, inventory costs, and production defects), total quality control (involving both workers and managers in maximizing productivity and quality), and close partnerships with reliable suppliers and subcontractors. However, this did not significantly improve Renault's productivity and product quality.

French-born and U.S.-educated Renault chairman Bernard Hanon (1981–1985) took the lead in expanding its product range by raising Renault's stake in American Motors Corporation (AMC) in North America from 22.5% stake at the beginning of the partnership in late 1979 to 46% by 1982. The French government dismissed Hanon after Renault lost $1.3 billion and its debt reached $6.0 billion. In 1985, the government installed Georges Besse, who had led several state-controlled French companies (e.g., Eurodif,

COGEMA, Pechiney-Ugine-Kuhlmann), as Renault chairman. Besse initiated a drastic restructuring plan that included 21,000 job cuts, sales of non-core assets, and withdrawal from most motorsports, which restored Renault's profitability. Besse's tenure was cut short, however, when he was assassinated by a far-leftist terrorist group in November 1986 (Tiberghien, 2007, p. 185). His successor, Raymond Levy (1986–1992) continued Besse's initiatives, including the closure of the Billancourt factory near Paris. Besse believed that Renault's partnership with AMC in the North American market was vital but, when both Renault and AMC faced losses in 1987, Levy sold AMC to Chrysler. Louis Schweitzer, who had been a bureaucrat at the French Treasury and Chief of Staff to Prime Minister Laurent Fabius, took over from Levy as Renault chairman in 1992 and held the position until 2005. In 1993, Renault and Volvo announced their plan to merge operations, but Volvo shareholders, suspicious of the French government's heavy involvement in the deal, rejected it (Tiberghien, 2007).

Renault was semi-privatized in 1994 when the French government reduced its stake in the automaker to 50%, at which point Schweitzer decided to create new bridgeheads outside Europe, examining a possible alliance with an automaker in Asia. In 1996, the French government privatized Renault while retaining a 15% stake. In the same year, Schweitzer hired Carlos Ghosn, who was already known for his cost-cutting prowess at Michelin's operations in North and South America, as Renault's chief operating officer. Ghosn was also well-known for his pursuit of American-style rationalist business management (Nikkei Business, 2019, pp. 48–49). The combination of Schweitzer and Ghosn at Renault epitomized France's hybridization of traditional state capitalism and American-style shareholder capitalism.

In February 1997, Renault announced a restructuring plan that, between 1998 and 2000, would close Belgium's Vilvorde factory (which had approximately 3,500 employees), standardize car platforms and parts, cut back purchasing costs by pitting suppliers against each other, and revise production processes to improve productivity. The announcement of the Vilvorde factory closure caused a political and social shock in both Belgium and France, triggering massive public demonstrations by French and Belgian people in Brussels, resulting in condemnation of the closure by the EU Commission and the European parliament. Despite these extraordinary political interventions, the factory was closed as planned in July 1997. In addition to these cost reductions, Renault also launched several successful new cars, including the Clio, Megane, Scenic, and Twingo in the 1990s, which improved its profitability (Freyssenet, 2009).

During the late 1990s, the success of their new models in the rapidly growing European market, together with the Asian financial crises, provided Renault with a golden opportunity to globalize in one fell swoop for its long-term survival (Freyssenet, 2009, pp. 271–274). Nissan Motor, the second-largest Japanese automaker, was in crisis due to a sales slump caused by the bursting of the bubble economy in the early 1990s, the banking crisis in the late 1990s, and excess production capacity, workforce, and debt. In the late 1990s, Nissan's main creditor bank, the Industrial Bank of Japan (IBJ, currently Mizuho Financial Group), faced a serious bad debt problem and could not provide additional financial assistance to the ailing automaker. Nissan negotiated, for its very survival, a possible alliance with three automakers: Renault, DaimlerChrysler, and Ford.

DaimlerChrysler wanted a majority stake in Nissan (which Nissan would not accept) and Ford had concerns about Nissan's high debt, which had reached $23.7 billion (Sato, 2012, pp. 347–371). In contrast, Renault was more willing to make an alliance with the Japanese automaker due to Nissan's advanced technology and presence in Asia and North America. In 1999, the French automaker paid $7 billion for new shares (equivalent to a 36.8% stake) and bonds with warrants issued by Nissan (which increased the former's stake in the latter to 43.4% in 2002), which was needed for the latter's survival, while Nissan took a 15% non-voting stake in Renault. However, Renault could have paid only $1.8 billion without the French government's guarantee of its debt financing (Inoue, 2019, pp. 353–370). Had Nissan gone bankrupt after this major investment, Renault would have fallen into a financial crisis itself, wiping out the French taxpayers' money. Renault was able to make this bold and risky investment because the French government was a major shareholder. If Renault had been 100% privately owned by shareholders, the investment would have been impossible (Tiberghien, 2007, p. 198).

Renault's investment in Nissan represents a typical example of moral hazard associated with state intervention. However, once Carlos Ghosn resuscitated Nissan in the early 2000s, Renault's own lackluster performance was compensated by the flow of enormous dividends and equity appreciation from Nissan, as well as the exploitation of Nissan's technology and R&D. In this respect, Renault's huge investment also had an element of Anglo-American-style moral hazard related to shareholder capitalism as the French automaker improved financial performance through the merger rather than its own product quality and technology improvement.

Section 2 Nissan constrained by "systemic support" and "industrious norms"

We contend that the cohesion of intermediary organizations (e.g., village, company) in Japan is underpinned by "systemic support" and "industrious norms." Although the original, narrow definition of systemic support refers to government and bank support for distressed financial institutions and companies, its broadened definition incorporates dominant elites/superiors' support and protection of subordinates in exchange for the latter's loyalty and obedience (Gotoh and Sinclair, 2017). Hayami (1992; 2015) argues that during the Edo period (1603–1868), Japan experienced a labor-intensive, capital-saving path of agricultural development – an industrious revolution that, given its scarcity of arable land and abundance of labor, enhanced living standards and formed modern Japan's work ethic and respect for labor. From the mid-16th century to the early Edo period, the government separated the samurai warriors/elites (the ruling class) from the farmers to establish a standing army in order to mitigate the risk of an agrarian revolt. They confiscated weapons from farmers and eliminated landlords who combined aspects of both samurai and farmer characteristics, promoting the independence of small farmers. These policies removed samurai control over farming operations, while the industrious revolution transformed inefficient traditional agriculture that relied on peasants in a state of servitude into highly efficient small-sized farming operations based on family labor, which provided more highly motivated workers due to their opportunity to retain the profits from increased production yields. The Japanese village worked as a membership community that provided vital mutual support for small farmers; in return for this support, all members were required to make a full commitment to the village. Villages sometimes rebelled against tax hikes and money lenders' farmland foreclosure to maintain their autonomy. Systemic support was witnessed within villages and between samurai elites and farmers in the same domain.

Industrious norms (an internalized work ethic, respect for labor and a negative view of financial profit) and systemic support have been carried forward to contemporary Japan (Gotoh, 2021). After WWII, U.S. occupation forces used agricultural land reform, dissolution of zaibatsu, a purge of top management, and a wealth tax to eliminate major Japanese capitalists, including landlords and executives of zaibatsu conglomerates and large firms. This greatly contributed to the maintenance of anti-capitalistic industrious norms in postwar Japan, allowing the formation of coalitions of anti-liberal management and labor against capitalists (mainly shareholders in pursuit of short-term profit) at most large firms. Furthermore, it has been Japanese postwar companies, rather than the state, that have provided a large (albeit declining over the last two decades) proportion of social welfare for their employees. Nishiyama (1992, p. 246) points out that large Japanese firms are dominated by managers (as supervisory workers) rather than by shareholders. Besides, claims that the postwar decline of capitalists and the dominance of firms by supervisory workers in Japan evolved from the perspective that only those who provide labor should be rewarded, while those who do not are unqualified for a reward. We contend that Japanese elites have promoted industrious norms to mobilize committed labor to enrich intermediary organizations and the nation. Moreover, in contrast to France's version of systemic support, which mainly exists between the government and the big businesses in which it has a stake, Japan's version is ubiquitous and can be witnessed within and between intermediary organizations.

Like Renault, Nissan Motor has long been intertwined with the government—in particular, it has had a long relationship with the Ministry of International Trade and Industry (MITI, now known as the Ministry of Economy, Trade, and Industry, METI). Before World War II, Nissan Konzern, led by Yoshisuke Ayukawa, was a zaibatsu conglomerate that mainly covered the mining, energy, chemical, and machinery industries. The Japanese automobile market was dominated by GM and Ford from the mid-1920s until 1938 but the Automobile Manufacturing Industry Act in 1936 forced the two American automakers to leave Japan in 1939. Thanks to the close ties between Nobusuke Kishi (Minister of Commerce and Industry in 1941–1943 and Prime Minister in 1957–1960) and Yoshisuke Ayukawa, who were from the same province and were both involved in the Japanese colonization of Manchuria, Nissan Konzern – which was close to the Ministry of Commerce and Industry, the predecessor to MITI – was permitted to confiscate most of the assembly machinery at Ford's Yokohama plant and ship it to Manchuria. Nissan also enjoyed strong financial backing from the IBJ, which had been governmental until the end of World War II and remained virtually quasi-governmental even after its postwar privatization. Under U.S. occupation, Nissan Konzern was broken up into Nissan Motor, Hitachi, and Nissan Chemical, among others, but Nissan Motor maintained its tight ties with the government (MITI/METI), the Liberal Democratic Party (LDP) – in which former bureaucrats were influential – and the privatized IBJ during the postwar period.

In the late 1940s, the Ministry of Transport, the Bank of Japan, and importers of foreign-made cars insisted that Japan did not need domestically-produced cars, whereas domestic automakers (e.g., Toyota, Nissan, and Isuzu) and MITI regarded the development of the domestic car industry as critically important. As of 1950, Japan's car production ranking was the ninth in the world. When the influx of foreign cars into Japan significantly increased in the early 1950s, MITI restricted foreign automakers from exporting finished vehicles to and investing in Japan unless the investment contributed to the domestic automotive industry. Japanese automakers learned automotive technology through the assembly of foreign cars and through alliances with their American and European peers (e.g., Willys-Overland Motors and Mitsubishi Heavy Industries, Austin Motor Company and Nissan Motor). The Japanese automotive industry developed rapidly under MITI protection.

In 1947, the IBJ dispatched its senior banker, Katsuji Kawamata, to Nissan as a managing director to tackle labor disputes between the All Japan Automobile Workers Union (JAWU) and automakers (particularly Nissan). Nissan's 1949 dismissal of 1,760 workers intensified the labor dispute, and during a 1953 Nissan labor dispute over wage hikes, Kawamata created a second union cooperative with management (Nissan Roren) to weaken the influence of the JAWU, which was defeated and dissolved in 1954. Kawamata, who had become known as "the emperor of Nissan," was its CEO from 1957 to 1973, when he became its chairman.

Until 1962, Nissan enjoyed the largest domestic market share, but from the following year onward, Toyota took over as the top carmaker. When Japan's car import restrictions were lifted in 1965, MITI was concerned about the survival of Prince Motor, Japan's sixth-largest automaker, as Prince Motor also had loss-making aerospace and forklift businesses. To remedy this concern,

Yoshio Sakurauchi, Minister of International Trade and Industry and a significant member of the LDP, proposed the merger of Nissan and Prince Motor to Kawamata (Shioji, 2012, p. 114). Meanwhile, Bridgestone, the largest Japanese tire manufacturer and the leading shareholder of Prince Motor, found itself facing a conflict of interest, as it aimed to expand its tire sales to Toyota and Nissan. In 1965, Sumitomo Bank, the main creditor bank of Prince Motor, dispatched its senior managing director, Hidehiko Kobayashi, to Prince Motor as the CEO and requested a merger with Toyota. Toyota, however, rejected this request. Nissan aimed to surpass Toyota's largest domestic market share, and with intermediation from MITI, the IBJ, and the LDP, Nissan acquired Prince Motor in 1966, which resulted in both excess production capacity and workforce at Nissan. This merger sowed the seeds of moral hazard: Nissan's acceptance of the merger was not driven by commercial rationality but governmental pressure and, more importantly, the expectation that the Japanese government would condone a future risky strategy.[2] It is not surprising that moral hazard materialized with Nissan's major investment in Sunderland (U.K.) in the 1980s. How did it happen?

The growing car exports from Japan caused trade frictions with the United States and the European Community in the 1970s. In the meantime, the revenue gap between Toyota and Nissan widened dramatically. Takashi Ishihara became the new CEO of Nissan in June 1977. Three months after his inauguration, Ishihara declared that Nissan's domestic market share would exceed that of Toyota in two years, but it would not provide sales incentives for dealers. Nissan's domestic market share, however, dropped from 31% (versus Toyota's share of 37.6%) in 1976 to 28.6% (versus Toyota's 38.2%) in 1978 (Japan Automobile Dealers Association, 1994). To avoid criticism of this domestic failure, Ishihara announced a new management policy called "Global 10" that was aimed at acquiring a 10% market share of global auto sales through international expansion (Sato, 2012, pp. 15–16). Coincidentally, Margaret Thatcher replaced James Callaghan (of the Labor Party) as British Prime Minister in May 1979. British Leyland had been nationalized under the Labor administration in 1975 and received a large amount of public funding, but under the Thatcher administration, HM Treasury wanted to reduce fiscal spending and force companies to compete, while the U.K. Department for International Trade wanted Japanese automakers to invest in the United Kingdom (Suzuki, 2015, pp. 50–51). In April 1980, the U.K. government requested Nissan provide equity capital for British Leyland, and although Nissan turned down the request, as it suspected British Leyland of having financial problems, they sounded out a possible greenfield investment into the United Kingdom.

In fact, the Japanese automaker intended to alleviate trade frictions with the European Community by producing vehicles in the U.K. To this end, Nissan's initial U.K. investment plan included beginning factory construction in 1982, opening the factory in 1984, the production of 200,000 units per year by 1986, using a workforce of 4,000 to 5,000, and involving a total investment of $420 million (Sato, 2012, p. 91). In addition, Nissan had plans for other overseas projects, including factory expansions in the U.S., Mexico, and Australia, as well as an investment into Motor Iberica (Spain). The aggregate amount of these overseas projects would exceed $4.2 billion (Sato, 2012, p. 98). A 1984 feasibility study on its U.K. investment revealed that loss-making would continue for seven years and accumulated losses of $270 million would remain in 1993 (Shioji, 2012, pp. 238–239). Nissan chairman Kawamata and Nissan Roren chairman Ichiro Shioji were concerned about the large risks inherent in these projects and opposed the U.K. investment. During the G7 summit held in Williamsburg, Virginia in the United States in May 1983, Thatcher requested Yasuhiro Nakasone (Japanese Prime Minister) push Nissan to invest in the United Kingdom. Nakasone and Ishihara leaked this information to Japanese media to overcome opposition (Sato, 2012, pp. 146–153). MITI also pressured Nissan not to cancel the U.K. investment (Suzuki, 2015, p. 123). The modified plan proposed by Kawamata involved sending knock-down kit exports from Japan to a pilot assembly plant in the U.K. as Phase 1, and then making a decision regarding whether Nissan would move to Phase 2 (fully-fledged local production with commitment to 100,000 units per year by 1990) by 1987.

Kawamata stepped down as chairman in 1983, and Nissan came to an agreement with the Thatcher administration over its investment in the U.K. in February 1984. Two years later, Ishihara forced Shioji, who opposed the U.K. project, to resign as Nissan Roren chairman by fabricating a scandal (Sato, 2012, pp. 293–297; Arimori, 2019, pp. 153–154). In July 1986, Nissan accelerated Phase 2 of their plan and initiated full operations at the Sunderland factory. However, following the burst of Japan's financial bubble in 1991, Nissan quickly encountered excess production capacity, labor, and debt as a result of their enormous U.K. investment (whose aggregate amount had reached $1.6 billion as of 1992), other overseas investments, and a sharp decline in their global market share (from 6.6% in 1991 to 4.9% in 1998). Japanese corporate executives, including those at Nissan, promoted industrious norms to ensure commitment to work from their labor force, which made it difficult for executives to conduct drastic restructuring such as layoffs.[3]

Systemic support from MITI, the LDP, and the IBJ contributed to Nissan's early postwar growth, but this support caused the automaker to not only be involved in large, politicized investments like Prince Motor and Sunderland, but bring about a level of complacency among its executives and union leaders who were overwhelmed by internal political struggles. The LDP was defeated in the 1993 general election, and the power of MITI's interventionist faction was weakened due to the prolonged economic slump and the rise of neoliberal thought during the 1990s. By the end of that decade, the IBJ was debilitated by financial deregulation and bad debt problems. The price of moral hazard paid by Nissan was extremely heavy. The ailing automaker could no longer turn to the LDP, MITI, and the IBJ in the circumstances. They had to turn to Renault.

Section 3 Clash of French and Japanese capitalisms

In this section, we examine the tensions between Renault and Nissan arising from France's and Japan's divergent capitalist models. Both France and Japan are often categorized as CMEs characterized by state interventionism, despite the differences in their government/business relations. The French government directly intervenes in the management decisions of the big businesses in which it has a stake, while the Japanese government is primarily a coordinator of interests among industries and companies, providing support for big business in crisis through the use of state/business networks. State interventionism in France and Japan led both Renault and Nissan each to take enormous but unsuccessful risks, which resulted in their alliance. Due to Carlos Ghosn's neoliberal restructuring at Nissan – which resolved the negative legacies of poor management constrained by systemic support and industrious norms – the Renault-Nissan alliance looked promising until 2004. Thereafter, however, a conflict of interests between the two automakers (i.e., Renault's state-backed extraction of money and technology from Nissan) and the negative aspects of Ghosn's short-termist management came to the fore. Starting in 2015, Emmanuel Macron sought to transform the alliance into a fully integrated automotive group, but this generated a clash between the two automakers, and more broadly, between French hybrid (state-led and shareholder) capitalism and Japanese stakeholder capitalism (centered on the people's strong attachment to intermediary organizations, systemic support, and industrious norms). We argue that the latter's communitarian nature (opposed to capitalist dominance) is at odds with the former's state-interventionist features.

The Renault-Nissan alliance was established in March 1999. A few months later, Renault purchased a 36.8% stake in Nissan while Carlos Ghosn became Nissan's Chief Operating Officer (COO), along with Thierry Moulonguet (a former bureaucrat at the French Treasury who was seconded from Renault) as its Chief Financial Officer (CFO). In 2002, the alliance created Renault-Nissan BV, an Amsterdam-based strategic management company to maximize synergy between the two companies.

Nissan announced the Nissan Revival Plan in October 1999, under the leadership of Carlos Ghosn. This plan consisted of a reduction of 21,000 workers, a 30% decrease in domestic production capacity (with the closure of five factories), cost reductions of $8.8 billion through a reduction in the number of suppliers and dealers. This was intended to reduce the cost of purchasing parts and materials, sales expenses, and use fewer car platforms. Debt cuts through inventory reductions and non-core asset sales were also part of the plan. The restructuring dramatically improved Nissan's performance between 1999 and 2001. Operating profit margin jumped from 1.7% to 7.9%, and the debt was cut from $23.7 billion to $5.8 billion.[4]

Ghosn focused on sales expansion in the North American market, where Nissan's profitability was higher than in Japan. Thus, he opened the Canton

(Mississippi) plant in 2003, in addition to the Smyrna (Tennessee) plant, in operation since 1983. He shook up traditional Japanese business practices, including lifetime employment, social commitment to local communities, and keiretsu networks with suppliers and affiliated companies, all of which exhibited industrious norms and systemic support and thereby constrained capital and labor mobility. From the mid-1990s until the early 2000s, neoliberal thought gained influence in Japan as its business community lost confidence in Japanese-style stakeholder capitalism, and Japanese investors and media praised Ghosn as a management guru. However, Nissan workers in Japan found it difficult to accept the opening of its new overseas plants and their increased production there (Stevens and Fujimoto, 2009, p. 107). A former president of Yokohama Kogyo, a second-tier subcontractor to Nissan that went bankrupt, criticized Nissan for ruthlessly demanding cost reductions from its subcontractors (Tiberghien, 2007, p. 190).

Ghosn and Renault chairman Schweitzer had stated that the Renault-Nissan alliance had been formed to avoid a cultural clash between the two automakers caused by full integration (Nikkei Business, 2019). However, some Japanese critics believed that Renault intended to colonize Nissan and deprive it of technology and money – as had happened with France's colonization of Indochina – while Ghosn took advantage of the alliance to maximize and maintain his power (Arimori, 2019). Ghosn was promoted to Nissan CEO in 2001, then chairman and CEO in 2003. He also obtained the two positions at Renault in 2005, seizing absolute power within the Renault-Nissan group. At the beginning, both sides emphasized a spirit of equality and partnership in the alliance but, in reality, Nissan was subordinated to Renault. Under French corporate law, due to Renault's 43.4% stake in Nissan, the Japanese firm was considered a subsidiary of Renault so that Nissan's 15% stake in the French automaker did not have voting rights. Nevertheless, Nissan's profitability and technology development subsequently outstripped those of its parent company.

With the implementation of an overseas sales expansion policy from 2002 onward, Nissan's operating profit margin reached 9–11% between 2002 and 2005, exceeding that of Toyota. However, despite the sales expansion, its subsequent profitability fell. Nissan's accumulated dividend payments to Renault during 2000–2018 amounted to $9.1 billion, including $3.4 billion between 2015 and 2018, and were particularly heavy burdens on Nissan's finances. Given its low profitability, Renault could not have paid large dividends to its shareholders, especially the French government. The equity in Nissan's net income accounted to a significant portion (e.g., around 50% in 2017 and 2018) of Renault's bottom line. Nissan employees criticized Renault for using the shared platforms funded by Nissan at no cost and for receiving the benefits of joint purchases of parts and materials given Renault's own lack of bargaining power with suppliers (Arimori, 2019, p. 208). Because of the massive dividend payments to Renault and Ghosn's short-termist management, Nissan could not secure a sufficient budget for research and development, which caused its product competitiveness to deteriorate and halted its development of hybrid cars (Arimori, 2019, p. 191).

This presents a clear example of one negative aspect of financial/shareholder capitalism. Ghosn resisted pressure from the French government to proceed with Renault's full acquisition of Nissan to maintain his power in the alliance. In 2015, however, Emmanuel Macron, Minister of the Economy, Trade and Digital Affairs, enhanced the French government's shareholding ratio in Renault from 15% to 19.7% in order to apply the Florange Act to Renault. Under the terms of this legislation, shareholders possessing shares for two years or more in a French company are awarded double voting rights. Although the French government reduced its shareholding ratio in Renault from 19.7% to 15% again in 2017, its control over the automaker remained very strong due to its enhanced voting rights ratio. These developments coincided with Nissan's sharply increased dividend payments to Renault between 2015 and 2018.

It could be argued that the Renault-Nissan group under Ghosn took excessive risks (e.g., race to gigantism, production of low-cost cars in which Chinese and Indian makers have a significant competitive advantage) as he knew that he was backed by the French government because of his grip on Nissan and that Renault was virtually "too-big-to-fail" (TBTF) for the French government.[5] The power of the group was concentrated in Ghosn as he made Nissan pay growing dividends to the French government, which also wanted Renault to become the top automaker in the world. After the retirement of Louis Schweitzer (Renault chairman during 1992–2005) and Thierry Moulonguet (Nissan CFO during 1999–2003 and Renault CFO during 2003–2010), nobody in the group could check and stop Ghosn's aggressive expansion strategy. The French government's interventionism and inadequate monitoring led to Renault's morally hazardous strategy; it also damaged the trust relationship between the two automakers.

Under the Koizumi administration (2001–2006), the influence of neoliberal thought aligned with financial/shareholder capitalism was at its peak in Japan (Teranishi, 2017). However, an anti-neoliberal backlash, which was epitomized by the so-called Livedoor-Murakami Fund incident and the revised money lending law, erupted in 2006, leading to Koizumi resigning from his premiership (Gotoh, 2020). Despite weak grounds for prosecution, the special investigative squad of the Tokyo District Public Prosecutors Office arrested both Takafumi Horie (CEO of Livedoor, an IT and financial group) and Yoshiaki Murakami (founder of the so-called "Murakami Fund," a shareholder activist fund), who were known to be outspoken neoliberal elites, on suspicion of security law violations. These allegations were politically motivated and designed to remove Anglo-American-style corporate raiders which may have disrupted Japan's stakeholder capitalism.[6] The special investigative squad can be considered a guardian of the Japanese system, which is centered on a strong attachment to intermediary organizations, systemic support, and industrious norms. The intention of the revised money lending law was to prevent consumers from excess borrowing and thereby destroying numerous consumer credit non-banks that had flourished since the Japanese financial Big Bang deregulation in 1996.

We contend that the prosecutors and lawmakers who made decisions in these cases were strongly influenced by industrious norms critical of the pursuit of short-term financial profits by capitalists and financiers. The global financial crisis of 2007–2009 accelerated anti-neoliberal sentiment in Japan. Since then, the influence of the proponents of Anglo-American-style capitalism – including Keizai Doyukai (a neoliberal-oriented industrial association), reformist politicians and bureaucrats, American and European financial institutions, as well as credit rating agencies – has weakened (Gotoh, 2019).

Macron's inauguration as President of France in May 2017 further intensified the tensions between Renault and Nissan. Although Ghosn was expected to step down as Renault's CEO due to his disagreement with Macron over the alliance, in February 2018, the Renault board asked Ghosn to stay in the position for another four years to pursue closer integration with Nissan.[7] This suggests Ghosn had succumbed to pressure from Macron, who had an ambition to "revitalize the French economy with major global French companies like a new Renault-Nissan entity" (Steel Advisory Partners, 2019). Furthermore, in March 2018, Bloomberg reported that Renault and Nissan were "in talks to merge, seeking to solidify their two-decade-old alliance under a single stock."[8] Ghosn's change of mind strained his relationship with those Nissan executives who opposed full integration, and they came to regard Ghosn as a traitor.

In a bid to oust Ghosn from Nissan and prevent closer integration, a small team of Nissan officials performed an investigation and discovered alleged malfeasance by Ghosn (i.e., misuse of corporate funds) and consulted with the special investigative squad of the Tokyo District Public Prosecutors Office (Nikkei Business, 2019, pp. 327–329). A dramatic public takedown of Ghosn at Haneda Airport and the public airing of the details of his alleged crimes might suggest Japanese elites (including those of METI, the LDP, Nissan, public prosecution and the media) sent an implicit warning to Renault and Macron regarding their disagreement with their plans (Steel Advisory Partners, 2019). An alternative interpretation was that METI, the special investigative squad, and the media had different motives for pursuing the Ghosn case. Unlike the French government, the Japanese government does not normally invest in private sector companies. The Japanese government (METI, in particular) did not want Nissan to be a French company, but they could not directly prevent the integration.[9] Meanwhile, the special investigative squad had lost public trust during the postal discount abuse case of 2011 and was seeking an opportunity to rebuild its public esteem (Suda, 2019).[10] The Japanese media have a close relationship with prosecutors, and to justify the prosecution and appeal to Japanese society's industrious norms they portrayed

Ghosn as a greedy, corrupt capitalist who had ruthlessly sacked thousands of employees (Suda, 2019).

Section 4 General Motors

General Motors was established in the shadow of the then-dominant Ford Motor Company in 1908. After World War II, GM became a key part of America's industrial, consumer, and financial infrastructure, employing 324,000 people directly worldwide by 2008, and supporting millions more who worked for suppliers (Vlasic, 2011, p. 10).

In 1908, GM was a holding company incorporating separate automobile manufacturing companies, including Cadillac, Buick, and others. In 1920, the separate companies were incorporated into GM as operating divisions (Sloan, 1963, p. 55). Although the first decade or so of GM's business activity was financially turbulent, things began to settle down with the replacement of GM's flamboyant founder William C. Durant as president by Pierre S. du Pont in 1918. Womack et al. (2007, p. 39) argue that strong financial controls at the center, the creation of a clear division of professional labor, and the co-ordination of a series of decentralized divisions "solved the last pressing problems inhibiting the spread of mass production."

But with success GM came to suffer from what we might call "corporate narcissism." Taylor (2010, p. 34) suggests the lack of real competition made the corporation increasingly focus on internal organizational processes rather than on the product. Following Michels (2001 [1911], p. 6), markets, like democracy, give rise to oligarchy. Inside GM, a very distinctive deliberate corporate culture emerged associated with the great success of the company in the middle decades of the 20th century. This induced a conceit, an over-confidence which increased risk on the assumption that the accumulated resources of the company would pay for poor execution. This is moral hazard in market terms.

Summing up the problems with GM in 1994, Taylor quotes CEO Roger Smith saying:

> Size and success…led to 'complacency, myopia, and, ultimately, decline.' Money became a substitute for innovation, past victories were turned into dogma, and maintenance of the status quo became the measure of success. A giant headquarters bureaucracy, under the paw of the accountants, attempted to coordinate everything but instead wound up stifling it. (Taylor, 2010, p. 130).

Section 5 The copper-cooled engine

The high profits of some divisions within GM, the problems with others, and the need to compete with the dominant Ford Motor Company led to a costly experiment with a revolutionary new engine design. This copper-cooled engine, as it was known, was actually an air-cooled engine using copper heat conducting components (which remove heat much more rapidly than other metals), allowing the engine to dispense with the complex design and heavy components associated with water cooling (Sloan, 1963, pp. 71–94 and Leslie, 1979).

In a pattern which is a familiar one in automobile innovation, GM rushed the product into production in 1923 before the technology was serviceable and had to buy back the vehicles and revert to water-cooled engines once it became clear these were not teething problems, but insurmountable obstacles given existing manufacturing techniques. The air-cooled engine, which in the early 1920s was intended to be the powerplant for all GM cars in future, only appeared again in a GM vehicle in the 1960s.

Alfred Sloan, president and chairman of GM during 1923–1956, details the conflicts within GM created by the championing of the new engine technology by du Pont, and how these conflicts, as much as the problems with the technology itself, were instrumental in destroying the prospects within GM for the air-cooled engine for almost two generations. Companies with similar assets and similar motivation to compete with incumbents, have produced equally problematic products in more recent times such as the Ford Pinto, Austin Allegro, Audi A2, and Pontiac Aztek.

Section 6 Unsafe at any speed

GM brought the air-cooled engine back into its lineup almost 40 years later with the compact Chevrolet Corvair in 1960. The Corvair was intended to compete with the Volkswagen Beetle which was selling strongly to young people and had become a style icon of the post-war era. The Corvair was faster, sleeker, more spacious, and comfortable than the VW product. The air-cooled engine worked well. Unfortunately, like the 1923 copper-cooled car, the Corvair had significant problems. The engine of the new car was mounted in the rear like the Beetle. The rear-weight bias of the car was a challenge for the suspension. GM chose to use a simple and cheap swing axle set-up in the rear which on cornering created increased camber of the wheels, causing the tyres to lose grip on the road, causing the car to go out of control and frequently flip over (Nader, 1965, p. 30). The Corvair's handling was not a result of cutting-edge automobile innovation or a blunder. “The tragedy was overwhelmingly the fault of cutting corners to shave costs” (Nader, 1965, p. 18). John DeLorean, senior GM executive later founder of the DeLorean Motor Company, agreed the Corvair was unsafe as originally sold (Wright, 1979, p. 53). Although GM corrected this issue in the 1965 model year with a fully independent rear suspension which stopped the rear wheels from tucking under, GM did not respond well to criticism of the Corvair, engaged in spying on Nader and had to settle many lawsuits. Nader suggests the fact that it took until 1964 before any substantial changes were made to the Corvair's suspension despite complaints and the possibility of legal action "can only be explained by bureaucratic rigidities and the abject worship of that bitch-goddess, cost reduction" (Nader, 1965, p. 36). Nader's 'bureaucratic rigidities' is synonymous with Michels' rise of oligarchy, or what we call "market-based moral hazard." GM sold 1.8 million Corvair 1960–1969, while VW sold 21 million original Beetles by the time production ended in 2003.

The problem for GM has never been innovation. GM's research resources were first rate and GM has provided many fundamental advances in automobiles such as exhaust catalyst technology (Womack et al., 2007, p. 130). A key problem has been the de-contenting of these innovations to reduce costs and increase margins, leading to weak implementation or execution of these improvements. Because GM dominated auto sales in the mid-20th century, the company did not have to prove anything and it could, it seemed, extract more profit and get away with not doing things as well as an aspirant competitor. In addition to the copper-cooled engine and Corvair issues, Womack et al. (2007, p. 131) cite the Vega project in the late 1960s, the X-car project ten years later, and the GM-10 factories in the late 1980s.

Section 7 Legacy costs

By the time GM was close to bankruptcy in 2008, it "looked more like a health care and pension provider than it did a car company" (Taylor, 2010, p. 215). The U.S. has not, unlike all the other advanced industrial societies, ever provided socialized medical care to all its citizens. One of the attractions of working at GM was that the company, like other major enterprises, provided this along with wages and other compensation. Much of this reward infrastructure was built up following the Flint sit-down strike of 1936–1937, which led to the unionization of the U.S. automobile industry. These costs were affordable when productivity growth was rising, when profit margins were high, and when auto sales were still expanding. In 2004 health care for GM's employees, retirees and dependents added $1,525 to the cost of every car and truck produced by GM in the U.S. and Canada. GM was buying more from health care provider Michigan Blue Cross than it was from steel, glass, and rubber providers. GM's medical costs rose 8.5% in 2004 and were expected to rise by 10.5% in 2005. After repeated downsizings GM had two and a half retirees for every worker (Taylor, 2010, p. 215). This meant once the costs of retirees were added to the compensation for workers, they cost $74 per hour. Because Toyota had few retirees, the cost of its U.S. workers was just $44 per hour (Taylor, 2010, p. 222).

GM and the other U.S. auto producers were targeted by foreign producers who could build more efficient and reliable vehicles, or more attractive and better performing cars. The U.S. automakers did, at times, respond well to these threats, such as when Ford introduced the Mustang in 1964, a compact and well-handling vehicle for the time. However, between 1970 and 1990,

Cadillac, which had been a highly profitable division, and the world standard in luxury automobiles, was eclipsed by imported luxury cars from Europe and Japan.

The de-contenting, the failure to reinvest and implement effectively to meet the competition, increasing dependence on discounting, and a high-cost base in Detroit, undermined the viability of GM compared with other sectors of American commerce. By 1993, GM, the former blue-chip company, was unable to access the capital markets and had to finance its activities via expensive bank borrowing (Sinclair, 2005, pp. 77–78). GM filed for Chapter 11 bankruptcy in June 2009 with $83 billion in assets and $173 billion in liabilities. Despite that, GM remained a "too-big-to fail" firm: it was thus able to secure U.S. Government cooperation in the worst financial crisis since the Great Depression, including billions of dollars in government funding (Manns, 2011, pp. 1360–1361).

Section 8 Conclusions

Moral hazard is typically thought of as bad behavior exploiting the reduction of perceived risk due to explicit or implicit insurance. In our chapter, the global automobile industry reveals different modalities of moral hazard, as shown by the cases of France and Japan. But in addition to the conventional understanding of moral hazard as predicated on government intervention, we think moral hazard can also be conceived as an inevitable byproduct of market failure, following Michels' discussion of the rise of oligarchy. The failure to implement innovation effectively and to deal with legacy costs are illustrated by this form of moral hazard in the case of General Motors.

Notes

1 P. Myners, "The Banker's Moral Hazard," *The Guardian*, 8 March 2010.
2 The risk that the pernicious relations between the state (or a state agency) and a private firm could give rise to moral hazard is also analyzed by Darbellay and Gaillard in Chapter 4 of this volume.
3 Nissan closed its Zama factory in the Kanagawa prefecture in 1995 due to its excess production capacity. It could not sufficiently improve its profitability.
4 This restructuring was regarded as exceptionally successful in Japan.
5 The TBTF issue and its moral hazard implications are addressed by Gaillard and Michalek in Chapter 7 of this volume.
6 S. Givens, "Murakami to Horie ni Omou Ki wo Tsukenaito "Yararechau" yo (A Lesson from the Murakami and Horie Cases: If You Are Not Careful, They Will Get You)," *Asahi Judiciary*, 21 May 2011; available at https://judiciary.asahi.com/fukabori/2011052000011.html.
7 L. Frost, "Renault Board Asks Ghosn to Stay, Pursue Closer Nissan Integration," *Reuters*, 15 February 2018, available at https://www.reuters.com/article/us-renault-board/renault-board-asks-ghosn-to-stay-pursue-closer-nissan-integration-idUSKCN1FZ2KM.
8 *Bloomberg*, "Nissan, Renault in Talks to Merge, Create New Company," 29 March 2018.

9 See A. Yamada, "Nissan Kudeta no Kage de Sasayakareru Keisansho no Shicchi Kaifuku no Omowaku (The Ministry of Economy and International Trade's Possible Intention to Recover Lost Ground behind the Nissan Coup d'état," *Diamond Online,* 11 December 2018 available at https://diamond.jp/articles/-/188028).

10 In July 2009, the special investigative squad of the Osaka District Public Prosecutors Office indicted Atsuko Muraki, a senior official of the Health, Labor, and Healthcare Ministry, on suspicion of abuse of the postal discount system. However, it was subsequently revealed that the prosecutors had tampered with data on a floppy disk they had confiscated in their investigation.

References

Arimori, T. (2019) *Nissan Dokusai Keiei to Kenryoku Koso no Masturo* [*Nissan: The Consequence of Autocratic Management and Power Struggle*]. Tokyo: Sakurasha.

Clift, B. (2014) *Comparative Political Economy: States, Markets and Global Capitalism.* Basingstoke: Palgrave Macmillan.

Commissariat Général du Plan (1990) *Du fordisme au toyotisme? Les voies de la modernisation du système automobile en France et au Japon.* Paris: La Documentation française.

Dowd, K. (2009) "Moral Hazard and the Financial Crisis," *Cato Journal*, Vol. 29, No. 1, pp. 141–166.

Freyssenet, M. (2009) "Renault, 1992–2007: Globalisation and Strategic Uncertainties," in Freyssenet, M. (Ed), *The Second Automobile Revolution.* Basingstoke: Palgrave Macmillan.

Fukuyama, F. (1995) *Trust: The Social Virtues and the Creation of Prosperity.* Glencoe (Illinois): The Free Press.

Gotoh, F. (2019) *Japanese Resistance to American Financial Hegemony: Global versus Domestic Social Norms.* Abingdon: Routledge.

Gotoh, F. (2020) "Industrial Associations as Ideational Platforms: Why Japan Resisted American-Style Shareholder Capitalism," *The Pacific Review*, Vol. 33, No. 1, pp. 125–152.

Gotoh, F. (2021) "Social Norms and (De-)Financialization: Japan's and China's Divergent Paths in Consumer Credit," *Contemporary Politics*, Vol. 27, No. 4, pp. 397–418.

Gotoh, F. and Sinclair, T. J. (2017) "Social Norms Strike Back: Why American Financial Practices Failed in Japan," *Review of International Political Economy*, Vol. 24, No. 6, pp. 130–151.

Hall, P. and Soskice, D. (2001) *Varieties of Capitalism: Institutional Foundations of Comparative Advantage.* New York: Oxford University Press.

Harvey, D. (2005) *A Brief History of Neoliberalism.* Oxford: Oxford University Press.

Hayami, A. (1992) "The Industrious Revolution," *Look Japan*, Vol. 38, No. 436.

Hayami, A. (2015) *Japan's Industrious Revolution: Economic and Social Transformations in the Early Modern Period.* Tokyo: Springer.

Inoue, H. (2019) *Nissan vs. Ghosn: Shihai to Anto no 20 Nen* [*Nissan vs. Ghosn: Two Decades of Dominance and Secret Strife*]. Tokyo: Bungeishunju.

Japan Automobile Dealers Association (1994) *Jidosha Tokei Deta Bukku* [*Automobile Statistical Data Book*]. No. 12.

Leaver, A. (2015) "Fuzzy Knowledge: An Historical Exploration of Moral Hazard and Its Variability," *Economy and Society*, Vol. 44, No. 1, pp. 91–109.

Leslie, S. W. (1979) "Charles F. Kettering and the Copper-Cooled Engine," *Technology and Culture*, Vol. 20, No. 4, pp. 752–776.

Manns, J. (2011) "Building Better Bailouts: The Case for a Long-Term Investment Approach," *Florida Law Review*, Vol. 63, No. 6, pp. 1349–1406.

Michels, R. (2001 [1911]) *Political Parties: A Sociological Study of the Oligarchical Tendencies of Modern Democracy*. Kitchener (Ontario): Batoche Books.

Nader, R. (1965) *Unsafe at Any Speed: The Designed-in Dangers of the American Automobile*. New York: Grossman.

Nikkei Business (Ed) (2019) *Karisuma Shittsui: Gohn Teikoku no 20 Nen* [*The Downfall of the Charisma: Two Decades of the Ghosn Empire*). Tokyo: Nikkei BP.

Nishiyama, T. (1992) *Nippon Kigyo-ron* [*A Study on the Japanese Company*]. Tokyo: Bunshindo.

Safire, W. (1978) *Safire's Political Dictionary*. New York: Random House.

Sato, M. (2012) *Nissan Sono Eiko to Kutsujoku* [*The Glory and Humiliation of Nissan*]. Tokyo: Bungeishunju.

Shioji, I. (2012) *Nissan Jidosha no Seisui: Jidosha Roren Kaicho no Shogen* [*Rise and Fall of Nissan Motor: Testimony of Japan Automobile Workers' Unions Chairman*]. Tokyo: Ryokufu Shuppan.

Sinclair, T. J. (2005) *The New Masters of Capital: American Bond Rating Agencies and the Politics of Creditworthiness*. London and Ithaca, NY: Cornell University Press.

Sloan, Jr., A. P. (1963) *My Years with General Motors*. New York: Currency Doubleday.

Steel Advisory Partners (2019) "Macron's Ambitions Sowed the Seeds of Discord within the Renault-Nissan Alliance," available at https://www.steeladvisorypartners.com/macron-ambitions-renault-nissan.

Stevens, M. and Fujimoto, T. (2009) "Nissan: From the Brink of Bankruptcy," in Freyssenet, M. (Ed), *The Second Automobile Revolution*. Basingstoke: Palgrave Macmillan.

Suda, S. (2019) *Naze Karisuma Keieisha ha "Hanzaisha" ni Saretaka?* [*Why Was the Charismatic Management Made a "Criminal"?*]. Tokyo: East Press.

Suzuki, H. (2015) *Saccha to Nissan Eikoku Kojo* [*Thatcher and Nissan UK Factory*]. Tokyo: Yoshida Shoten.

Taylor III, A. (2010) *Sixty to Zero: An Inside Look at the Collapse of General Motors – and the Detroit Auto Industry*. New Haven, CT: Yale University Press.

Teranishi, J. (2017) "Neo-liberalism and Market-Disciplining Policy in the Koizumi Reform in Japan," in Backhouse, R. E., Bateman, B. W., Nishizawa, T. and Plehwe, D. (Eds), *Liberalism and the Welfare State*. Oxford: Oxford University Press.

Tiberghien, Y. (2007) *Entrepreneurial States: Reforming Corporate Governance in France, Japan, and Korea*. Ithaca, NY: Cornell University Press.

Tocqueville, A. (1955) *The Old Regime and the French Revolution*. New York: Doubleday Anchor.

Vlasic, B. (2011) *Once Upon a Car: The Fall and Resurrection of America's Big Three Automakers – GM, Ford, and Chrysler*. New York: William Morrow.

Vogel, S. K. (2018) *Marketcraft: How Governments Make Markets Work*. New York: Oxford University Press.

Womack, J. P., Jones, D. T. and Roos, D. (2007) *The Machine that Changed the World: How Lean Production Revolutionized the Global Car Wars*. New York: Simon & Schuster.

Wright, J. P. (1979) *On a Clear Day You Can See General Motors: John Z. De Lorean's Look Inside the Automotive Giant*. London: Sidgwick & Jackson.

9 Design and cost of U.S. responses to the 2007–2009 financial crisis and the 2020 Covid-19 pandemic

Cheryl D. Block

This chapter addresses unique design and cost-estimation challenges regarding U.S. emergency responses to the 2007–2009 financial crisis and the 2020 COVID-19 pandemic. More specifically, it illustrates that the fragmented and insufficient U.S. emergency response infrastructure often requires rushed, ad hoc solutions to crisis, resulting in inefficient and sloppy solutions. This chapter compares relief and bailout-like intervention designs implemented by the Federal Reserve, other government agencies, and Congress in response to both crises, focusing in particular on the 2008 Emergency Economic Stabilization Act (EESA) and the 2020 Coronavirus Aid, Relief, and Economic Security Act (CARES Act). It also considers specific budget costs that cannot be readily quantified, including potential moral hazards, indirect relief from special tax breaks, and relief from burdensome regulation.

Many U.S. citizens were angered by the extraordinary scope of government interventions during the devastating "Great Recession" of 2007–2009. Much of this anger surely was triggered by news of staggering government expense incurred to assist some private businesses and industries while others were left to struggle – or even fail – on their own. Though most of the anger focused on the so-called $700 billion Troubled Asset Relief Program (TARP),[1] this legislation represented only a fraction of the government's overall interventions. In the end, the U.S. government actually profited from most interventions to rescue private financial entities (Webel and Labonte, 2018). Of course, no one knew at the time that most of the financial sector interventions would be profitable. Indeed, total amounts for which the federal government was *potentially* at risk were extraordinary. According to one estimate, the "magnitude of guarantees and bailouts approached 80% of U.S. GDP, some $12 trillion."[2]

To be sure, accurately estimating the ultimate budget cost of government rescue at the time of the initial intervention is almost impossible. Even retrospectively, measuring overall government costs depends on one's perspective. Mere profit and loss accounts do not measure broader costs and benefits, including, for example, the extent to which government interventions may have mitigated – or perhaps exacerbated – the severity of the financial crisis itself. In addition, they do not account for longer term effects on economic growth. Many experts apparently agree that large-scale interventions during the Great

DOI: 10.4324/9781003139249-9

Recession were effective in fostering economic recovery. Others, however, believe that inconsistent government signals – particularly the Federal Reserve's rescue of Bear Stearns while failing to assist Lehman Brothers – exacerbated financial market panics. Even though the Fed's overall interventions in 2007–2009 were relatively low cost, experts generally agree that "government actions to assist the financial sector may have increased moral hazard... [which] could result in future costs if reduced private sector incentives to manage risks contribute to a future crisis" (United States Government Accountability Office, 2013, pp. 28–29). Some say that the U.S. government's COVID-19 interventions do not raise similar moral hazard concerns, arguing that since the pandemic is a once-in-a-century event, no one would have deliberately taken additional risk based upon expectations that the Fed would bail them out. The contrary position is that this time the Federal Reserve

> chose to make some facilities available to "fallen angels" – firms who have been downgraded to junk... Although those firms could not have been expected to foresee that they would be downgraded to junk because of the pandemic, they were less prudent than more highly rated firms, yet received the same access to Fed facilities. Because the Fed's response to COVID-19 was more extensive than its previous interventions, it may fuel expectations of similar interventions in the future... (Labonte, 2020, p. 15).

In other words, even though the COVID-19 pandemic itself was unforeseen, the expansive U.S. government response to it may signal future assistance at moments of crisis, thereby providing incentives for businesses to take on greater risk.

Despite congressional "no more bailout" declarations in the 2010 Dodd-Frank Wall Street Reform Act,[3] the U.S. government again is in the rescue business little more than a decade later. Indeed, COVID relief expenditures could exceed the Great Recession intervention costs by an almost unthinkable magnitude. In four separate pieces of legislation, including the CARES Act,[4] Congress had authorized appropriations of approximately $2.6 trillion as of June 2020 (US GAO, 2020). These are scary numbers for those who care about budget deficits.

Of course, budgeting is challenging and uncertain even in the best of times, and the massive cost estimates making headlines are not especially helpful. As an initial matter, one should note that funds *authorized* are not necessary funds actually spent. Nonetheless, what is certain is that the COVID-19 response will substantially increase the U.S. federal deficit; it is unlikely that the government this time will be pleasantly surprised by profits.

One particular challenge to identifying, understanding, and measuring the true cost of U.S. government rescue activities is the multiplicity of government agencies involved, sometimes alone and sometimes in partnership.

Though related, another problem is transparency. Given the use of multiple programs and agencies, numbers are reported in different places, making it difficult to develop an estimate of aggregate costs; and the numbers sometimes are hidden. Some agencies, such as the Federal Reserve,[5] are off-budget altogether. Others, though on-budget, may use different accounting methodologies to compute budget expenses and receipts. Moreover, Congress sometimes uses budget gimmicks to make costs harder to see. As explained further below, for example, use of the Exchange Stabilization Fund (ESF) as a source of some funding makes some expenditures less visible for U.S. budget purposes. The section that follows addresses the challenges presented by fragmentation.

Section 1 U.S. institutional structure for crisis response

1.1 The fragmented U.S. financial regulatory system and the 2007–2009 crisis

The U.S. has an emergency management system created by Congress in 1974, and amended over several decades,[6] which identifies responsible agencies and establishes protocols to ensure quick federal government emergency response to natural and humanitarian disasters without need for immediate congressional action. This overall system is headed by the Federal Emergency Management Agency (FEMA), now housed within the Department of Homeland Security. Yet, the United States has no parallel centralized regime for handling financial or economic crises. The problem is not simply the absence of such regime. Part of the problem is that the highly fragmented U.S. financial regulatory system itself includes multiple state and federal regulators, many with overlapping jurisdictions. National banks, for example, are chartered and regulated by the Treasury Department's Office of Comptroller of the Currency (OCC), but they are also required to join the Federal Reserve System. State-chartered banks may choose whether or not to join this system. Those that opt to join are subject to primary regulation by the Fed but remain secondarily subject to state bank regulation. The Federal Deposit Insurance Corporation (FDIC) is the primary regulator for non-Federal Reserve member state banks. Even when it is not the designated primary federal regulator, the FDIC has secondary – and sometimes overlapping – regulatory authority over all depository institutions participating in the federal deposit insurance system. Finally, the Federal Reserve regulates non-member state banks, and Bank Holding Companies (BHCs) with over $5 billion in consolidated assets (Congressional Research Service – CRS, 2020b, p. 8). Another complicating factor is that even this patch-work financial regulatory quilt – with modest exceptions added by the Dodd-Frank Act – applies only to banks.

Indeed, investors in modern markets have taken advantage of regulatory gaps, inventing creative new investment vehicles technically not subject to the jurisdiction of any existing regulator. This "shadow banking" industry has allowed investment vehicles to mutate over time, outpacing regulatory reforms. Many believe, for example, that the government's failure to regulate certain derivatives, swaps, and other financial instruments commonly issued or traded by these shadow banks contributed substantially to the 2007–2009 financial crisis (see Gaillard and Michalek, 2019).

In part, the chaotic, ad hoc response to the 2007–2009 financial crisis highlighted regulatory inadequacies and gaps and exposed the consequence of having no central agency with oversight responsibility for a coherent, coordinated government response. Absent a coherent institutional framework, regulatory agencies during the financial crisis found themselves scrambling – sometimes alone and sometimes in partnership – to invent ad hoc remedies. Writing a decade later about lessons learned from the financial crisis, three key financial regulatory officials contend that the crisis would have been less intense and the firefighting less apparently inconsistent and unfair "[i]f the regulatory system had been less balkanized and more capable of addressing risks to outside commercial banks" (Bernanke et al., 2019, p. 111). While conceding that Dodd-Frank improved financial sector regulators' fire prevention tools, these officials argue that constraints on the Fed's discretion to provide emergency assistance to individual firms – among other restrictions imposed by the Act – simultaneously weaken the Fed's response tools.

Congress established some regulatory improvements with Dodd-Frank, one of which is the new Financial Stability Oversight Council (FSOC), an interagency body with members representing multiple financial regulators.[7] The FSOC's primary function was to provide advanced monitoring of potential systemic risks to financial stability, and to classify certain non-banks as "systemically-important financial institutions" (SIFIs), which would then be subject to enhanced supervision.[8] FSOC has little role to play in responding to economic problems such as those triggered by the COVID crisis; it has taken no major action and has remained relatively silent with respect to pandemic emergency responses.

1.2 The fragmented U.S. government pandemic response

What the U.S. – and the world – experienced with COVID is far more than simply a *financial crisis.* In fact, the economic downturn to date has not substantially harmed large banks or the financial system. Instead, COVID's impact has been much more widespread and sudden. Unemployment numbers have skyrocketed, health care facilities are overwhelmed, and small businesses are closing in record numbers. Just as the United States had to resort to ad hoc measures in handling the 2007–2009 financial crisis, it similarly has been poorly equipped to deal with the pandemic. In fact, the COVID response involved an even greater number of federal agencies than the financial crisis response. Ultimately, the response triggered by both crisis events can be broken into at least three, sometimes overlapping, categories: stimulus, bailout, and relief.

1.3 Classifying crisis responses

Loose use of the terms "stimulus" and "bailout" might lead to the impression that the two are synonymous. Although the definitional boundary can be fuzzy, I see stimulus and bailouts as different. First, bailouts typically are immediate, emergency efforts to prevent the imminent collapse of private firms or industries (see also Gaillard and Michalek, Chapter 7 of this volume).[9] Stimulus, on the other hand, tends to be forward-looking, designed to spark economic growth or redevelopment. Second, economic stimulus typically has a broader target. It is hard to imagine describing stimulus as a "general economic bailout," for example. Moreover, government bailout-type actions may be specific to particular business entities in a way that stimulus is not. It makes sense, for instance, to refer to "bailing out," but not to "providing a stimulus for," AIG or the Chrysler Corporation.

Stimulus interventions themselves can take many different forms. As described further below, for example, the Federal Reserve can create stimulus by using its monetary policy tools to increase money supply. Even in a strong economy, Congress also may enact general stimulus legislation, such as broad-based tax cuts, simply to spur general economic growth. Stimulus legislation also may be designed to ease the overall impact of an economic downturn or crisis. In addition to its specific bailout-type responses to the 2007–2009 crisis, Congress included outright government spending on infrastructure or government works projects as part of a $787 billion stimulus package.[10] Finally, stimulus legislation may be enacted immediately after a crisis to spur redevelopment of the general economy,[11] or areas hard hit by specific disasters. For example, Congress created special "New York Liberty Zones" to spur investment in lower Manhattan following the collapse of the World Trade Towers,[12] and special "Gulf Opportunity Zones" to spur investment in areas of the Gulf Coast affected by the devastating 2005 hurricane season.[13]

In a third response category, Congress sometimes extends "relief subsidies" to provide reasonably immediate help to those who have suffered from natural, man-made, or economic disasters. Victims of the 9/11 terrorist attacks, for example, received direct subsidies from the September 11th Victim Compensation Fund of 2001.[14] Congress also provided immediate financial relief after the devastating 2005 Gulf Coast hurricanes.[15] Like bailout-type interventions, relief subsidies may prevent financial collapse of businesses suffering losses triggered by disaster. Unlike bailouts, however, post-disaster relief assistance usually is not limited to businesses facing imminent collapse. Instead, relief subsidy measures recognize that disasters can strike arbitrarily, imposing costs on victims from which others are spared. To my mind, stimulus provisions are distinct from other relief efforts designed to offer more immediate assistance to disaster victims, and from bailouts meant to prevent a potentially imminent collapse of specific businesses or industries in the interest of preserving economic stability.

Bailouts are especially controversial because they often are triggered not by humanitarian considerations, but instead by the perceived need to rescue certain businesses in order to protect against system-wide economic harm. As a result, bailouts sometimes provide benefits to firms considered too-big-to-fail (TBTF), and even to some regarded as culpable in creating the crisis in the first place. As such, moral hazard is a major concern. Bailout expectations may cause large firms to believe that they can act with impunity because their survival is assured.

At the margins, one might debate whether particular legislation represents bailout, stimulus, or relief. I contend that the three crisis response categories serve different functions. Bailouts do *not* equitably provide assistance to all similarly struggling businesses, but instead, help specific businesses whose failure would otherwise trigger systemic harm. As such, I believe it is especially important to be transparent about reasons for individual bailouts, and – to the extent possible – to separately account for associated costs. Moreover, once the crisis resolves, those who directly benefitted from government bailouts, thereby regaining their financial health, should be expected to repay the government for benefits received.

Of course, separately accounting for different types of government response can be challenging when government action includes aspects of more than one response category. The government's response to the 2007–2009 crisis, for example, included stimulus and bailouts designed to avoid systemic economic harm. The key concern then was a potential – and apparently imminent – economic breakdown. Thus, bailout interventions at the time effectively were designed to *prevent* or *mitigate* widespread economic collapse.

The COVID pandemic too might ultimately produce systemic economic harm. Unlike immediate threats to the very financial institutions underpinning funds transmission and payment systems throughout the economy, however, COVID's potential systemic economic harm is a longer-term concern. The more immediate impact of the pandemic has not been evenly distributed throughout the economy. Though some large companies – particularly in the transportation and hospitality sectors – have suffered, COVID's more immediate economic impact has been on owners and employees of small businesses, state and local governments, and the health care industry. Not surprisingly, a substantial proportion of the government's COVID response provides relief to individuals, and to specifically impacted sectors. For example, the CARES Act authorized tax rebate checks for qualifying taxpayers,[16] and provided a temporary weekly federal supplement to state-level unemployment compensation payments.[17] These relief components of the U.S. COVID response – as important as they are – are not the primary focus of this chapter. To my mind, tax rebates, supplemental unemployment compensation, and funding to assist the health care sector to purchase testing equipment and other necessary emergency costs should not be classified as bailout expenditures. Rather, they seem closer to humanitarian disaster relief.

That said, some COVID-related assistance to small businesses may be tricky to classify. For example, even though the federal disaster relief program does not focus primarily on *economic* disruptions or downturns, the system does recognize that businesses in federally declared disaster areas can suffer disastrous economic impact. In fact, one of Congress's first COVID responses before the CARES Act was to appropriate supplemental funding to the Small Business Administration (SBA) for assistance under its disaster loan program. Notably, the legislation explicitly *deemed* the coronavirus to be a disaster eligible for the program without the prior presidential declaration that would otherwise be required.[18] Though these disaster loans may prevent a potentially imminent business failure, I see this SBA program – on balance – as providing relief subsidies rather than bailout.

Another set of CARES Act small business provisions created a new Paycheck Protection Program (PPP), also administered by the SBA.[19] PPP loans offer extremely generous terms, including fee waivers, low interest, and even loan deferrals and forgiveness under certain conditions (see Dilger et al., 2020). As another illustration of crisis intervention partnership among agencies, the Fed assisted the SBA with the PPP by creating a new Paycheck Protection Program Liquidity Facility, providing liquidity to financial institutions, thereby enabling them to make loans to small businesses that banks otherwise might find difficult to fund. The Fed is taking the PPP loans themselves as collateral, but it faces no risk of loss because the federal government is guaranteeing the loans through the SBA.

Though the program was intended for small business, many large firms rushed to be first in line, overwhelming the SBA and leaving few resources for smaller businesses, who were the intended beneficiaries. The SBA stopped accepting new applications after less than two weeks as the program neared its authorization limits.[20] As news of PPP loans to large healthy companies spread, some – but not all – of these companies were shamed into returning the funds.[21] In addition to revealing glitches that may result from rushed, ad hoc interventions, this story also illustrates moral hazards that can arise when unintended beneficiaries exploit hurriedly enacted legislation, sometimes improperly diverting resources meant to address emergencies.

Because the PPP program too may rescue small businesses otherwise doomed to fail as a result of the COVID pandemic, it could be thought to provide bailouts. This assistance to small businesses confronting an unprecedented, once-in-a-century event might more accurately be described as providing humanitarian relief. In the end, the U.S. government's COVID response includes substantial relief and some stimulus, with very little bailout. In contrast, the government's 2007–2009 financial crisis actions were largely bailout and stimulus. In both cases, the Federal Reserve played an unprecedented role.

Section 2 Federal Reserve as first responder

2.1 The Fed's authority

Though born in the aftermath of the 1907 financial panic, the Federal Reserve was not envisioned as a rescue agency. Rather, it was charged with i) conducting monetary policy; ii) promoting financial stability; iii) promoting individual bank safety and soundness; and iv) fostering safe and efficient payments and settlements (see United States Federal Reserve System, 2016, pp. 1–2). As amended in 1977, the Federal Reserve Act also charges the Fed to pursue "maximum employment, stable prices, and moderate long-term interest rates."[22]

Ordinarily, the Federal Reserve's lending is limited to depository institutions, and must be collateralized to the satisfaction of the Bank.[23] As a result, the Fed's transactions are not very risky. During the 2007–2009 financial crisis, however, the Fed used its Federal Reserve Act §13(3) emergency power under "unusual and exigent circumstances," first authorized during the Great Depression,[24] to create unprecedented new emergency facilities and programs, playing almost a first responder role in addressing the crisis. Perhaps most important, the Fed's §13(3) authority expands its lending authority beyond depository institutions.[25] Until the latter part of 2008, the Fed had not used this extraordinary power since the Great Depression. As then Federal Reserve Chairman Bernanke observed in 2009: "[e]xtraordinary times call for extraordinary measures. Responding to the very difficult economic and financial challenges we face, the Federal Reserve has gone beyond traditional monetary policy making to develop new policy tools..."[26] – to my mind, a rather dramatic understatement.

As described further below, the Fed relied on its §13(3) emergency authority numerous times during the 2007–2009 economic crisis. A decade later, the Bank again used this authority to play an important role in the government's COVID-19 pandemic response. The sections that follow first briefly illustrate the differences between the Fed's traditional and more aggressive monetary policy tools, and then describe the Fed's moves into uncharted territory during both the 2007–2009 and COVID-19 crises.

2.2 Federal Reserve: basic monetary policy

The Federal Reserve uses three traditional monetary policy tools, the first of which is open-market purchase and sale of U.S. Treasury securities, which are designed to indirectly manage the supply and demand for money and credit. When it purchases government securities, the Bank effectively increases the money supply. In this respect, the Fed is often described as having the power to "print" money. The resulting increased supply of liquid funds theoretically makes credit more readily available and should result in decreased interest rates.

A second monetary policy tool is the "discount window," through which the Fed extends short-term, typically overnight loans to eligible depository institutions. This discount window is based upon the lender of last resort (LOLR) concept, common to most central banks. Traditional LOLR authority is designed to extend fully collateralized penalty-rate government loans, which provide reasonable assurance that borrowers will repay. The logic of such penalty rates is that they should be attractive only as a last resort to solvent banks otherwise unable to obtain quick access to funds at regular rates in private credit markets.[27] Discount window lending generally is intended to address temporary cash flow or *liquidity* problems of otherwise healthy banks; it is not meant to assist *insolvent* banks. Third, the Fed is empowered to increase and decrease cash reserve amounts required to be maintained at the Bank by depository institutions, thus also effectively contracting or expanding the money supply. With a few exceptions, further discussed below, the Fed generally does not use its traditional monetary policy tools for major stimulus, bailout, or relief.

In addition to its traditional monetary policy responsibilities, the Fed is charged with promoting financial system stability and minimizing and containing systemic risks (United States Federal Reserve System, 2016). Even in difficult times, however, the Bank typically turns first to its monetary policy toolbox. As a first effort to increase money supply, the Fed can push interest rates down through regular daily purchases of short-term Treasury securities, or by encouraging more borrowing from the discount window. When financial crisis persists despite traditional efforts, the Fed can employ more visible and aggressive measures to increase the money supply, thereby pumping up a lagging economy. The Fed took such actions during the Great Recession by purchasing large quantities of longer-term Treasury securities, bonds, and other financial instruments, actions typically referred to as quantitative easing (QE). As the Federal Reserve becomes increasingly aggressive, I contend that its actions move along a continuum from traditional monetary policy to substantial stimulus through monetary policy, to major emergency stimulus, and finally to fiscal policy intervention. At the extreme, some of the Fed's rescue interventions effectively serve as bailouts.

2.3 Federal Reserve responses to the financial crisis and to COVID

2.3.1 2007–2009 financial crisis

ASSISTANCE TO INDIVIDUAL BANKS AND PRIVATE FIRMS

Before the 1970s, the Fed's discount window had been used only for short-term liquidity support; it had not been a source of ongoing assistance for troubled banks. From the 1970s through the early 1990s, however, the Fed contravened the traditional injunction to lend to *illiquid* banks, not to *insolvent* ones (see Schwartz, 1992). Similarly, contrary to general discount window lending practices, 2007–2009 discount window loans were extended to seriously troubled banks. For example,

> Washington Mutual, which was on the verge of collapse in September 2008, borrowed $2 billion for several consecutive days before being taken over by J.P. Morgan Chase. IndyMac, another mortgage lender, borrowed $500 million just before regulators seized it in July 2008.[28]

As Manns (2011, pp. 1380–1381) notes,

> the expansion of the Federal Reserve's lending window into a de facto bailout fund during the early stages of the crisis placed the Federal Reserve in the contradictory position of propping up the financial institutions that it was supposed to regulate.

Among its more controversial interventions during the 2007–2009 crisis, the Fed also used its §13(3) emergency authority under unusual and exigent circumstances to provide assistance to specifically targeted individual, noncommercial bank entities. As the potential bankruptcy of Bear Stearns – then the nation's fifth-largest investment banking firm – loomed in March 2008, the Federal Reserve determined that "a disorderly failure of Bear Stearns would [threaten] overall financial stability and would most likely have significant adverse implications for the U.S. economy" (Board of Governors of the Federal Reserve System, 2009, p. 50). Rather than a direct loan to facilitate J.P. Morgan's purchase of the troubled Bear Stearns, the Fed created a new wholly owned Limited Liability Company (LLC). The LLC received a $29 billion nonrecourse loan from the Fed and a $1 billion subordinate loan from J.P. Morgan, which the LLC then used to purchase $30 billion in troubled assets from Bear Stearns. Although the Fed did not hold a *direct* interest in the high-risk assets, it held them indirectly through its 100% ownership interest in the LLC.[29] As a result of this transaction structure, the first $1 billion in risk of loss was borne by J.P. Morgan, and the remaining $29 billion by the Federal Reserve.

The Fed's decision to intervene on Bear Stearns' behalf was unprecedented. First, the Bank had not previously "committed to 'bailing out' a financial entity that was not a commercial bank." Second, it had not previously agreed to take an interest in troubled assets as collateral for a loan. Third, the Bank had not previously used an intermediary through which to funnel loans. The Bank subsequently used this Special Purpose Vehicle (SPV) approach more broadly for other new lending programs. In part, such convoluted transactions were used by the Fed to bypass restrictions otherwise imposed by the Federal Reserve Act.

In another intervention on behalf of a single private firm, the Fed authorized a loan of up to $85 billion, receiving in exchange an approximately 80% *equity interest* from AIG, the first time the Fed ever took equity in exchange for lending funds.[30] Still, the Bank was careful not to take a *direct* equity interest, instead lending to a newly created intermediary trust, which in turn made the loan to AIG in exchange for substantial equity. Even though the Fed's intervention effectively kept the company alive, AIG's primary shareholder had the temerity to sue the U.S. government, arguing that the Fed's taking of equity went beyond its §13(3) emergency authority, thereby constituting an illegal exaction. The Federal Court of Claims ultimately agreed with the illegal exaction claim but found that the plaintiff had suffered no damages.[31] On appeal, the Federal Circuit Court held that the plaintiff, as an individual, had no standing to assert claims on behalf of AIG,[32] thus rendering the illegal exaction claim moot.

The extent to which the Fed exceeded its lawful §13(3) emergency authority during the 2007–2009 financial crisis remains controversial. While some believe the Fed's actions were illegal (e.g., Posner, 2018, pp. 59–65), others argue that "there can be little doubt that the Fed acted within its statutory authority" (Blinder and Zandi, 2015). Few would disagree, however, that the Fed was in uncharted waters. As former Federal Reserve Chair Paul Volcker observed, the Fed took "actions that extend to the very edge of its lawful and implied powers, transcending certain long embedded central banking principles and practices."[33]

Regardless of how this debate over the Fed's legal authority is resolved, it seems clear that the Fed's rescue of individual firms and its discount window lending to insolvent banks effectively served a bailout function. Public awareness of such government interventions by the Fed and other U.S. government agencies probably increased expectations that similar safety nets would be extended in the future. In other words, the intervention precedents likely exacerbated the moral hazard that large private sector firms will engage in higher-risk activities under the assumption that they will be rescued in the event of major economic hardship. In any event, Congress later expressed its displeasure at the Fed's ad hoc measures to rescue individual non-bank firms, deleting language in the Bank's §13(3) "unusual and exigent circumstances" authority, which *had* permitted intervention with respect to an "individual, partnership, or corporation," and replacing it with language authorizing such emergency power only with respect to programs or facilities with broad-based eligibility, adding the new constraint that the Fed can no longer use its emergency power "for the purpose of assisting a single and specific company avoid bankruptcy."[34]

BROAD-BASED FACILITIES

In addition to assisting individual entities, the Fed acted alone under the auspices of its §13(3) emergency authority and used its own resources in 2008 and 2009 to create many new broad-based lending programs or facilities. Notable patterns reflected in these new programs included i) an expansion of the class of institutions to which assistance is offered; ii) a move from extremely short-term (i.e., overnight) loans to longer-term loans; and iii) a dramatic expansion of the types of collateral that the Bank was willing to accept (Board of Governors of the Federal Reserve System, 2009). In other words, the new programs involved taking on greater risk. By dramatically expanding access to lending and taking on greater risk, the Fed's new facilities during the financial crisis may have exacerbated moral hazard.

Among the most significant of the Fed's early programs was the Commercial Paper Funding Facility (CPFF), created to assist *non-banks* as a backstop to rapidly deteriorating commercial paper markets. Though acting on its own, the Fed's press release further announced that "[t]he Treasury believes this facility is necessary to prevent substantial disruptions to the financial markets and the economy and will make a special deposit at the Federal Reserve Bank of New York in support of this facility."[35] This marked the beginning of the Fed's increasing partnership with the Treasury Department and other agencies during the financial crisis.

FEDERAL RESERVE PARTNERSHIPS WITH OTHER U.S. AGENCIES

As conditions worsened in 2008, it became increasingly clear that the scope of the problem was greater than the Fed should or could handle on its own. Moreover, as noted earlier, the Fed was already testing even the limits of its existing statutory emergency powers. Thus, it joined the Treasury Department, the FDIC, and other agencies to develop joint programs. In November 2008, for example, Citigroup received an assistance package including Treasury Department funds through TARP, along with guarantees from the FDIC and the Federal Reserve (Board of Governors of the Federal Reserve System, 2009, p. 51).

One of the most dramatic of these joint new programs was the Term Asset-Backed Securities Loan Facility (TALF). Under expanded eligibility rules, this facility was made available to any U.S. companies – including non-banks.[36] In this case, the U.S. Treasury explicitly provided $20 billion in credit protection to the New York Federal Reserve Bank using funds authorized under TARP.[37]

2.3.2 The Federal Reserve's response to COVID

Though the 2020 pandemic did not begin as a financial crisis, it surely presented potentially serious risk to the financial sector and to broader economic stability. In response, the Fed has acted quickly, again first using its traditional tools. For example, the Bank lowered the federal funds rate target in March of 2020, ultimately reaching the zero-lower bound rate for the second time ever.[38] It also announced a reduction in bank reserve requirements to zero, thus eliminating reserve requirements for thousands of depository institutions, thereby increasing risk to the federal deposit insurance fund.[39]

As before, the Fed took major stimulus action, expanding its balance sheet with large purchases of long-term Treasury securities, mortgage-backed securities (MBS), and government debt, thereby expanding the money supply and making credit more readily available, and again acquiring assets beyond those that it would ordinarily purchase. This round of quantitative easing, however, was massive compared to similar actions during the 2007–2009 financial crisis. While the Fed's three quantitative easing rounds during the financial crisis never increased its securities holdings by more than $100 billion, *in April 2020 alone,* its holdings increased by about $1.2 trillion" (Labonte, 2020, p. 18).

The Fed in 2020 also created new and revived several old emergency lending facilities from the 2007–2009 financial crisis, all of which had terminated by 2010.[40] Given restrictions imposed by Dodd-Frank, however, the Bank can no longer extend assistance to individual firms, and it must get the Treasury Secretary's permission even before creating new or re-opening financial crisis-era broad-based facilities.[41] Despite similarities to 2007–2009, the Fed's COVID-19 response is quantitatively and qualitatively different, standing apart even from its actions during the Depression and the Great Recession.[42] Among the qualitative differences, the Fed's 2020 lending facilities include a Main Street Lending Program, offering loans to businesses too small to qualify for other credit facilities, and a lending facility for state and local governments.

Moreover, as Labonte (2020, p. 10 – emphasis added) explains:

> [i]n some cases, assistance has been *unsecured and on a nonrecourse basis.* The Fed has extended its lending function to include the purchase of securities, which typically cannot be secured or collateralized. It has created lending facilities for nonfinancial firms and municipalities that have seen their revenues collapse. It has made facilities broadly accessible; in some cases, it has opened facilities to firms or securities that are no longer investment grade or are too small to have credit ratings. It has committed assistance preemptively, before a lack of access to private credit has been established.

In other words, the emergency actions in 2020 involve even greater risks to the Fed than those taken in response to the financial crisis. Some might even argue that the 2020 facilities again stretch the limits of the Bank's emergency authority, as revised by Dodd-Frank, which now restricts the Fed to "providing liquidity to the financial system, and not to aid a failing institution, and [requiring that] the security for emergency loans is sufficient to protect taxpayers from losses…"[43]

At some point, higher-risk loans with a lower probability of repayment begin to resemble spending more than lending. Recognizing this higher risk to the Fed, Congress – in an unprecedented provision included in the CARES Act – explicitly provided for the investment of Treasury Department funds in Federal Reserve emergency lending facilities.[44] In a recent speech, Federal

Reserve Chair, Jerome Powell expressed his concern about blurring boundaries between lending powers, which traditionally are within the Fed's domain, and spending powers, which belong to Congress. He noted that the Fed

> can provide bridges across temporary interruptions to liquidity... But the recovery may take some time to gather momentum, and the passage of time can turn liquidity problems into solvency problems. Additional fiscal support could be costly, but worth it if it helps avoid long-term economic damage and leaves us with a stronger recovery. This tradeoff is one for our elected representatives, who wield powers of taxation and spending.[45]

Indeed, to the extent that the Treasury Department provides funding, and the Fed's COVID-19 response begins to resemble spending, there may be serious implications for the Fed's political independence.

Raising similar concerns, Labonte (2020) noted that

> [t]raditionally, financial assistance that goes beyond short-term liquidity to solvent financial firms has been the purview of the federal government, not the Fed. Congress decided in the CARES Act to provide most of the $500 billion for economic stabilization to support Fed – instead of Treasury – programs, however.

One possible explanation for Congress's reliance on the Fed for a significant portion of the government's COVID response might be that Fed actions appear less costly. In fact, Representative Lloyd Doggett (Dem., Texas), suggested just this at 2009 House Budget Committee hearings, where he noted that "[r]elying upon the Federal Reserve instead of the Treasury for bailouts can... mask the true cost to the public in terms of our soaring national debt."[46]

2.3.3 Congressional appropriations through the Exchange Stabilization Fund (ESF)

Two particularly unconventional features of the Federal Reserve-Treasury Department partnerships spawned by the 2007–2009 financial crisis and the 2020 COVID pandemic are the effective pooling of Treasury Department and Federal Reserve resources,[47] and the source of Treasury Department funds. For example, CARES Act funds authorized to backstop Federal Reserve emergency lending facilities are not direct appropriations from the Treasury Department to the Fed. Instead, the statute appropriates Treasury funds to the Exchange Stabilization Fund (ESF), to then be transferred by the ESF to the Fed.[48]

The ESF statutory provisions, enacted in 1934, authorize the Treasury Secretary, upon the President's approval, to access the fund "for the purposes of stabilizing foreign exchange rates."[49] The Treasury Department used this unconventional funding source once before in the aftermath of the 2008 Lehman Brothers bankruptcy. Upon news of Lehman's collapse, investors rushed to withdraw assets from money market funds, causing one such funds' net asset value to fall "below the hallowed $1-per-share level," [i.e., "to break the buck"].[50] Though somewhat analogous to bank deposits, money market accounts are not insured by the FDIC. Fearing that it had little time to stop dislocations in credit markets, the Treasury announced its *own* Money Market Mutual Fund Guarantee Program (MMMF).[51] In a novel and controversial move, Treasury Secretary Henry Paulson, Jr. received the President's approval to access the ESF to finance any program losses. Though some question the legality of the Treasury Department's using the ESF for such purposes (see Posner, 2018, p. 68), the Treasury Department justified the Fund's use on the grounds that "[m]aintaining confidence in the money market fund industry is critical to protecting the integrity and stability of the global financial system."[52]

The program expired in 2009, and no claims were ever made against the guarantee. Even before the program expired, however, Congress expressed its displeasure at the Treasury Department's use of the ESF, insisting that Treasury reimburse the ESF for any funds used in connection with the MMMF program, and explicitly prohibiting the Treasury Secretary from using the ESF "for the establishment of any future guaranty programs for the United States money market mutual fund industry."[53] This congressional prohibition seems warranted. After all, ESF funds are meant for stabilizing foreign exchange rates; using the fund for other purposes diminishes amounts available for the fund's primary purpose. Moreover, ESF withdrawals are not reflected in the annual federal budget, which makes use of the Fund less transparent. Some even refer to the ESF as the Treasury Department's "slush fund" (Belz and Wessel, 2020).

Absent legislative changes, the Treasury Department could not have used the ESF in 2020. Yet, Congress temporarily reversed itself, explicitly providing in the CARES Act that previously imposed restrictions on Treasury's use of the ESF shall *not* apply through the end of 2020.[54] Congress's decision to use ESF funds in 2008 and again in 2020 is curious. Perhaps one explanation is that these amounts are not reflected in the Treasury Department's annual spending. On the other hand, appropriations to backstop the Fed against potential loss ultimately may not result in any actual spending if the Fed receives profits, as it did when it used similar programs during the financial crisis. In other words, Congress might not be especially concerned with this particular use of funds for budget expenditure purposes.

In a November 2020 letter to J. Powell, Treasury Secretary Steve Mnuchin, controversially – and contrary to the Fed's wishes – requested that the Fed return unused funds appropriated under the CARES Act so that they can be re-appropriated for other uses.[55] In other words, the Treasury Department is no longer backstopping the Fed for potential losses resulting from its high-risk 2020 emergency facilities. Though it is hard to imagine that this was Secretary Mnuchin's motivation for the request, if these returned funds are put directly to use by other agencies, the expenditures may be more visible in budget documents.

2.4 Measuring the cost of Federal Reserve emergency interventions

Not only is the Federal Reserve uniquely self-supporting and independent, but it typically generates a surplus, which is remitted to the Treasury and reflected in the federal budget as revenue; it has not had a net operating loss since 1915. In fact, for fiscal years 2000 through 2008, annual remittances by the Federal Reserve to the Treasury ranged between $19 billion and $34 billion (Congressional Budget Office – CBO, 2010, p. 4). When the Fed makes large asset purchases and lends significant amounts through its facilities during economic downturns, it pumps cash into the economy, and simultaneously expands total assets reflected on its balance sheet. In 2007, for example, the Fed's total assets were approximately $870 billion. Resulting in part from financial crisis interventions, the Fed's total assets dramatically grew to a high of $4.5 trillion in 2015, dropped in 2017, and began increasing again in August 2019. As of November 2020, the balance sheet remarkably had grown to over *$7 trillion.*[56]

Notably, the assets in Fed's expanded balance sheet during and after the financial crisis were much riskier than those it would ordinarily hold. Had the Fed suffered losses, its remittances to the Treasury would have fallen, and the amount lost to general revenues from reduced remittances would represent real taxpayer cost. Moreover, if the Bank *had* incurred substantial losses, taxpayers would be on the line to cover them through general revenues. Potential costs to taxpayers from Federal Reserve bailout-type actions – though remote – are less visible than other government interventions but still quite real.

At the same time, substantially expanded balance sheets have the potential to generate substantial profits. When total assets reached their 2015 peak, for example, the Fed remitted record profits to the Treasury Department.[57] Though the Fed is taking even greater risks in connection with its COVID-related lending programs than it did during the financial crisis, one recent estimate projected that profits from the Fed's huge 2020 asset balance could top $140 billion.[58] Though uncertain, it appears that the Federal Reserve's COVID crisis interventions may cost the government little or nothing – and may again even result in profits.

Section 3 Other agency intervention costs

3.1 Direct and discretionary spending

One challenge to interpreting federal agency budget costs is that even straightforward outlays for federal programs can appear very differently. For one thing, the GAO and the CBO tallies for the same programs can differ because they use different calculation methods (Painter, 2020, pp. 6–7). Besides, the government's COVID response includes a mix of discretionary and direct spending. *Discretionary spending*, which results from "budget authority provided in and controlled by *appropriations* acts," appears relatively visibly in the budget. *Direct spending*, which is an "appropriation or other budget authority made available to agencies in an act other than an appropriation act" can be harder to identify (see United States Government Accountability Office, 2005b, pp. 44–46). This can occur, for example, when non-appropriation, substantive legislation makes changes to an agency's obligations for existing programs, which simply increase or decrease the agency's direct spending obligations. Thus, "it takes a certain level of expert analysis to project how much more (or less) spending over an extended time may result from a particular change" (Painter, 2020, p. 4). One example from the financial crisis was the increase in the FDIC insurance coverage cap from $100,000 to $250,000.[59]

3.2 Federal loans and loan guarantees

Much of the government's financial crisis and COVID response has been structured as federal loans or loan guarantees. Budget accounting for such programs is complicated by the absence of a crystal ball identifying borrowers who will fail to repay and the guarantees that the government ultimately will be required to satisfy. Before the Federal Credit Reform Act (FCRA) of 1990,[60] the federal budget generally recorded expenditures for credit programs using a cash method of accounting, under which expenditures are recorded for the budget year in which funds are paid and income is recorded for the year in which funds are received. Thus, direct government loans were reflected as cost when funds were disbursed, even if they were likely to be repaid. On the other hand, even if the borrower was likely to default, a government loan guarantee did not appear as budget cost until the government was required to make good on the guarantee. As a result, direct government loan costs were overstated, and loan guarantee costs were understated. Moreover, the apparently lower price tag for loan guarantees created a policy bias in favor of guarantee over direct loan programs, without genuine policy consideration of the advantages and disadvantages of the different approaches.

Concern over these budgetary distortions led to the FCRA, which requires accrual accounting for most loan and loan guarantee programs.[61] Under this method, the value of a loan or loan guarantee is determined first by estimating all expected cash inflows and outflows for the duration of the transaction. Those projections are then consolidated and expressed as a single present-value calculation. Computing present value requires use of an interest – or discount – rate to determine the value today of an expected future payment, or the amount that must be set aside today to meet a future obligation.

Most probably agree that accrual-basis reforms mandated by FCRA have improved the accuracy of federal budget reporting for loans and loan guarantees. Still, some accuracy and consistency issues remain. First, FCRA was not comprehensive. Though most credit programs today are governed by accrual accounting rules, FCRA does not apply to credit or insurance activities of the FDIC and certain other deposit insurance programs.[62] In the end, different budget accounting rules may apply depending on the specific agency source of the federal lending or guarantee activity. Moreover, even though all Treasury Department programs are governed by FCRA's accrual reporting requirements, TARP expenditures that were used for some Treasury Department bailout-type interventions were subject to special risk-based accounting rules that did not apply to other Treasury Department expenditures. At the same time, FDIC bailout-type actions were reported for budget purposes through cash-method accounting.[63] At a minimum, these different approaches created consistency problems, making it difficult to compare the budget consequences of lending activities undertaken by different government agencies. In turn, these difficulties complicate policy choices regarding the most efficient use and source of government loans and guarantees.

Another potential accuracy and consistency problem under FCRA relates to setting appropriate interest or discount rates to compute net present value. Although the concept of discounting to net present value is straightforward, choosing the appropriate rate requires insight into future general economic conditions and market risk. For purposes of the TARP program, Congress required that discount rate calculations be adjusted for market risk.[64] But conceptualizing is far easier than implementing risk-based net-present-value discounting. Ideally, each investment should be analyzed on a case-by-case basis, taking default and other risk details into account for particular investments. The Congressional Oversight Panel established to conduct monthly reviews of Treasury Department activity under the TARP program reported that the "Treasury paid substantially more for the assets it purchased under TARP than their then-current market value." Instead of a case-by-case analysis, the Treasury Department adopted a "one-size-fits-all investment policy," making investments on similar terms in both so-called "healthy" and "weaker institutions" (Congressional Oversight Panel, 2009a, pp. 2–8). One concern with a "one-size-fits-all" approach is that it creates differential subsidy rates. For example, the Congressional Budget Office (2009, pp. 3–4) estimated a 73% subsidy for auto-related government assistance, but only a 2% subsidy for bailout transactions with certain financial institutions. Differential subsidy rates are not necessarily wrong as a policy matter. The problem with the TARP investment approach is that subsidy differences did not appear to result from measured policy judgments, but instead were an almost accidental outcome of different accounting methodologies used for different government programs and a one-size-fits-all approach to valuation for very different transactions within the same programs.

Congress must refine its budget accounting by using market-risk analysis to more systematically compute net present value. To do this, Congress could establish an independent valuation entity with expertise in market-based risk assessment. To make informed decisions about the most efficient allocation of resources, Congress must be able to compare the extent to which different government interventions involve different "subsidy rates."

3.3 Covert bailouts and relief[65]

3.3.1 Tax breaks

In addition to more obvious forms of bailout and relief, Congress often provides indirect, more hidden assistance. One common example is special tax breaks. Reductions in tax liability for struggling businesses represent revenue foregone and, hence, a burden on general taxpayers. In response to the financial crisis, for example, Congress enacted temporary rules allowing financial institutions to deduct otherwise impermissible losses from Fannie Mae and Freddie Mac preferred stock investments against their ordinary income.[66] The congressional Joint Committee on Taxation (Joint Committee on Taxation, 2008) estimated the 2008–2012 revenue foregone from this specifically targeted tax break at $3.4 billion. The Treasury Department indirectly provided substantial assistance to failing firms by expanding the number of years to which small businesses were entitled to carryback their net operating losses (NOLs). Carrying current losses back to prior profitable years results in tax refunds for those earlier years, thus providing struggling businesses with much-needed cash. By expanding the number of prior years to which taxpayers can carry back losses, Congress can put more cash in eligible taxpayers' hands. This is precisely what Congress did in 2009, when it permitted small business taxpayers to carry back 2008 net operating losses for up to five, rather than two, years.[67] As Citizens for Tax Justice noted, although the legislation was billed as a "stimulus" package, the NOL provision simply made it "easier for corporations to use tax losses to get a refund of taxes paid in prior years (i.e., to get a check from the IRS) while doing nothing to change companies' incentives to invest or create jobs."[68] The NOL extension provision was more bailout than stimulus. In fact, the inclusion of a special provision disallowing the expanded five-year carryback to those otherwise receiving TARP assistance confirms the bailout focus of this legislation.[69] The government's COVID-19 response included similar assistance in the form of tax breaks, including a tax credit for employers who retained employees while they were otherwise shut down due to the coronavirus, a delay in required payroll tax payments, and – similar to financial crisis response provisions – a relaxation of certain NOL restrictions.[70]

Since 1974, federal budget rules have required that the president's budget and the congressional budget resolution include estimates of revenue foregone by tax expenditures. Still, this information is not otherwise incorporated into the federal budget, making tax expenditures more hidden than other budgetary costs. In itself, this is troublesome. A true measure of aggregate costs demands better budgetary incorporation of bailout-type costs incurred through tax expenditures. Along these lines, the GAO (2005a, p. 73) has recommended generally that tax expenditures be presented "in the budget together with related outlay programs to show a truer picture of the federal support within a mission area."

Of special concern in the bailout setting is that most bailout-type tax expenditures are targeted provisions, designed to assist businesses or industries in economic distress. Although always important, transparency and accounting accuracy should be emphasized especially when individual businesses or select industries receive targeted assistance. Moreover, the addition of tax expenditure bailout-type relief to the already-fragmented assortment of other direct spending bailout programs makes it even more difficult for Congress or the Treasury Department to fully appreciate how much is being spent on related efforts. Before providing additional assistance, those with power over the various purses should have information on aggregate government resources already devoted through tax expenditures and other devices. Absent such information, different units of government effectively issue checks on different accounts without the ability to balance the overall checkbook.

3.3.2 Relaxed agency interpretations

Government bailout-type assistance can also be provided through regulatory or interpretive actions of administrative agencies. This more covert type of bailout raises dual concerns. First, the existence of such government intervention is less visible to the public. Second, the costs of such intervention can be difficult to measure and will not be reflected in budgetary and agency financial documents. Unlike legislatively enacted tax expenditures, for which there is at least *some* budgetary information, nothing in the budget captures the costs of such administrative action.

The Treasury Department is probably the agency most able to provide economic assistance to struggling businesses through administrative action. By relaxing its interpretation or application of rules in the taxpayer's favor, the Treasury Department can – and often does – reduce tax liability for certain taxpayers, thus offering bailout-type relief. Particularly during the latter part of 2008 through 2009, an empathetic IRS issued a number of pronouncements that significantly reduced tax liability for some taxpayers. In some cases, the IRS went beyond simply choosing between plausible, alternative meanings of statutory language, instead making pronouncements that were inconsistent with the statute and contrary to congressional intent (see Zelenak, 2009). One controversial illustration was an IRS Notice facilitating Citigroup's acquisition of the failing Wells Fargo by permitting Citigroup to deduct Wells Fargo pre-acquisition losses against post-acquisition income, contrary to loss limitation rules.[71] Responding to a Washington Post reporter, one Treasury Department spokesman described the notice as "part of our overall effort to provide relief" and conceded that the Department did not estimate costs of the tax change.[72] Assuming that these comments accurately reflect IRS views, it seems clear that the Treasury Department deliberately provided bailout-type relief through changes in its interpretation of the tax law – a "hidden" bailout.

At the time this notice was released, Congress was debating emergency bailout legislation, and Citigroup and Wells Fargo were competing to acquire control of Wachovia. Before the Notice, it appeared that Wells Fargo's bid had failed, and that Citigroup would acquire Wachovia.[73] One observer noted the tax savings from this dramatic change in IRS interpretation of the § 382 loss limitation rules "could be worth about $25 billion for Wells Fargo."[74] Whether or not the IRS, in fact, exceeded its authority, these recent events provide an important reminder of the ways in which administrative action can provide bailout-type assistance.

Section 4 Conclusion

Throughout U.S. history, political reactions in the aftermath of emergency government intervention reveal striking patterns. First, once the immediate crisis abates, policymakers shift their attention from emergency response to reform mode. The latter often results in reactive legislation addressing the perceived causes of the most recent crisis and attempting to prevent recurrences. Looking backward, legislators may be addressing a problem that no longer exists. Thus, reactive backward-looking legislation may not offer workable solutions as future emergency conditions arise. Second, as memories of the last crisis fade, deregulatory pressures inevitably increase. This deregulation response, in turn, often plants seeds for the next crisis. Third, Congress sometimes responds to public frustration and anger over perceived federal agency overreach during the previous emergency by imposing new limits. Though such new limits can be an effective tool in reducing moral hazard perhaps unleashed by the last round of rescues, they also can tie government officials' hands, making it more difficult to respond to the next crises. Indeed, the U.S. government's 2020 emergency response was slowed as Congress found it necessary to quickly undo some restrictions imposed in 2010 by the Dodd-Frank Act.

In addition, the United States has been challenged for the second time in a decade by its fragmented and – some might say incoherent – crisis response infrastructure, resulting in the need for ad hoc reactions. Though precise details of the COVID-19 pandemic and its impact could not have been predicted, the government should have been better prepared for *some* unforeseen, massively disruptive event. Having to invent new ad hoc programs when urgency requires quick action can be a recipe for incoherence and confusion. Fortunately, the Federal Reserve had emergency lending facility prototypes from the 2007–2009 financial crisis that it was quickly able to retool for use in 2020. Unfortunately, new programs to assist small businesses, particularly the PPP, were so rushed and ill-defined that many small businesses who might have used it chose not to, and some large firms that did not need it rushed in to take advantage. Again, the government's crisis response was slowed by the need for further legislation to clarify and limit misuse. As the U.S. recovers from its second major economic crisis in two decades, Congress should develop and improve a federal disaster relief infrastructure with less fragmentation, and one that would more directly respond to *economic* crisis events.

Notes

1 Emergency Economic Stabilization Act of 2008 (EESA), Pub. L. No. 110-343, tit. I, §§ 101–136, ("Targeted Asset Relief Program," or TARP), 122 Stat. 3765 (codified at 12 U.S.C. §§ 5211–5241).
2 Stiglitz (2010, p. 110), citing M. Pittman and B. Ivry, "Fed's Strategy Reduces U.S. Bailout to $11.6 Trillion," *Bloomberg News*, 25 September 2009.
3 Pub. L. No. 111-203, 124 Stat. 1376 (2010) (preamble).
4 Coronavirus Aid, Relief, and Economic Security Act (CARES Act), Pub. L. No. 116-136, 134 Stat. 281 (2020).
5 This chapter uses the terms Federal Reserve, the Fed, and the Bank interchangeably.
6 Disaster Relief Act of 1974, Pub. L. No. 93-288, as amended by the Robert T. Stafford Relief and Emergency Assistance Act of 1988, Pub. L. No. 100-707 (1988) (codified at 42 U.S.C., ch 68, §5121 et. seq.).
7 Dodd Frank Act, §111, 124 Stat., at 1392–93 (codified at 12 U.S.C. §5321). Congress also created an Office of Financial Research (OFR) as a centralized office to generate and share data with the and other government agencies. *Id.*, at §152 (codified at 12 U.S.C. §5342).
8 *Id.*, at §113, 124 Stat, at 1398–1403 (codified at 12 U.S.C. §5323).
9 I define "bailout" as "a form of government assistance or intervention specifically designed or intended to assist enterprises facing financial distress and to prevent enterprise failure." See Block (1992, p. 960).
10 American Recovery and Reinvestment Act of 2009, Pub. L. No. 111-5, 123 Stat. 115.
11 Though TARP was closer to a bailout than stimulus, Congress's label for the legislation was the "Emergency Economic Stabilization Act." This emphasis on stabilization was probably to avoid the "bailout" taint.
12 Job Creation and Worker Assistance Act of 2002, Pub. L. No. 107-147 § 301(h), 116 Stat. 21, 39 (codified at 26 U.S.C. § 1400L(h) (2006)).
13 Gulf Opportunity Zone Act of 2005, Pub. L. No. 109-135, § 101(a), 119 Stat. 2577, 2578 (codified at 26 U.S.C. § 1400M(1) (2006)).
14 Air Transportation Safety and System Stabilization Act of 2001, Pub. L. L. 107-42, tit. IV, 115 Stat. 230.
15 Emergency Supplemental Appropriations Act to Meet Immediate Needs Arising from Consequences of Hurricane Katrina, Pub. L. No. 109-61, 119 Stat. 1988 (2005).
16 CARES Act, at §2201, 134 Stat, at 335-40 (codified at 26 U.S.C. §6328).
17 *Id.,* at §2012, 134 Stat., at 313-17 (codified at 15 U.S.C. §9021).
18 Coronavirus Preparedness and Response Supplemental Appropriations Act, Pub. L. No. 116-123, 134 Stat. 146, tit. II (Small Business Administration) (2020).
19 CARES Act, §1102, 134 Stat., at 286-94 (codified at 15 U.S.C. §9001).
20 J. Silver-Greenberg, D. Enrich, J. Drucker, and S. Cowley, "Large, Troubled Companies Get Government Bailout Money in Small Business Loan Program," *New York Times*, 26 April 2020. Two subsequent legislative acts were necessary to provide additional appropriations, expand eligibility, and address concerns about program misuse.
21 See P. Rudegeair, H. Haddon, and R. Simon, "Ruth's Chris to Repay Loan Amid Outcry Over Rescue Program," *Wall Street Journal*, 23 April 2020.
22 Federal Reserve Reform Act, Pub. L. 95-188, 91 Stat. 1387–91 (1977) (codified as amended in scattered sections of 12 U.S.C.).
23 The Fed has detailed regulations specifying collateral and other requirements for its discount window lending based upon §10B of the Federal Reserve Act (codified at 12 U.S.C. §347(b)). Fed. Reserve Bd., Reg. A, 12 C.F.R.§201.
24 Emergency Relief and Construction Act, P. L. No. 72-302, §210, 47 Stat. 709, 715 (1932) (adding §13(3) to the Federal Reserve Act of 1913, Pub. L. No. 63-43, 38 Stat. 251 (codified, as amended, at 12 U.S.C. § 343 (2006)).

25 For a review of the history of §13(3), see Sastry (2018).
26 Ben S. Bernanke, Chairman, Federal Reserve, "Federal Reserve Policies to Ease Credit and Their Implications for the Fed's Balance Sheet," Speech at the National Press Club Luncheon, 18 February 2009, available at http://www.federalreserve.gov/newsevents/speech/bernanke20090218a.htm.
27 The LOLR concept is frequently attributed to Bagehot (1873). See Ugolini, Chapter 3 of this volume.
28 N. Irwin, "Files Shed Light on Fed Lending Activity," *Washington Post*, 1 April 2011.
29 For a description of events surrounding assistance to Bear Stearns and the transactions themselves, see Shorter (2008).
30 For a description of initial Federal Reserve loans, and later TARP-related loans, to AIG, see Webel (2017).
31 Starr Int'l Co. v. United States, 121 Fed. Cl. 428, 466 (2015), *rev'd*, 856 F.3d 953 (Fed. Cir. 2017), *cert. denied,* 138 S. Ct. 1324 (2018) (mem.).
32 Starr Int'l Co. v. United States, 856 F.3d 953 (Fed. Cir. 2017), *cert. denied,* 138 S. Ct. 1324 (2018) (mem.).
33 P. A. Volcker, Speech before the Economic Club of New York, 8 April 2008, available at https://econclubny.org/documents/10184/109144/2008VolckerTranscript.pdf. For a balance analysis, see Wallach (2015).
34 Dodd-Frank Act, at §1101(a) (codified at 12 U.S.C. §343).
35 Board of Governors of the Federal Reserve System, "Board Announces Creation of the Commercial Paper Funding Facility (CPFF) to Help Provide Liquidity to Term Funding Markets," 7 October 2008, available at https://www.federalreserve.gov/newsevents/pressreleases/monetary20081007c.htm.
36 See http://www.newyorkfed.org/markets/talf_terms.html.
37 Id.; see also http://www.federalreserve.gov/monetarypolicy/bst_lendingother.htm.
38 Board of Governors of the Federal Reserve System, "Federal Reserve Issues FOMC Statement," 15 March 2020, available at https://www.federalreserve.gov/newsevents/pressreleases/monetary20200315a.htm. The first time was during the 2007–2009 crisis.
39 Board of Governors of the Federal Reserve System, "Federal Reserve Actions to Support the Flow of Credit to Households and Businesses," 15 March 2020, available at https://www.federalreserve.gov/newsevents/pressreleases/monetary20200315b.htm.
40 For an overview of the six new and revived lending facilities opened by the Fed in 2020 under its §13(3) emergency authority, see CRS (2020a, pp. 7–9).
41 Dodd-Frank Act, at § 1101(a) (codified at 12 U.S.C. §343).
42 For analysis of the 2020 differences, see Sablik (2020).
43 Dodd-Frank Act, at § 1101(a) (codified at 12 U.S.C. §343).
44 CARES Act, §4003(a), 134 Stat., at 470 (codified at 15 U.S.C. §9042) authorizes a total of $500 billion, which includes $29 billion for the airline and air cargo industries, $17 billion for loans or loan guarantees to businesses critical to national security, and the remaining $454 billion to support Federal Reserve emergency liquidity lending facilities.
45 Jerome Powell, Speech at the Peterson Institute for International Economics, 13 May 2020, available at https://www.federalreserve.gov/newsevents/speech/powell20200513a.htm.
46 See https://www.congress.gov/event/111th-congress/house-event/LC4197/text?s=1&r=1749.
47 The CRS suggests that the pooling of funds may have been designed to avoid legal restrictions that would otherwise have applied to the Fed under the Federal Reserve Act. See Labonte (2020, p. 7).
48 CARES Act, §4003(a), 134 Stat., at 470 (codified at 15 U.S.C. §9042).
49 Gold Reserve Act of 1934, Pub. L. No. 73-87, 48 Stat. 337, ch. 6, §10 (1934) (codified, as amended, at 31 U.S.C. §5302).
50 D. Gullapalli, S. Anand, and D. Maxey, "Money Fund, Hurt by Debt Tied to Lehman, Breaks the Buck," *Wall Street Journal*, 17 September 2008.

51 See Webel and Labonte (2018, pp. 25–26) for MMMF details.
52 See https://www.treasury.gov/press-center/press-releases/pages/hp1147.aspx.
53 Emergency Economic Stabilization Act of 2008 (EESA), Pub. L. No. 110-343, 122 Stat. 3765, 3797-98, §131 (codified at 12 U.S.C. §5236).
54 CARES Act, §4015, 134 Stat. 281, 481 (2020).
55 See https://home.treasury.gov/system/files/136/letter11192020.pdf.
56 See https://www.federalreserve.gov/monetarypolicy/bst_recenttrends.htm.
57 K. Davidson, "Fed Sent Record $97.8 Billion in Profits to U.S. Treasury in 2015," *Wall Street Journal*, 18 March 2016.
58 G. Friesen, "Profits from Fed Balance Sheet Expansion Could Top $140 Billion," *Forbes*, 3 May 2020.
59 EESA, §136, 122 Stat., at 3799. Although the increase was originally scheduled to expire at the end of 2009, the $250,000 cap was extended through the end of 2013, Helping Families Save Their Homes Act of 2009, Pub. L. No. 111-22, § 204(a)(1), 123 Stat. 1632, 1648–49, and later made permanent by the Dodd-Frank Wall Street Reform and Consumer Protection Act of 2010, Pub. L. No. 111-203, § 335, 124 Stat. 1376, 1540 (codified as amended at 12 U.S.C. §1821(a)(1)(E)).
60 Federal Credit Reform Act of 1990, Pub. L. No. 101-508, 104 Stat. 1388 (codified at 2 U.S.C. § 661 (2006)).
61 2 U.S.C. § 661a(5)(A) (2006) (defining "cost" as "the estimated long-term cost to the Government of a direct loan or loan guarantee or modification thereof, *calculated on a net present value basis…*") (emphasis added).
62 2 U.S.C. § 661e(a) (2006) (exempting the FDIC).
63 Congressional Oversight Panel (2009b, p. 9, noting different types of budget treatment for the Treasury Department, the Federal Reserve, and the FDIC).
64 EESA, §123(b)(1), 122 Stat., at 3790 (codified at 12 U.S.C. §5232).
65 For more detailed analysis of covert bailouts, see Block (1992 and 2010).
66 Emergency Economic Stabilization Act of 2008, Pub. L. No. 110-343, § 301(a), 122 Stat. 3765, 3802 (codified at 12 U.S.C. § 5261 (2006)).
67 EESA, § 1211, 123 Stat., at 335 (codified at 26 U.S.C. § 172(b)(1)(H) (2006)).
68 See http://www.ctj.org/pdf/sixworsttaxcuts.pdf.
69 Worker, Homeownership, and Business Assistance Act of 2009, § 13(f), 123 Stat., at 2992.
70 CARES Act, at §§2301-2303, 134 Stat., at 347-356 (codified at 26 U.S.C. §3111).
71 I.R.S. Notice 2008-83, § 2, 2008-42 I.R.B. 905.
72 A. R. Paley, "A Quiet Windfall for U.S. Banks: With Attention on Bailout Debate, Treasury Made Change to Tax Policy," *Washington Post*, 10 November 2008.
73 See E. Dash and B. White, "Wells Fargo Swoops In," *New York Times*, 4 October 2008.
74 A. R. Paley, "A Quiet Windfall for U.S. Banks: With Attention on Bailout Debate, Treasury Made Change to Tax Policy," *Washington Post*, 10 November 2008.

References

Bagehot, W. (1873) *Lombard Street: A Description of the Money Market*. London: Henry S. King & Co.

Belz, S. and Wessel, D. (2020) *What is the Exchange Stabilization Fund? And How is it Being Used in the Coronavirus (COVID-19) Crisis?* Washington, DC: Brookings Institution Press.

Bernanke, B. S., Geithner, T. F. and Paulson, H. M. (2019) *Firefighting: The Financial Crisis and Its Lessons*. New York: Penguin Books.

Blinder, A. S. and Zandi, M. (2015) "The Financial Crisis: Lessons for the Next One," *Center on Budget and Policy Priorities, Policy Futures*. Washington, DC: Center on Budget and Policy Priorities.

Block, C. D. (1992) "Overt and Covert Bailouts: Developing a Public Bailout Policy," *Indiana Law Journal*, Vol. 67, No. 4, pp. 951–1038.

Block, C. D. (2010) "Measuring the True Cost of Government Bailout," *Washington University Law Review*, Vol. 88, No. 1, pp. 149–228.

Board of Governors of the Federal Reserve System (2009) *Monetary Policy Report to the Congress*. 24 February. Washington, DC: Board of Governors of the Federal Reserve System.

Congressional Budget Office (2009) *The Troubled Asset Relief Program: Report on Transactions Through June 17, 2009*. Washington, DC: Congressional Budget Office.

Congressional Budget Office (2010) *The Budgetary Impact and Subsidy Costs of the Federal Reserve's Actions During the Financial Crisis*. Washington, DC: Congressional Budget Office.

Congressional Oversight Panel (2009a) *February Oversight Report – Valuing Treasury's Acquisitions*. Washington, DC: Government Printing Office.

Congressional Oversight Panel (2009b) *November Oversight Report – Guarantees and Contingent Payments in TARP and Related Programs*. Washington, DC: Government Printing Office.

Congressional Research Service (2020a) *Federal Reserve: Emergency Lending*. Report R44185. Washington, DC: Congressional Research Service.

Congressional Research Service (2020b) *Who Regulates Whom? An Overview of the U.S. Financial Regulatory Framework*. Report R44918. Washington, DC: Congressional Research Service.

Dilger, R. J., Lindsay, B. R. and Lowry, S. (2020) *COVID-19 Relief Assistance to Small Businesses: Issues and Policy Options*. CRS Report R46284. Washington, DC: Congressional Research Service.

Gaillard, N. and Michalek, R. J. (2019) "How and Why Moral Hazard Has Distorted Financial Regulation," in Hira, A., Gaillard, N. and Cohn, T. H. (Eds), *The Failure of Financial Regulation – Why A Major Crisis Could Happen Again*. International Political Economy Series. Cham: Palgrave Macmillan.

Joint Committee on Taxation (2008) *Estimates of Federal Tax Expenditures for Fiscal Years 2008–2012*. Washington, DC: Government Printing Office.

Labonte, M. (2020) *The Federal Reserve's Response to COVID-19: Policy Issues*. CRS Report R46411. Washington, DC: Congressional Research Service.

Manns, J. (2011) "Building Better Bailouts: The Case for a Long-Term Investment Approach," *Florida Law Review*, Vol. 63, No. 6, pp. 1349–1406.

Painter, W. L. (2020) *Tallying Federal Funding for COVID-19: In Brief*. Report R46449. Washington, DC: Congressional Research Service.

Posner, E. A. (2018) *Last Resort: The Financial Crisis and the Future of Bailouts*. Chicago: University of Chicago Press.

Sablik, T. (2020) "The Fed's Emergency Lending Evolves," *Federal Reserve Bank of Richmond, Econ Focus*, Second/Third Quarter, Vol. 25, No. 2, pp. 14–17.

Sastry, P. (2018) "The Political Origins of Section 13(3) of the Federal Reserve Act," *FRBNY Economic Policy Review*, Vol. 24, No. 1, pp. 1–33.

Schwartz, A. J. (1992) "The Misuse of the Fed's Discount Window," *Federal Reserve Bank of Saint Louis Review*, Vol. 74, No. 5, pp. 58–69.

Shorter, G. (2008) *Bear Stearns: Crisis and "Rescue" for a Major Provider of Mortgage-Related Products*. CRS Report for Congress RL34420. Washington, DC: Congressional Research Service.

Stiglitz, J. E. (2010) *Freefall – America, Free Markets, and the Sinking of the World Economy.* New York: W. W. Norton.

United States Federal Reserve System (2016) *The Federal Reserve System: Purposes & Functions.* Washington, DC: Federal Reserve System Publication.

United States Government Accountability Office (2005a) *Government Performance and Accountability – Tax Expenditures Represent a Substantial Federal Commitment and Need to Be Reexamined.* GAO-05-690. Washington, DC: Government Accountability Office.

United States Government Accountability Office (2005b) *A Glossary of Terms Used in the Federal Budget Process.* GAO-05-734SP. Washington, DC: Government Accountability Office.

United States Government Accountability Office (2013) *Financial Regulatory Reform – Financial Crisis Losses and Potential Impacts of the Dodd-Frank Act.* Report to Congressional Requesters GAO-13-180. Washington, DC: Government Accountability Office.

United States Government Accountability Office (2020) *COVID-19 – Opportunities to Improve Federal Response and Recovery Efforts.* Report to the Congress GAO-20-625. Washington, DC: Government Accountability Office.

Wallach, P. A. (2015) *To the Edge: Legality, Legitimacy, and the Responses to the 2008 Financial Crisis.* Washington, DC: Brookings Institution Press.

Webel, B. (2017) *Government Assistance for AIG: Summary and Cost.* Report R42953. Washington, DC: Congressional Research Service.

Webel, B. and Labonte, M. (2018) *Costs of Government Interventions in Response to the Financial Crisis: A Retrospective.* Report R43413. Washington, DC: Congressional Research Service.

Zelenak, L. (2009) "Can Obama's IRS Retroactively Revoke Massive Bank Giveaway?," *Tax Notes*, Vol. 122, 16 February, pp. 889–893.

10 Remarks and policy recommendations to fight moral hazard

Norbert Gaillard and Rick Michalek

This chapter summarizes the main arguments and findings presented in Chapters 2–9. Next, it advances recommendations to eliminate the roots of moral hazard, going beyond the "fine tuning" of macroprudential and microprudential policies. First, the Federal Reserve should include the evolution of financial assets' prices in its monetary policy. Second, the strict separation of the deposit-taking function of universal banks from their capital markets activities is advocated. Third, "too-big-to-fail" banks could be compelled to hold a certain percentage of the securities they originate. Fourth, the number of times a security can be used as collateral should be cut dramatically. Fifth, a micro tax on all electronic payments could be implemented to penalize speculative transactions. Sixth, certain types of financial products must be prohibited. Seventh, some "safe harbors" embedded within laws and regulations that facilitate morally hazardous behavior should be revisited.

Moral hazard has been, and continues to be, a pervasive issue and a major threat to capitalism and liberalism. In the past decades, moral hazard has thrived on the growing distortions and flaws of liberal capitalism: it may be driven by the failure of the "insurer" to control the behavior of the "insured" (e.g., loose regulation and supervision, or poor monitoring), the exploitative and deceptive strategy developed by the "insured" (e.g., hard lobbying, disproportionate capacity to obtain subsidies, abuse of an oligopolistic, monopolistic, or privileged position), or a strained, complex, and opaque environment resulting in hasty, ad hoc discretionary policies by the "insurer." These drivers of moral hazard have been investigated at various degrees in this collective book.

A key argument advocated by R. Claassen (Chapter 2) – and implicit in several other chapters – is the moral dimension of moral hazard. Insurance schemes are socially beneficial because they enable economic players to increase their risks while optimizing returns net of costs. Any excessive risk taking is unethical and unsustainable in the long term unless the costs are borne (at least partly) by the delinquent "insured." The lack of cost internalization obliges the "insurer" to raise "insurance premiums" and induces other insured entities to "re-optimize" their net returns by increasing their risk exposure. Ultimately, the very principle of insurance is jeopardized.

Cost internalization remains contingent on the profile of the parties and thus may take many forms. A central bank acting as lender of last resort

DOI: 10.4324/9781003139249-10

(LOLR) to rescue distressed – but solvent – financial institutions should ensure that solvency before lending freely at high rates against good collateral (see Chapter 3 by S. Ugolini). An international LOLR (ILOLR) committed to supporting a failing country will impose a set of conditions on such support (see Chapters 5 and 6 by J. Flores and N. Gaillard, and G. Bianco, respectively). Such conditionality is designed to help the country recover, preserve the credibility of the "insurer", and fight against moral hazard. The bailouts announced by governments are by far the most controversial measures, precisely because the managers, shareholders, and creditors of the rescued firms may escape their responsibility. This issue is frequently overlooked by governments who see bailouts as policy tools designed primarily to prevent imminent systemic risk (see Chapters 7 and 9 by N. Gaillard and R. Michalek, and C. Block, respectively).

It seems clear that bailouts encourage moral hazard. However, the firms that take advantage of these ad hoc measures have a long track record of influencing lawmakers and absorbing public funds prior to their crossing the event threshold requiring a bailout. They have succeeded in obtaining subsidies (such as export credits and subsidized loans) and signing governmental contracts. Despite that, they are unable to preserve their competitiveness and ultimately turn to their government to get rescued. These firms look like the "semi-obsolete corporate leviathans that are unable to live and unable to die," which Lippman (1937, p. 224) once described. Identified by A. Darbellay and N. Gaillard (Chapter 4) and F. Gotoh and T. Sinclair (Chapter 8), these "leviathans" are mainly concentrated in extensively regulated aircraft, energy, and automotive sectors.

****

Since the COVID-19 outbreak, moral hazard problems have been exacerbated. Governments worldwide have stepped in to provide support to banks and firms but the burden to taxpayers and public finances will increasingly force authorities to identify those having inappropriately taken advantage of this support (see Public Citizen, 2020). Next, the very accommodative monetary policies implemented in many countries, especially in the United States, have become a source of concern. The lowering of the Fed funds rate to nearly zero, the massive purchases of low-rated private sector securities,[1] and the acceptance of those securities as collateral for repurchase agreements and discount window operations have sustained stock exchange indices but also encouraged leverage and supported zombie firms. These two policies have combined to accelerate the misallocation of resources. More than ever, it is time to wonder, as Minneapolis Fed President N. Kashkari did a few months ago, whether a financial system that needs bailouts every decade is efficient and consistent.[2]

As a result, we provide here some recommendations to fight moral hazard and restore a more resilient and efficient financial system at the domestic and international levels. We will, in turn, tackle several problems analyzed in the previous chapters and advance possible solutions.

The reform of the export credit industry seems to be relatively manageable. Wherever export credit agencies (ECAs) or export-import banks (EIBs) are wholly or partly owned by the State, export credit schemes should be granted to small- and medium-sized enterprises (SMEs) exclusively. Larger firms have easier access to capital markets and financial instruments; they should not be allowed to "crowd-out" available export credit support. Second, the selection of SMEs should be based on their competitive advantages, the credit position of their importer, and the country risk rating of the importing economy.[3] Third, export credit schemes should never be involved in debt relief. Fourth, public authorities should require exhaustive transparency regarding the projects, the beneficiaries, the amounts, and the ex-post costs of the loans, guarantees, and insurance contracts granted by ECAs or EIBs.

Turn now to central banks, and the Federal Reserve in particular. The so-called "Great Moderation" (1987–2006) and the accommodative monetary policy implemented since 2007 have not only facilitated leverage and risk-taking (see Cecchetti et al., 2017) but also nurtured moral hazard. Our view is that monetary policy should be "normalized." However, the pace and the scope of this process are tortuous as they involve many connected issues. Our recommendations focus on the Federal Reserve's policy and the financial regulatory environment at large in *non-crisis times* because both fundamentally condition the last-resort measures announced *in crisis times*.

Perhaps the most iconic misjudgment regarding the alleged desirable (and actual) monetary policy of the Federal Reserve since the late 1980s is found in Bernanke and Gertler (1999, p. 18) when they write that "in the context of short-term monetary policy management, central banks should view price stability and financial stability as highly complementary and mutually consistent objectives, to be pursued within a unified policy framework." In an era of both disinflation and growing financial sophistication and liberalization, this "complementarity" was dubious and explains why the inflation-targeting approach promoted by A. Greenspan and B. Bernanke is outdated.

The inflation-targeting approach did not *and does not* grasp that the globalization era we had entered entailed a durable, low inflation rate.[4] Besides, it was said to "ignore movements in stock prices that do not appear to be generating inflationary or deflationary pressures" (Bernanke and Gertler, 1999, p. 22). One could say that such pressures were insulated from the real economy, as evidenced by the long-lasting decoupling between the stratospheric growth of financial assets' prices and the moderate inflation rate observed during the past three decades (see Figure 10.1). However, this decoupling conceals a more complex situation.

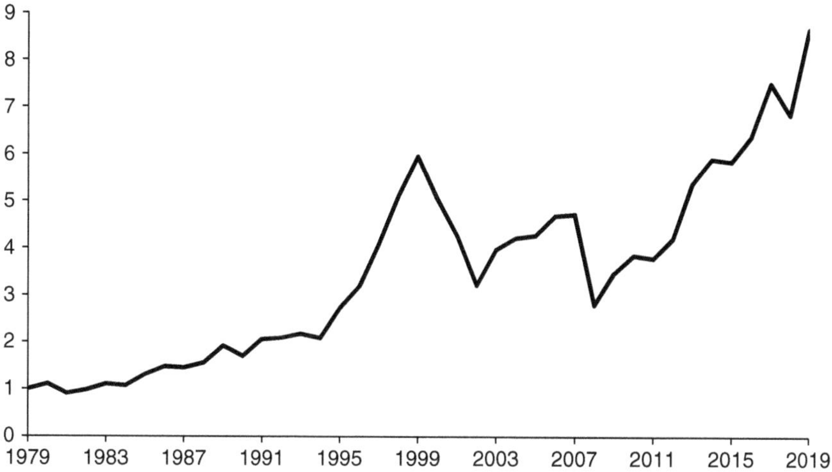

Figure 10.1 Ratio S&P 500/CPI, 1979–2019.

Source: Authors calculations based on Federal Reserve's data and www.measuringworth.com. Note: Index 100 for the 1979 S&P 500 Index and the 1979 consumer price index (CPI).

In fact, the Federal Reserve acts in an asymmetrical manner: it does not react to the booms in the housing and equity markets on the ground that they do not generate inflationary pressures in the real economy. In doing so, the central bank fails to prevent the *latent expansion of moral hazard* in noncrisis times. In contrast, the Federal Reserve implements last-resort measures when an asset bubble bursts, the objective being to eliminate systemic risk. In doing so, the central bank is reacting to the *materialization of moral hazard*.

The inflation-targeting policy leads to low real interest rates and encourages leverage. The borrowed funds feed financial asset bubbles and inflates what Minsky (1986) calls the "financial layering." It is the growing doubt about the validity of the expected asset prices that risks a systemic crisis. The only solutions consist of lowering the Fed funds rates dramatically and providing massive liquidity to financial institutions.

What is at stake in such Minsky moments was described by Bill Gross, founder of Pacific Investment Management (PIMCO). At the dawn of the subprime crisis in January 2007, he warned that when "the cost of capital (Fed Funds) moves above the return on capital (Nominal GDP) then assets dependent on leverage (stocks, houses) suffer negative or more restrictive cash flows and are liquidated at the margin."[5] B. Gross' advocacy for dovish monetary policy illustrates how and why major investors thrived during the "Great Moderation." In the reaction to the subprime crisis that erupted in July 2007, the Federal Reserve's monetary policy became increasingly accommodative and even more conducive to moral hazard. As Hogan et al. (2015) showed, the central bank acted as LOLR but violated the Bagehot rules: it lent to insolvent institutions, did not charge high penalty rates of interest, and accepted low-rated collateral for its last-resort loans. The same recipe has been used responding to the Covid-19 crisis with similar morally hazardous effects.

We consider that the Federal Reserve cannot reduce moral hazard unless it conscientiously revises its policy tools. A prerequisite is to admit that, in a world where i) financial institutions are highly leveraged and interconnected and ii) liquidity is the keystone of the financial system, movements in bond, equity and housing markets should be taken into account by monetary authorities when setting Fed funds rates. Such an updated approach would be consistent with two key duties of the central bank: namely, ensuring the safety and soundness of the nation's banking and financial system and containing systemic risk.[6]

Concretely, several indicators should be scrutinized. For example, real estate prices and stock exchange indices that rise at least three times as fast as GDP growth for more than two consecutive years are relevant indicators of speculation. A prolonged surge in the ratios of private sector credit to GDP and bank assets to GDP should also be cause for alarm. In addition, the Federal Reserve should similarly address any persistent tightening of spreads between risk-free and speculative-grade bonds. This would restore credit risk analysis and cut the excessive number of zombie firms.[7]

However, we agree with Bernanke and Gertler (1999, p. 17) when they state that "monetary policy is not by itself a sufficient tool to contain the potentially damaging effects of booms and busts in asset prices." This entails a greater cooperation between the Federal Reserve and other U.S. agencies.[8] In our view, the main area that requires enhanced regulation and supervision is certainly shadow banking. The Financial Stability Oversight Council, established by the Dodd-Frank Act, should have an extensive rulemaking authority to regulate and oversee major nonbank financial companies and identify and reduce systemically risky activities across the shadow banking system (for an excellent analysis, see Gelzinis, 2019).

Turn now to the reforms that are in the ambit of the Congress: the fight against the "too big to fail" (TBTF) problem and the necessity to revise bailout schemes.

Chapters 3, 7, and 9 have shown how bailouts – and their inherent *discretionary application* – can become the politically preferable default choice.[9] The relative failure of Dodd-Frank legislation to "end bailouts as we know them" underscores the difficulty of extracting the benefits of morally hazardous behavior from the deeply interlocking worlds of Washington and Wall Street. The literature is replete with possible improvements, if not "solutions" and their very number demonstrates the remaining distance to consensus.[10]

Successful reform will require the explicit acknowledgment of the existing co-dependence between the lawmakers and the clientele of the lobbyists. Insofar as regulation entails biting the hand that feeds (the campaigns), policy proposals will need to include both the internalization of the foreseeable costs of, and inducements for reducing the opportunity for, exploitative morally hazardous behavior. Just as there are restrictions limiting the prospect of future employment in the private sector for former federal officials (18 U.S. Code § 207), so should there be more exhaustive prohibitions on the acceptance of campaign donations from entities affiliated with regulatorily sanctioned violators.

For so long as the existence of TBTF firms and systemically important financial institutions (SIFIs) persists, there may be room for a *hybridization* of the dichotomous paradigm "rescue or bailout."[11] Such an approach might include a government-sponsored agency such as the FGIC proposed by Manns (2011) acting as both the source of *rescue* financing, and *bailout*, or *supplemental "bail-in"* funding,[12] for the distressed firm whose complete failure can reasonably be seen as having systemic costs greater than the then-current market-based cost of required rehabilitative funding.[13] The rescue financing would be provided (at rates consistent with Bagehot's rules) for those elements of the firm reasonably believed to be viable post-rescue, while *bailout* funding would be provided (subject to stringent conditions, and with the agency retaining a "vertical" slice of the capital structure) to those elements of the firm that may be successfully sold once bailed out. Any remaining elements of the firm would be passed into the bankruptcy regime for either Chapter 11 or Chapter 7 treatment (see Ayotte and Skeel, 2010). The funding for such an agency would be provided first by profits from successful rescues and sales, a usage tax,[14] penalties for noncompliance imposed on licensed shadow bank entities, and lastly by taxpayer funds.

The world of shadow banking and complex structured and derivative instruments in the capital markets is one area where the asymmetry of information as between structurer and end user opens wide the door to moral hazard.[15] The (slow) development of recognized exchanges for swap clearance at least introduces the ability to require and subsequently maintain improved disclosure and data. To the extent that economic rents have been obtained primarily, if not solely, by the exploitation of information asymmetry, shadow banks and the world of complex derivatives remain a significant source of economic inefficiency in our capital markets as well as a systemic risk to financial markets generally. So long as the employment of off-balance sheet liabilities (to say nothing of the interconnectedness as between institutions employing and exploiting off-balance sheet structures) extends the exposure of the TBTF institution beyond the application of quantifiable rules and regulations, the likelihood of further bailouts increases. The burden of qualifying for "permission *ex ante*" (to use and rely on off-balance and shadow bank financing) must be shifted more transparently to the structurer and issuer in order to increase the accuracy of the risk assessment performed by the end user and its agents. Violations of regulatory conditions to issuance must similarly result in sanctions not only to the issuer but to the experts and agents (including any credit rating agency) upon whom the issuer and structurer can reasonably be said to have relied.[16]

But the foregoing suggestions are reactionary to the world in which TBTF and SIFI firms, and the institutionalization of bailouts, exist. As moral hazard unavoidably inhabits opportunistic and competitive finance capitalism, the more direct solution to the problem of the externalized costs of moral hazard continues to be the reduction as well as the disentanglement of the SIFIs.[17] As suggested above, this challenge is largely political and will require answering any criticism insisting that federal constraints on size or interconnectedness will invariably generate a competitive disadvantage and consequent capital flight that could trigger the very failure intended to be avoided.

So far, microprudential and macroprudential regulations have had mixed results in terms of stabilization of the international financial system, curtailment of the funding cost advantages enjoyed by SIFIs, and reduction of moral hazard problems.[18] There are at least three reasons for these mixed results. First, the efficiency of Basel II and Basel III rules has been undermined by the very accommodative European and U.S. monetary policies. Second, microprudential and macroprudential tightening has led lenders to develop their activities in the shadow banking system. Third, macroprudential policies have failed to mitigate the excessive interconnectedness between SIFIs, a persistent key driver of systemic risk.[19] This last point requires unprecedented structural reforms, involving a progressive de-financialization and reintermediation of the U.S. economy, which would inevitably spread to other developed economies and reshape the world financial system. Several proposals can be advanced; they differ, in their philosophy as well as in their scope, from the reforms implemented so far to reduce the systemic and moral hazard risks (see Financial Stability Board, 2021).

A radical set of proposals includes reducing the size of SIFIs. Dismantling these TBTF banks by reinstating a new Glass-Steagall Act is politically unlikely but deserves consideration (see Wilmarth, 2020). Narrow banking, defined as the strict separation of the deposit-taking function of universal banks from their capital markets activities (Wilmarth, 2014), is another option. This would prevent SIFIs from using the federal safety net to subsidize their derivatives and securities activities. Systemic risk would be reduced and confined to nonbank affiliates.

Another set of reforms (perhaps even more crucial) tackles liquidity glut.[20] Our view is that increasing financial sophistication combined with the persistently low interest rates throughout the boom cycle caused the last-resort rescue lending and bailouts observed over the past three decades. The Fed has been constrained to resort to increasingly unorthodox means and ever-increasing liquidity injections to eliminate and prevent systemic risk. This has resulted in massive liquidity flows among highly interconnected investors. Accordingly, we contend that some reforms should be launched to lessen the liquidity accumulated in the financial system during low risk-aversion periods. In addition to the normalization of the monetary policy (stressed above), we would highlight three priorities: the reduction in the circulation of securities in capital markets, the prohibition of certain types of financial products, and what we call "economic disincentivization."

To limit the circulation of capital market securities, regulators must act to "contain" the "originate-and-distribute" model by obliging SIFIs (and possibly other, smaller banks) to hold a certain percentage of the securities they originate. This new rule would entail an update of present microprudential and macroprudential policies. A second option would be to reduce the collateral multiplier (i.e., the number of times a security is used as collateral through contracts, including rehypothecation). Infante et al. (2020) find that this multiplier is around 7 for Treasury securities. We could imagine a financial system where T-bonds and T-bills would be pledged no more than twice and all other securities just once. Only the actual holder of the securities would be allowed to pledge them. Thus, "collateral chains" would be shorter and less likely to exacerbate market stress. Lastly, a complementary measure would be to implement a micro tax on all electronic payments, which would penalize speculative transactions (see Ekeland and Rochet, 2020).[21]

Direct intervention through the prohibition of certain types and classes of financial products is another key issue. Both structurers and users pursue perceived economic advantage, and that advantage is largely determined by an analysis of risk. Products that are, by design, so complex and opaque as to make meaningful risk assessment unacceptably variable should be susceptible to prohibition. Synthetic CDOs (collateralized debt obligations) of ABS (asset-backed securities) is but one example of a financial product where the variability of performance is contingent upon the occurrence (or non-occurrence) of many levels of antecedent risks.[22]

So-called "economic disincentivization" requires revisiting some of the *politically sensitive* "safe harbors" that have been embedded within the myriad legislation that determines and directs Wall Street creativity. Among the many examples of such safe harbors, we would list the exception given to the rating agencies from the liability attaching to experts when advising the structurers.[23] We would similarly insist on revising the safe harbor purportedly given to swap transactions that would otherwise be subject to a stay in bankruptcy proceedings.[24] But apart from reversing or revising previously provided accommodations to the other side of the revolving door, Washington can add requirements that will simply alter the economics in a way that will redirect the generation of new financial products away from uncontained and unknown risk. Existing regulatory efforts in that direction include the requirement to clear swap transactions on regulated exchanges, increased monitoring for the necessary posting of adequate collateral when swap counterparties are downgraded, and the requirement for senior management to sign off on the adequacy and completeness of information disclosure.

History has so far shown us that "fine tuning" of macroprudential and microprudential policies has not reversed the rising tides of excess liquidity and morally hazardous exploitation of politically generated equity imbalances, it has in some cases accelerated it. The time has passed when marginal improvements to existing structures can suffice; aggressive reform is essential to redirect the momentum that has led to financial services dominating rather than serving our economies.

Notes

1 Note that the Federal Reserve's total assets increased from $4.4 trillion in February 2020 to $7.7 trillion in March 2021. See https://www.federalreserve.gov/monetarypolicy/bst_recenttrends.htm.
2 G. Robb, "Fed's Kashkari Decries 'Absurd' U.S. Financial System That Needs Bailout Every ten Years," *MarketWatch*, 18 September 2020.
3 Country risk ratings should include environmental, social and governance (ESG) criteria.
4 Starting in the 1980s, disinflation was driven by the booming of international trade and the extraordinary capacity of China to produce and export a massive quantity of cheap manufacturing goods.
5 R. Shaw, "The Bond Yield Curve as an Economic Crystal Ball," *Seeking Alpha*, 7 January 2007; available at https://seekingalpha.com/article/23597-the-bond-yield-curve-as-an-economic-crystal-ball.
6 https://www.federalreserve.gov/aboutthefed.htm
7 L. Lee and T. Contiliano, "America's Zombie Companies Rack Up $1.4 Trillion of Debt," *Bloomberg*, 17 November 2020; available at https://www.bloomberg.com/news/articles/2020-11-17/america-s-zombie-companies-have-racked-up-1-4-trillion-of-debt.
8 Such cooperation will not be fruitful unless regulatory leniency and regulatory capture are reduced beforehand (see Gaillard and Michalek, 2019, and Cohn, 2019, respectively).
9 The government's decision to allow Lehman to file for bankruptcy, instead of providing a government rescue, was, in the standard account, the primary cause of the severe economic and financial contraction that followed. See Ayotte and Skeel Jr. (2010).
10 See, inter alia, Manns (2011) arguing for a new agency, the Federal Government Investment Corporation (FGIC), to serve as the 'investor of last resort' to act as the private enterprise "bailout complement" to the FDIC's role viz., banks; L. Pedersen and N. Roubini ("A Proposal to Prevent Wholesale Financial Failure," *Financial Times*, 29 January 2009) calling for mandatory insurance on all financially related institutions; Schwarcz (2010) proposing the creation of a market maker liquidity provider role for individual stocks to support debt markets as a whole, by ensuring emergency liquidity for the liquidation of illiquid debt securities.
11 Although the terms somewhat overlap, they can be distinguished on the basis of illiquidity and solvency, and on the basis of anticipated consequences; see Diamond and Rajan (2005) discussing liquidity and solvency problems. *Rescue* funding forestalls the suspension of obligations to creditors (otherwise resulting from a bankruptcy filing), the need for which may result from either a distortion in current capital market conditions (precluding a market source of funding) or a time and information constraint that makes third party financing impractical or not cost-efficient. While the rescued firm may be technically insolvent (given illiquid assets against known liabilities), there is an expectation that closing the (temporary) liquidity gap will enable viability. *Bailout*, in contrast, is generally the term used in connection with government financial assistance to clearly insolvent firms with a large liquidity shortfall in order to forestall expected and foreseeable extensive consequential failures (i.e., systemic risk). See Ayotte and Skeel Jr. (2010).
12 See Chennells and Wingfield (2015) discussing and explaining the use and purpose of "bail-ins" and answering typical criticisms thereof.
13 See Block, Chapter 9 of this volume. See also Block (2010) discussing the use of off-budget accounting that obscures the true costs of bailouts, calling for greater transparency and on-budget accounting.
14 See Federal Reserve Bank of Minneapolis (2017, p. 74) discussing systemic risk charges and shadow banking tax.

15 See Federal Reserve Bank of Minneapolis (2017, p. 28): "we have very little data describing the balance sheets of the firms in the shadow banking sector."
16 Gaillard and Waibel (2018) analyze the greater vulnerability of credit ratings agencies to litigation since the late 2000s.
17 Antill and Sarkar (2018) focus on the importance of size, complexity, and interconnectedness.
18 For an array of literature criticizing the present design of macroprudential frameworks, see Tonveronachi (2018), Aikman et al. (2019), and White (2019).
19 In a remarkable analysis, Campbell and Minsky (1987, pp. 255–256) insist that bank failures "occur mainly because of the interdependence of payment commitments and position-making transactions across institutions and units." They add that "depression bankruptcies arise from systemic conditions that make entire classes of institutions vulnerable."
20 Several proposals designed to decrease liquidity glut would concern banks as well as non-bank financial intermediaries.
21 While beyond the scope of this Chapter, the asymmetry as between the aggrieved end user suffering, on an individual basis, an extremely marginal and insignificant harm (thereby lacking any meaningful legal recourse outside of aggregation within class actions), and the advantaged structurers, originators and distributors who can exploit that marginal harm across many investors or many millions of dollars (per transaction) represents something of an irreducible challenge to the regulators. The imposition of a micro tax, and similar "benefit adjusting" measures should be explored through the lens of "optimizing" overall equity.
22 A "synthetic" CDO is one where the issuing entity does not own, but instead *references* underlying assets; in a synthetic CDO of ABS, the underlying assets are *asset backed securities* that are issuances supported by the cashflows from aggregated securities. Thus, the ability to "look through" to the risk contained in the cashflow generating security requires the assessment of hundreds or even thousands of underlying securities, each of which is presenting dynamic risk.
23 Despite the clear language of the Dodd-Frank Act in Section 939g, the SEC delivered, and has refreshed, the "No Action" letter delivered to Ford Motor Credit Company LLC (available at https://www.sec.gov/divisions/corpfin/cf-noaction/2010/ford072210-1120.htm) exempting the rating agencies from expert liability under Section 11 of the Securities Act of 1933, 15 U.S.C. § 77k for their rating opinion letters, used and relied upon by investors and by structurers involved with complex derivative transactions.
24 For a comprehensive discussion of the "flip clause" used in the rated ABS and structured finance sector worldwide and involving swap agreements, see Gaillard and Harrington (2016) and Harrington (2019).

References

Aikman, D., Bridges, J., Kashyap, A. and Siegert, C. (2019) "Would Macroprudential Regulation Have Prevented the Last Crisis?," *Journal of Economic Perspectives*, Vol. 33, No. 1, pp. 107–130.

Antill, S., and Sarkar, A. (2018) "Is Size Everything?," *Federal Reserve Bank of New York Staff Report No. 864*, August.

Ayotte, K. M. and Skeel Jr., D. A. (2010) "Bankruptcy or Bailouts?," *Journal of Corporation Law*, Vol. 35, No. 3, pp. 469–498.

Bernanke, B. and Gertler, M. (1999) "Monetary Policy and Asset Price Volatility," *Federal Reserve Bank of Kansas City, Economic Review*, Vol. 84, Fourth Quarter, pp. 17–51.

Block, C. D. (2010) "Measuring the True Cost of Government Bailout," *Washington University Law Review*, Vol. 88, No. 1, pp. 149–228.

Campbell, C. and Minsky, H. P. (1987) "How to Get Off the Back of a Tiger, or, Do Initial Conditions Constrain Deposit Insurance Reform?," in Federal Reserve Bank of Chicago (Ed), *Merging Commercial and Investment Banking – Risks, Benefits, Challenges*. Proceedings, A Conference on Bank Structure and Competition. Chicago: Federal Reserve Bank of Chicago.

Cecchetti, S., Mancini-Griffoli, T. and Narita, M. (2017) "Does Prolonged Monetary Policy Easing Increase Financial Vulnerability?," *IMF Working Paper 17/65*.

Chennells, L. and Wingfield, V. (2015) "Bank Failure and Bail-In: An Introduction," *Bank of England, Quarterly Bulletin 2015 Q3*, pp. 228–241.

Cohn, T. H. (2019) "The Effects of Regulatory Capture on Banking Regulations: A Level-of-Analysis Approach," in Hira, A., Gaillard, N. and Cohn, T. H. (Eds), *The Failure of Financial Regulation – Why A Major Crisis Could Happen Again*. International Political Economy Series. Cham: Palgrave Macmillan.

Diamond, D. W. and Rajan, R. G. (2005) "Liquidity Shortages and Banking Crises," *Journal of Finance*, Vol. 60, No. 2, pp. 615–647.

Ekeland, I. and Rochet, J-C. (2020) *Il faut taxer la spéculation financière*. Paris: Odile Jacob.

Federal Reserve Bank of Minneapolis (2017) *The Minneapolis Plan to End Too Big to Fail*. December. Minneapolis: Federal Reserve Bank of Minneapolis.

Financial Stability Board (2021) *Evaluation of the Effects of Too-Big-To-Fail Reforms – Final Report*. Basel: Financial Stability Board.

Gaillard, N. and Harrington, W. J. (2016) "Efficient, Commonsense Actions to Foster Accurate Credit Ratings," *Capital Markets Law Journal*, Vol. 11, No. 1, pp. 38–59.

Gaillard, N. and Michalek, R. J. (2019) "How and Why Moral Hazard Has Distorted Financial Regulation," in Hira, A., Gaillard, N. and Cohn, T. H. (Eds), *The Failure of Financial Regulation – Why A Major Crisis Could Happen Again*. International Political Economy Series. Cham: Palgrave Macmillan.

Gaillard, N. and Waibel, M. (2018) "The Icarus Syndrome: How Credit Rating Agencies Lost Their Quasi Immunity," *Southern Methodist University Law Review*, Vol. 71, No. 4, pp. 1077–1116.

Gelzinis, G. (2019) *Strengthening the Regulation and Oversight of Shadow Banks – Revitalizing the Financial Stability Oversight Council*. Washington, DC: Center for American Progress.

Harrington, W. J. (2019) *Harrington Independent Flip Clause Assessments*, 3 November, available at https://www.sec.gov/comments/265-30/26530-6383231-197808.pdf.

Hogan, T. L., Le, L. and Salter, A. W. (2015) "Ben Bernanke and Bagehot's Rules," *Journal of Money, Credit and Banking*, Vol. 47, No. 2–3, pp. 333–348.

Infante, S., Press, C. and Saravay, Z. (2020) "Understanding Collateral Re-use in the US Financial System," *AEA Papers and Proceedings*, Vol. 110, May, pp. 482–486.

Lippman, W. (1937) *The Good Society*. Boston: Little, Brown & Cy.

Manns, J. (2011) "Building Better Bailouts: The Case for a Long-Term Investment Approach," *Florida Law Review*, Vol. 63, No. 6, pp. 1349–1406.

Minsky, H. P. (1986) *Stabilizing an Unstable Economy*. New Haven (CT): Yale University Press.

Public Citizen (2020) *Covid Lobbying Palooza*. 6 July. Washington, DC: Public Citizen.

Schwarcz, S. (2010) "Too Big to Fail?: Recasting the Financial Safety Net," in Mitchell, L. E. and Wilmarth, Jr., A. E. (Eds), *The Panic of 2008: Causes, Consequences and Implications for Reform*. Cheltenham (U.K.) and Northampton (MA): Edward Elgar.

Tonveronachi, M. (2018) "Ending Laissez-Faire Finance," in Corsi, M., Kregel, J. and D'Ippoliti, C. (Eds), *Classical Economics Today – Essays in Honor of Alessandro Roncaglia*. London: Anthem Press.

White, W. R. (2019) "The Limits of Macroprudential Policy," *The International Economy*, Winter, pp. 52–55.

Wilmarth, Jr., A. E. (2014) "Narrow Banking as a Structural Remedy for the Problem of Systemic Risk: A Comment on Professor Schwarcz's Ring-Fencing," *Southern California Law Review*, Vol. 88, No. 1, pp. 1–10.

Wilmarth, Jr., A. E. (2020) *Taming the Megabanks: Why We Need a New Glass-Steagall Act*. New York: Oxford University Press.

Index

For Product Safety Concerns and Information please contact our EU
representative GPSR@taylorandfrancis.com
Taylor & Francis Verlag GmbH, Kaufingerstraße 24, 80331 München, Germany

www.ingramcontent.com/pod-product-compliance
Ingram Content Group UK Ltd.
Pitfield, Milton Keynes, MK11 3LW, UK
UKHW020008200926
475702UK00015B/2530
9780367688349